D0941287

LAWNS

The American Horticultural Society
Illustrated Encyclopedia of Gardening

LAWNS

The American Horticultural Society
Mount Vernon, Virginia

For the American Horticultural Society

President
Dr. Gilbert S. Daniels

Technical Advisory Committee
Everett Conklin
Mary Stuart Maury
Dr. John A. Wott

Lawns Staff for The Franklin Library/Ortho Books

Editorial Director
Min S. Yee

Supervisory Editor
Lewis P. Lewis

Editor
Ken Burke

Art Directors
John Williams
Barbara Ziller

Creative Director
Michael Mendelsohn

Assistant Creative Director
Clint Anglin

Written by
Michael MacCaskey

Contributing Writers
Lance Walheim
Scott R. Millard

Photography by
William Aplin
Michael Landis

Additional Photography by
Fred Lyon
Kent Kurtz

Illustrations by
Ebet Dudley

Additional Illustrations by
Ron Hildebrand
Rik Olson

Production Director
Robert Laffler

Production Manager
Renee Guilmette

Production Assistant
Paula Green

For Ortho Books

Publisher
Robert L. Iacopi

For The Franklin Library

Publisher
Joseph Sloves

Consultants

Dr. E. O. Burt
University of Florida
Fort Lauderdale, FL

Dr. Jack Butler
Colorado State University
Fort Collins, CO

The cover photograph shows a beautiful lawn of Kentucky bluegrass dappled with the shade cast by a large oak tree.
Photograph copyright © by Derek Fell.

Dr. Henry Indyk
Soils and Crops Department
Cook College, Rutgers University
New Brunswick, NJ

Dr. Jeff Krans
Mississippi State University

Prof. Kent Kurtz
California State
Polytechnic University
Pamona, CA

Patricia Kurtz
Pomona, CA

Dr. William Meyer
Turf-Seed Inc.
Hubbard, OR

Robert C. O'Knefski
Cooperative Extension Agent
Nassau County
Garden City, NY

J. F. Shoulders
Extension Specialist
Turf Department of Agronomy
Virginia Polytechnic Institute and
State University
Blacksburg, VA

Ralph White
Southern Turf Nurseries
Tifton, GA

Dr. V. B. Youngner
Botany and Plant Sciences Department
University of California
Riverside, CA

Acknowledgments

Dr. Glenn Burton
Tifton, GA

Big 4 Rents
Santa Rosa, CA

Boething Treeland Nursery
Woodland Hills, CA

Cal Turf
Camarillo, CA

Bob Cowden
Walnut Creek, CA

The De Georgios
Rutherford, CA

Ed Fack
Ventura, CA

Ferry-Morse Seed Co.
Mountain View, CA

Four Seasons Landscaping
St. Helena, CA

The Grass Farm
Morgan Hill, CA

Irv Jacobs
Albany, OR

Howard Kaerwer
Minneapolis, MN

Frank Mackaness
Corbett, OR

Jean T. Michels
St. Helena, CA

Mr. Miller
New Orleans, LA

James F. Miller
Athens, GA

Ken Vander Molen
Grand Rapids, MI

Pat Montandon
Rutherford, CA

Ellie and Lem Osborne
Marysville, CA

Pacific Weather Center
Richmond, B.C., Canada

Jim Patterson
Atascadero, CA

Ralph Pinkus
Dallas, TX

Richard Post
Reno, NV

Pursley Grass Sod Farms
Palmetto, FL

Rutgers University
New Brunswick, NJ

Silverado Country Club
Napa, CA

Dr. C. Richard Skogley
Kingston, RI

Chester Spiering
Napa, CA

Southern Turf Nurseries, Inc.
Tifton, GA

Dr. Avril L. Stark
Salt Lake City, UT

Dr. K. D. Taylor
Agassiz, B.C., Canada

Bill Titus
Long Island, NY

Mr. and Mrs. C. J. Traverse
Napa, CA

Dr. A. J. Turgeon
Urbana, IL

Van Winden Landscaping
Napa, CA

Warrens Turf
Fairfield, CA

F. Wiebel
El Paso, TX

Alfred Wilsey
Rutherford, CA

Dr. Frank Wooding
Fairbanks, AK

Produced under the authorization of The American Horticultural Society by The Franklin Library and Ortho Books.

Copyright © 1979, 1981 by Ortho Books. Special contents © 1982 by The American Horticultural Society. All rights reserved under International and Pan-American Copyright Conventions.

Every effort has been made at the time of publication to guarantee the accuracy of the names and addresses of information sources and suppliers and in the technical data contained. However, the subscriber should check for his own assurance and must be responsible for selection and use of suppliers and supplies, plant materials, and chemical products.

No portion of this book may be reproduced in any form or by any means without permission first being requested and obtained in writing from The American Horticultural Society, c/o The Franklin Library, Franklin Center, Pennsylvania, 19091. Portions of this volume previously appeared in the Ortho Books *All About Lawns*, *All About Bulbs*, and *How to Select, Use & Maintain Garden Equipment*.

Library of Congress Catalog Card Number 81-71122

Printed in the United States of America

12 11 10 9 8 7 6 5

A Special Message from
The American Horticultural Society

A lawn is a unifying element in the landscape and, along with shrubs and hedges, strongly influences how the landscape as a whole will be viewed and the effect it creates. A lawn does not demand a great deal of work, but it does require regular, balanced maintenance. There is more to it than just mowing. *Lawns* tells you how to achieve and maintain an outstanding lawn in the informative, reassuring way that we feel is most helpful in our *Illustrated Encyclopedia of Gardening*.

Basic lawn care is fully covered. Watering, mowing, fertilizing, what to do with grass clippings, how to get rid of thatch, how to renew an old lawn, how to control weeds, pests, and diseases—it's all here. The range of equipment that you can rent or buy is reviewed. If the varieties and styles of lawn mowers available today have ever left you bewildered, you'll find out which one is best for your needs.

Even putting in a new lawn is not as much of a challenge as it may seem at first, and *Lawns* almost does it for you. Each step in the process, even down to installing an irrigation system if you want one, is explained in a clear, orderly fashion so that you can't go wrong. There is a wealth of information about the various grasses available—which ones are better adapted to what climate, which are fast growing, which are slow growing, which wear well, which require frequent fertilizing, which ones tolerate heat, shade, or drought, which ones are disease resistant. These fundamental facts will make it easier for you to choose the right grass for your lawn and keep it healthy after it's established.

A beautiful lawn is a pleasure to behold and a great satisfaction to the gardener. But we also feel that almost any lawn looks better than no lawn at all. This is why we believe that lawns don't have to be perfect—only appealing and functional in the overall landscape. This book can be your guide to achieving the lawn you want, within the amount of time you can devote to it. Once you see the results, you'll understand why we consider *Lawns* such an important volume in our *Illustrated Encyclopedia of Gardening*.

Gilbert S. Daniels
President

CONTENTS

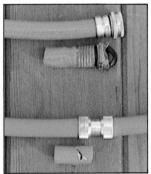

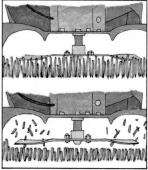

Lawn Maintenance   40

Lawn care can be adjusted to the amount of time you can spend on it as long as you keep a balanced program of lawn maintenance. Mowing, watering, fertilizing, and pest and disease control all should be done in the proper proportion to each other. This chapter explains each of these aspects of maintaining a well-groomed lawn.

Renovating a Lawn   54

Renewing an old or inherited lawn is not as lengthy a process as installing a new one. The six basic steps for renovating a lawn are given in this chapter, and there is also a section on the most common problem in old lawns requiring renovation—thatch buildup, and what to do about it. Patching a damaged portion of a lawn and overseeding warm-season grasses are also covered.

Lawn Problems   60

Anyone with a lawn should know what to do about weeds, insects, and diseases. This chapter covers all the problems you are likely to encounter, how to identify them, how to control them, and how to avoid them. Problems associated with lawns in the shade are also discussed, and the basics of proper lawn maintenance are reviewed, since that reduces problems, particularly disease.

	TOTAL INCHES RAIN	INCHES JULY/AUG.	JULY % SUNSHINE
Michigan			
Alpena	28	5.2	68
Detroit	31	6.0	70
Flint	30	6.2	70

Grasses for Your Region 88

This chapter is a guide to the grasses that are better adapted to specific climatic conditions, which should help you choose the right grass for your area. Grasses are also rated according to such important qualities as drought tolerance, disease resistance, shade tolerance, wearability, heat tolerance, and fertilizer requirements.

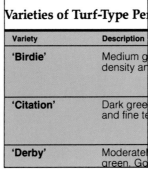
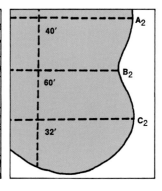

Varieties of Turf-Type Pe...	
Variety	**Description**
'Birdie'	Medium g... density an...
'Citation'	Dark gree... and fine te...
'Derby'	Moderate... green. Go...

Encyclopedia of Major Grasses 132

This is an examination of the fifteen major grasses that lists strengths and weaknesses, gives general watering and fertilizing requirements, and indicates growth habits and climatic adaptation. Specific cultivars of five grasses, as well as native grasses, are described in detail to further help you choose the right grass.

LAWNS

LAWNS OF NORTH AMERICA

Sixteen frequently asked questions, and their answers, show that good sense helps make good lawns.

What can equal the serene beauty of a healthy, well-maintained lawn? Whether yours is an expanse that stretches as far as the eye can see, or just a small plot of green separating house from sidewalk, the pleasure that comes from looking at (as well as smelling and walking on) a lawn of your own is just as satisfying.

Lawns are not for everyone, however—they *do* require upkeep, more so than ground covers, and far more than decks or paving. But if you want a handsome, often practical, lawn of lush grass, and if you are willing to take care of it, you can use the information in this book to make yourself a thriving, gratifying one.

What Do You Need to Know?

Lawn growers and nurserypeople all over the country have said, "Tell us about the 'how' and the 'when' of growing lawns." An extensive survey revealed that people care about their lawn, regarding it as more important than a mere hobby, whether it's a soft playground for children, a pleasant backdrop for the landscape, or a uniform-textured treat for the eye.

Here are the questions that were asked most often, along with the answers.

"Should I have my soil tested? If so, where?" Having your soil tested reduces some of the guesswork involved in preparing a planting site. As with any other project, eliminating possible problems before starting a lawn makes success more likely.

Most of the land-grant colleges and universities will test soil samples for state residents. Sometimes this is coordinated by the local Cooperative Extension Office. In states that don't offer soil-testing programs, there are numerous private laboratories. Look for them in the yellow pages, or ask your County Extension Agent for help.

Directions for taking a soil sample are on page 19. See also the addresses of state-provided soil testing, beginning on page 104.

"Experts use the words 'straight,' 'blend,' and 'mixture' when talking about lawn seed. What do they mean, and which should I use?" A *straight* is simply one type of seed of the same species and variety. An example is 'Adelphi' Kentucky bluegrass. Straights can be used for making your own mixture. However, think twice before planting an entire lawn with one kind of grass; disease or insect infestation can wipe it out.

A *blend* is two or more varieties of a single type of grass. A hypothetical blend of three Kentucky bluegrasses would combine 'Fylking', 'Adelphi', and 'Baron'. Blending combines grasses' strengths, and can produce quality, picture-perfect show lawns.

A *mixture* combines more than one species of grass. A typical mixture will have Kentucky bluegrass, fine fescue, and turf-type perennial rye grass.

A Bahia grass lawn near Tampa, Florida.

Mixtures are best for the average lawn. For most climates, they have the best insect resistance, disease resistance, and overall adaptability.

"Should I buy seed or sod?" Both have advantages and disadvantages. Improved varieties of cool-season grasses and warm-season grasses are frequently available as either seed or sod. A wider range of blends and mixtures is available in seed form than as sod. St. Augustine grass and the improved Bermuda grasses are sold as sod, sprigs, or plugs; they are not available as seed. Starting from seed is less expensive, but many home-owners have trouble getting a seeded lawn established—the critical period of initial care is longer. Also, many weeds may start at the same time as the lawn seed, particularly with inexpensive, low-quality mixtures (see pages 91–98). More likely, however, the weeds were already in your soil, not in the mix.

Sod provides an instant, usually weed-free lawn, and of course germination is no problem. Sod can be excellent for starting a lawn on a slope (where seed can wash away), or for limited areas (e.g., sod near an entryway will keep mud from being tracked inside the house).

"What type of grass should I buy?" Plant a grass that grows well in your area. The North is Kentucky bluegrass country. A blend of varieties, each with desirable characteristics, makes a more adaptable, disease-resistant lawn than does a single variety. Or use a mixture of Kentucky bluegrass with fine fescue and turf-type rye grass. Zoysia grass is often recommended, but it grows quite slowly and is dormant much of the year (up to seven or eight months), except around Long Island and south along the Atlantic Coast and in the southern edge of the midwestern states.

In the South, Bermuda grass is easy to grow in most states. Tall fescue makes a hardy lawn in transitional areas. Where the growing season is long, zoysia grass will make a good, shade-tolerant lawn. Another shade-tolerant grass is St. Augustine grass. Bahia and centipede grass make low-maintenance lawns. Carpet grass will thrive in wet, soggy soils. Kentucky bluegrass is often grown at higher elevations and inland. Mixed with turf-type rye grass, it is more disease resistant.

In the hot, dry areas of the Southwest and California's Central Valley, Bermuda grass is consistently successful. Kentucky bluegrass—particularly if mixed with turf-type perennial rye grass and fine fescue—is widely adapted throughout the West. In the cool, humid Northwest, bent grass or turf-type rye grass is often practical.

Most packaged lawn seed available in garden centers is not made up of a single grass variety but of mixtures of three or more different kinds. A mixture will make a lawn more adaptable to a variety of situations and generally more disease resistant.

One tip: Look around your neighborhood for the kind of lawn you like. If you find one that appeals to you, ask its owner about it. Also see pages 132–141 for more extensive information on grass varieties.

"Do I need to improve the soil if I buy sod?" Preparing the soil is the most important step in building any good lawn. Cultivate the soil as deeply as possible (at least 6 to 12 inches) and add plenty of amendments (see page 18). Good soil promotes a healthy, deep-rooted lawn that will need water less often. It will tend to be more resistant to disease or insect damage. In short, the better the soil before planting, the easier your lawn will be to take care of in the future. This is true whether you are starting a lawn from seed, sod, sprigs, or plugs.

"How do I know when my lawn needs water?" There are many ways to check—visible signals, soil-moisture meters, and coring tubes that actually let you see and feel the subsurface soil. Each offers guidance rather than iron-clad rules, and each requires some experience and observation to use.

Probably the simplest and most reliable signal is a change in turf color from bright green to a dull blue-green. This color change occurs first in the most drought-prone spots, especially beneath trees. Water as soon as you notice it.

Another way of checking for water need is to walk across the lawn. Look to see whether your footprint impressions remain visible for more than a few seconds. If the grass doesn't spring back quickly, especially in the morning, your lawn needs water.

"How soon after seeding should I mow the lawn?" Mow a new lawn for the first time after it has grown 30 to 40 percent higher than the regular mowing height. For example, a lawn that will be maintained at 2 inches should be mowed when it reaches 2½ to 3 inches.

The mower blades should be sharp—a dull blade can easily pull young grass plants from the soil. The same thing happens if the lawn is mowed when it is too tall. Try a manual push-reel mower or rotary mower for new lawns; they are lightweight, and therefore safer for new grass and less disturbing to soft soil.

New lawns from sprigs, stolons, plugs, or sod should be mowed with care the first time. However, they are much quicker to establish (especially sod) and don't need the delicate treatment that a newly seeded lawn requires.

"How often and how much should I water my lawn?" Overwatering can be wasteful, so wait until the lawn shows signs of needing water. Then water thoroughly—enough to wet the soil down to the depth of the roots (usually, about 6 to 8 inches). How often your lawn needs water will depend on your climate, soil, the time of year, the type of grass you have, how deeply rooted it is, and even how high you mow.

Wetting the soil to this 6- or 8-inch depth (assuming there is no runoff) will require about an inch of water in a loam soil, more if the soil is clay, and less if it is sandy.

An inch of water over 1,000 square feet is about 625 gallons. A ½-inch-diameter hose 50 feet long will deliver 350 gallons per hour (50 pounds of water pressure). Thus it would take a little less than 2 hours to water 1,000 square feet.

"What type of mower should I buy?" Power reel and rotary mowers are commonly used for home lawns. For either type, make sure that the mowing height is adjustable to the height your lawn requires, and that safety features are adequate. Older-design rotaries do not have the important safety improvements of the newer models. Push-reel types are the safest mowers.

The type of grass you have and the kind of lawn you want are very important considerations. Reel mowers, if properly cared for, give a mani-cured, golf-course look. They are *required* for low-growing grasses such as hybrid Bermuda and bent grass. Rotaries are better for taller-growing, less intensively maintained lawns. They are also lighter in weight, easier to handle, and less expensive; however, they do require more frequent sharpening.

"Should I remove clippings or let them filter down?" There is no definite "yes" or "no" answer to this. If your lawn is mowed frequently so that its height is reduced only by one-third or less, it's all right to leave the clip-pings, as long as they do not accumulate on the lawn surface. New types of mulching rotary mowers help dissipate clippings.

Clippings of cool-season grasses do not contribute significantly to thatch and do return some nutrients to the soil, thus enabling you to apply less fertilizer. But a lot of clippings become unsightly and may suffocate grass that's trying to grow underneath them. In such situations, remove the clippings.

Beautiful lawns are possible even with many shade trees, provided you choose the right grass and the right trees. See page 87 for information on trees in the lawn.

This field of mixed perennial rye and bluegrass is 3 weeks old.

"How much fertilizer does my lawn need? When should I apply it?" How much fertilizer a lawn needs depends on the type of grass, the season, and the weather. Some grasses require much more fertilizer than others for proper growth. Lawn experts talk in terms of "actual" nitrogen per 1,000 square feet. For instance, a 30-pound bag of 20 percent nitrogen (the first number of the analysis) has 6 pounds of actual nitrogen.

Spring and late summer to fall are the best times to fertilize cool-season grasses. Subsequent applications through spring and into summer are determined by the amount your lawn needs and the type of fertilizer you use. Fast-release fertilizers should be used sparingly (usually, no more than 1 pound of actual nitrogen per 1,000 square feet) and more frequently. Slow-release types can be used more heavily (up to 2 or 3 pounds of actual nitrogen per 1,000 square feet) and less frequently.

"What is thatch?" Thatch is the layer of grass stems, dead roots, and debris that accumulates above the soil and below grass blades. The name is well deserved—like the thatched roof on a tropical hut, thatch stops water (as well as fertilizer and almost everything else) from reaching the soil.

Thatch is not a problem until it becomes too thick. A thatched lawn will feel spongy underfoot. Insects and disease may develop in the thatch layer, and getting enough water and fertilizer into the soil becomes difficult.

Grasses with a horizontal or runner growth habit are notorious thatch formers. These include St. Augustine, Bermuda, and bent grass.

Because zoysia grass and fine fescue are wiry, tough, and slow to decompose, they also tend to form thatch.

"How do I tell the difference between insect damage and disease damage?" When you see a symptom such as a dead spot in your lawn, think like a "lawn doctor"—eliminate the most likely problems first. Spilled gasoline, fertilizer or chemical misuse, or even visits from the neighborhood dog can cause dead spots that look suspiciously like insect or disease damage.

Close examination of turf and soil will often reveal the presence of insects, or at least areas where insects have fed. Diseases may produce definite symptoms—spots, banding, or discoloring. In many cases, grass that has died from disease is firmly attached to the ground (one exception is root and crown rot, in which the grass pulls up easily). Grass killed by insect damage often is attached loosely. Also consider the season. The disease that looks most like the offender may not be active at that time of year.

"How do I know crabgrass when I see it? And what can I do about it?" Crabgrass is well known by name but little known by sight. It has been confused with other weeds such as tall fescue, timothy, and nimblewill. However, crabgrass differs from the stiffly upright, tall fescue; its blades are wider and softer than those of timothy; and nimblewill forms dense patches and is perennial (lives through winter). Crabgrass thrives wherever summers are quite hot and particularly when very moist.

Crabgrass is an annual—that is, it completes its entire life cycle in one season. It starts over from seed each spring, which is the key to its control. Use a "pre-emergence" crabgrass killer. This establishes a short-lived chemical barrier on the soil, which kills crabgrass seedlings just as they begin to grow. Timing is important: Crabgrass can be killed once it has gained a foothold, but with much more difficulty.

"What can I do about spurge, oxalis, and Bermuda grass in my dichondra lawn?" Weeds in dichondra lawns are not nearly as simple to eliminate as weeds in a grass lawn. Dichondra is itself killed by most of the common broadleaf weed killers.

Bermuda grass (sometimes aptly called devil grass) can be eventually eradicated by a chemical called dalapon. It's widely available and effective, but don't use too much or the dichondra will be damaged as well.

The standard approach for spurge, oxalis, and other weeds in dichondra is to use products containing pre-emergent chemicals—diphenamid, monuron, or neburon. Be patient—they will not work overnight.

Ammonium sulfamate is another kind of spray that is designed to rid dichondra of spurge and oxalis. Basically it's a fertilizer that selectively kills oxalis and spurge; however, repeat sprays will be necessary.

"What is brown patch? Can I prevent it?" Brown patch is really two things: (1) a symptom (a patch of dead grass), and (2) the common name of a specific disease caused by the fungus *Rhizoctonia solani*. It can be confusing when "brown patch" is used to name both problems.

Brown patch can be the result of a multitude of causes. Insects, fertilizer burn, and spilled gasoline are typical.

The fungus that causes brown patch is most damaging in transition-zone areas during midsummer. Bent grass can be severely damaged and, in the Southwest, St. Augustine grass is often attacked. It's rare in cool-summer areas such as the Pacific Northwest. Kentucky bluegrass is rarely bothered by the disease; rye grass and fescue are bothered only moderately.

Brown patch disease is promoted by warm, humid weather. You can discourage it by fertilizing properly and by improving drainage of surface water. Several fungicides will prevent this disease. (See pages 78–85.)

About This Book

The information in this book not only answers all the above questions and many others that gardeners have about lawns, but it also gives you all you need to know to grow a healthy, beautiful lawn whether you are starting from scratch or improving an existing lawn. Reading the entire book will give you a good working knowledge of the details that go into the growing and maintenance of a satisfying carpet of grass on your property.

"New Lawns" (pages 16–39) tells you what to do if you are planning a lawn where none exists now.

Once your lawn is established, it needs to be maintained. "Lawn Maintenance" (pages 40–53) outlines methods of mowing the different varieties of grasses; how often and close to mow according to the type of grass, the season, and the locality; and what to do about grass clippings.

If you are improving an existing lawn that is not doing as well as it could, read "Renovating a Lawn" (pages 54–59).

No matter how carefully you have tended your old lawn, or how carefully you have nursed along a newly planted one, sooner or later weeds and pests are bound to be a problem. "Lawn Problems" (pages 60–87) shows you how to look for insect and pest damage, and fungus diseases that affect grasses. Treatment for damage and methods of prevention are discussed.

Which grass to plant? "Grasses for Your Region" (pages 88–99) provides information and compares the different varieties of grass commercially available, with suggestions as to which types of grass are best suited for both your needs and your locality.

"Regional Grasses" (pages 99–131) gives regionalized information about the grasses that grow best in your area. Climate, the deciding factor, is discussed in terms of total inches of rain, inches of rain in July and August, percentage of sun in July, number of July days above 90°F., and average maximum/minimum temperatures. Also included are addresses, by state, of where to write for local publications and soil-testing information.

"Encyclopedia of Major Grasses" (pages 132–141) lists in alphabetical order the grasses most often used by gardeners. The grass varieties are classified in terms of strengths, weaknesses, shade tolerance, water needs, fertilizer needs, wearability, proper mowing height, soil requirements, varieties, and scientific name. Consult this listing as reference before you buy grasses, and to become better acquainted with the varieties available.

A 90-day-old lawn of turf-type perennial rye grasses: 'Citation', 'Birdie', and 'Omega'. See page 137 for additional varieties.

NEW LAWNS

In creating a lawn, planning counts. How well you know your soils, and the temperature and climate of your area, will contribute to lasting results.

If you're starting a new lawn from scratch, rather than inheriting someone else's old one, you may be impatient to see some green. But go slowly—the future of your lawn depends on your initial decisions and procedures.

Before you start working, ask yourself, "Which grass should I plant?... Do I want to sow seed or use sod, sprigs, stolons, or plugs?... How will I water?" It's a good idea to look through this entire book before beginning work. A little forethought will save you a lot of future headaches.

Starting from Scratch

There are many different ways of getting from bare ground to a new lawn. Some people simply spread seed over their existing ground without preparing the soil. However, few lawns that are started this way succeed or even reach their optimum level of appearance. New techniques such as hydromulching are becoming increasingly popular. Regardless of the planting method, success is still measured by long-term results.

Here are the steps of site preparation that lead to a long-lasting, beautiful lawn. If you do these in their logical order, you'll avoid the cost of having to backtrack and do these steps as a remedy.

1. Test the soil.
2. Remove debris.
3. Control persistent weeds.
4. Rough-grade the site.
5. Add high-phosphorus starter fertilizer and lime or sulfur (if necessary).
6. Add amendments or topsoil, if needed.
7. Cultivate thoroughly.
8. Install underground irrigation (optional).
9. Final-grade the site and settle excavation areas.
10. Roll lightly.

What you should know about soil. Much of the success of your lawn will depend on how you prepare the soil. Unlike vegetables, for which the soil can be rebuilt each year, grass roots use the same soil year after year. Although most nutrient deficiencies can be corrected after the lawn has been established, changing the soil structure under growing grass is difficult and expensive. The time and effort you put into preparing the growing medium will be reflected in the health and beauty of your lawn for years to come, both for lawns grown from seed and for vegetative plantings such as sod. Even though sod has some soil already attached, site preparation is still critical to success.

Gardeners describe soil types in many ways—heavy, light, clay, sandy, loamy, rich loam, poor soil, lean soil. Scientists and horticulturists classify soils by the proportion of sand, silt, and clay they contain. These designations are based on the size of the soil particles (clay is the smallest, silt is

bigger, and sand is the largest). A soil's texture is determined by the blend of these various particles.

For proper growth, plants need air in the soil, available moisture (but not standing water), and a supply of mineral nutrients. A soil with plenty of clay has no problem holding on to nutrients but the small clay particles that cling closely together hold water and leave little room for air. If squeezed into a ball, clay soil clings together tightly, slowing down water penetration. Drainage is the main problem; lack of drainage often results in suffocation of plant roots. You know you have a clay soil if it's rock-hard when dry and gummy when wet.

Sandy soils have lots of room for air, but moisure and nutrients disappear quickly. Water sinks right into sandy soil without spreading, and dries up in just a few days after watering. When a sandy soil is squeezed into a ball, as soon as the ball is released it quickly falls apart.

A loam soil is best for plant growth. Loam is between the extremes of a sandy soil and a clay soil. It contains a combination of clay, silt, and sand, and retains nutrients and water while still allowing sufficient room for air.

Your soil, like most soils, is probably not the perfect loam. Therefore it would benefit from the addition of organic matter. And even if it is an ideal soil, heavy foot traffic or construction activity around new homes can severely compact it, closing air spaces and restricting the penetration of water and nutrients. You've seen the effects of compaction in footpaths worn across a lawn.

If your soil's structure isn't quite right. The best way to change heavy clay soil or light sandy soil into a substitute for a rich loam is to add organic matter—not just a little, but a lot.

The addition of organic matter—for example, compost, peat moss, manure, sawdust, or shredded ground bark—makes clay soils more friable and easier to work. Organic matter opens up tight clay soils, improves drainage, and allows air to move more readily into the soil. In light sandy soils, organic matter holds moisture and nutrients in the root zone. The more organic matter you add to a sandy soil, the more you increase its moisture-holding capacity.

Add enough organic matter to physically change the structure of the soil to a depth of 6 to 8 inches—the area where most grass roots grow. The final soil mixture should be 30 percent organic matter by volume; about 2 inches of organic matter mixed into the top 6 inches of soil is usually sufficient. A common problem for many homeowners is determining how much total organic matter is needed to amend their entire lawn area. The chart on page 20 will assist in that calculation.

What type of organic material is used depends largely on what is locally available. While decomposed barnyard manure and compost are very good, they often contain troublesome weed seeds. Peat moss is generally problem-free and available, but it is also expensive.

There are other types of easy-to-find organic materials. In the West these include ground fir bark, straw, and grape pomace. In the South, peanut hulls, cotton screenings, shredded tobacco stems, and ground pine bark are inexpensive and readily available. In the North buckwheat hulls, ground bark, apple or grape pomace, and composted leaves are plentiful.

First test the soil. Before you prepare your soil to grow a lawn, have your soil tested. Many state universities test soils for a nominal fee. If your area has no such facility, you can go to a private soil-testing laboratory.

A soil test eliminates the need to guess the amounts of nutrients and lime to be added, and often provides useful information on the soil's texture. Some testing labs give specific recommendations; others supply instructions on how to interpret results and take appropriate steps. If you have any unanswered questions, consult your County Extension Agent.

How to Take a Soil Test

Test individual areas separately. The above areas are examples of the soil differences a lawn area will have; most areas will usually have only one or two different soil types.

½ inch slice from center

Using a spade or sampling tube, take separate samples of individual areas at a 6- to 7-inch depth.

Mix soil well. (Do not mix soil from separate sampling areas.) Place about one pint of this soil into labeled container. Repeat the process for each specific area.

Doing the test yourself. First obtain any necessary forms and question-naires from your local Cooperative Extension Service office or private soil lab. The information you supply through these forms will help the lab make specific recommendations for your site. Typical questions are: "How large is the sample area? Has fertilizer or lime ever been added? To what degree is the land sloped?"

To collect the soil, you will need: A clean nonmetal bucket or container; a soil sampler or a garden trowel or spade; a pencil and paper; and a mailable container that will hold about a pint of soil.

To get reliable soil test results, you must take a representative sample. This means that you need to gather the soil from 15 to 20 spots in any sampling area. Treat low spots, trouble spots, and areas with obvious soil-type differences as separate sampling areas.

Take soil samples to a depth of 6 to 7 inches—ideally, with a soil-sampling tube. The hollow shaft of an old golf club or curtain rod will usually do. If you don't have a sampler, dig a V-shape hole 6 to 7 inches deep with a spade or garden trowel. Remove a ½-inch slice from the smooth side. In the bucket, thoroughly mix together soil samples from one sampling area. Allow them to dry before proceeding.

Place about a pint of this soil in a sturdy carton or plastic bag, label it properly, and mail it to the soil lab. Record where each sample was taken from. Also provide any additional information on the history of the land, if pertinent.

Soil problems in the West. Because many parts of the West usually have low annual rainfall, this part of the country has unique soil problems. Here are some brief descriptions of those problems and ways to correct them. For more information, consult with your County Extension Agent or a soil-testing company.

Too high pH. The ideal pH for grasses is between 6.0 and 7. Where rainfall is low, soil pH may rise well beyond this range and significantly reduce growth. The basic cause is an overabundance of calcium carbonate (lime). Where rainfall is low, lime is not regularly washed from the soil, and soil alkalinity becomes a problem.

Ordinary powdered sulfur (also called flowers of sulfur) will reduce soil pH. The accompanying table shows the approximate quantities needed. Other acidifying materials are ferrous sulfate, lime-sulfur solution, and fertilizers containing ammonium.

Too much soluble salts. Arid-region soils are normally high in soluble salts. In most desert areas the irrigation water is high in salts. Fertilizers also add their share. Water, carrying salts, evaporates, and the salt accumulation builds up. High salinity greatly reduces plant growth. Most methods of dealing with salinity involve leaching the salts away from the root zone, where they do the most harm. Soil tests in arid regions routinely check the amount of salinity.

Gypsum. A clay soil with a large amount of sodium salt has poor physical structure. When wet, it is sticky and water penetration is slow. When dry, it becomes hard and difficult to work. Soil in this condition is called "deflocculated," meaning that the soil structure is destroyed. The poor soil structure makes leaching impossible because water does not penetrate. Adding organic matter and other acidifying materials helps, but gypsum is the most effective. However, when hard soil is not caused by excess sodium, gypsum will have little effect.

Mulch Coverage in Cubic Yards

Sq. Ft. of Area	Thickness of mulch						
	⅛"	¼"	½"	1"	2"	3"	4"
1,000'	.39	.78	1.56	3.12	6.24	9.36	12.48
2,000'	.78	1.56	3.12	6.24	12.48	18.72	24.96
3,000'	1.17	2.34	4.68	9.36	18.72	28.08	37.44
4,000'	1.56	3.12	6.24	12.48	24.96	37.44	49.92
5,000'	1.95	3.90	7.80	15.60	31.20	46.80	62.40
10,000'	3.90	7.80	15.60	31.20	62.40	93.60	124.80
20,000'	7.80	15.60	31.20	62.40	124.80	187.20	249.60
40,000'	15.60	31.20	62.40	124.80	249.60	374.40	499.20

Three cubic feet will cover 36 square feet to a depth of one inch.
There are 27 cubic feet in a cubic yard.

Approximate Amounts of Ground Limestone Needed to Raise pH

Change in pH desired	Pounds of ground limestone per 1,000 square feet*				
	Sand	Sandy loam	Loam	Silt loam	Clay loam
4.0 to 6.5	60	115	161	193	230
4.5 to 6.5	51	96	133	161	193
5.0 to 6.5	41	78	106	129	152
5.5 to 6.5	28	60	78	92	106
6.0 to 6.5	14	32	41	51	55

*In the southern and coastal states, reduce the application by approximately one-half.

Approximate Amounts of Soil Sulfur to Lower pH

Change in pH desired	Pounds of sulfur per 1,000 square feet		
	Sand	Loam	Clay
8.5 to 6.5	46	57	69
8.0 to 6.5	28	34	46
7.5 to 6.5	11	18	23
7.0 to 6.5	2	4	7

Preparing the planting site. How much work you'll have to do to prepare the soil prior to seeding or sodding obviously depends on its present condition. If you are lucky enough to have a rich loam soil and a proper grade, you may need to do little beyond thorough tilling, fertilizing, and raking. Usually, however, more work will be required.

To start with, clear all debris from the planting area. Rotting wood can cause low spots as it decomposes, and it can serve as a food source for termites. Stones and cement can damage tillers and other equipment.

Also, determine the dimensions of your lawn area with a tape measure. Methods for figuring lawn dimensions are explained on page 142. These figures will be useful later in deciding the quantities of amendments to add to the soil.

Next, establish a rough grade by filling low spots and leveling hills. Most lots have fixed grade points such as house foundations, sidewalks, driveways, and trees. When grading, be sure to distribute both rough and finished soil so that elevation changes between fixed points are gradual.

The ideal grade is a 1 to 2 percent slope away from the house; this prevents water from draining toward the foundation. That's about a 1- to 2-foot drop per 100 feet. A long string, a stake, and a level will be useful in determining the slope.

If the slope is not made to order, do the rough grading before adding topsoil or amendments. This will ensure good uniform soil to the depth of the root zone, once the soil has been improved. If the original soil is acceptable but the grade is wrong, remove the top 6 inches, correct the grade, and put back the soil.

In areas where underlying hardpan or heavy clay soils prevent proper drainage, you may need to install drain tiles. If so, consult a competent drainage contractor for advice. Drainage work should be done after the rough grade has been established, but before topsoil and amendments have been added for the final grade.

If the soil is to be moved or placed around trees, take care not to disturb roots. Trees in the lawn deserve special care. For further advice, see page 87.

While working on the rough grade, you should also begin thinking of ways to make later lawn care easier. Header boards and mowing strips help contain vigorous grass species as well as accent landscaping lines.

Once the grade is sloped the way you want it, add the organic material so that the final 6 to 8 inches of soil is about 30 percent organic matter. If topsoil is replaced or added, spread half of it over the area and thoroughly till it in. This creates a transition zone between underlying soil and new soil. After you have done this, add the rest of the topsoil.

If you plan to lay sod, remember that the final grade should be about 1 inch lower than the grade for a seeded lawn so that the sod will fit flush against any sprinklers and sidewalks.

Next, add starter fertilizer (high-phosphorus) and, if the soil test indicates, lime or sulfur. Till the soil thoroughly.

It's important to carefully mix the top 6 to 8 inches of soil. Make several passes with the tiller in opposite directions to ensure that the soil, organic matter, and fertilizer are properly blended.

Once everything is mixed, it's time to install underground irrigation, if that is what you have decided upon. Waiting until all the tilling is finished will avoid potential damage to pipes.

Controlling weeds. You'll save yourself time and trouble later on if you take steps to eliminate weeds now. There are several methods; most will take at least a month to be effective and safe.

Methyl bromide completely sterilizes the soil. However, it is very dangerous and should only be used by professionals.

Metham, known under the trade name Vapam, is a useful pre-planting fumigant that requires 30 days to pass after treatment before you can seed.

If time is not a factor, you can keep the prepared seedbed wet, allowing weed seeds to germinate, and then kill them with a contact herbicide. Or allow the soil to dry, and then lightly rake the surface to kill new seedlings as they emerge. Let the soil dry completely before watering again. If this is done three or four times, most of the weeds will be killed, leaving fewer weeds to compete with the grass seedlings.

Be sure to read the labels of all chemicals carefully. Do not sow any seed until the chemicals have dissipated. Check to see if the soil is safe by planting some quick-germinating seeds, such as radishes. If they sprout and begin normal growth, it is safe to sow seed or lay sod.

Be very careful around trees and shrubs. Many of these chemicals will kill them as well. Read the label!

Don't neglect the final grading. Do the final grading just prior to planting. The smooth bed can be ruined if it is left too long.

Take your time raking and smoothing the area—be sure it is free of rocks and as level as possible. Later on, it will be hard to correct high and low spots. In large areas, a chain or wooden drag can be helpful.

Starting from seed. Even though sodding gives more immediate results, starting a new lawn from sprigs, stolons, or seed has its rewards. Few colors are as bright yet as soft as young green grass. Growth occurs so quickly that the feeling of actually growing something is more intense; the part you play seems more important. To be sure that planting your lawn from seed is a pleasant experience, become familiar with lawn seed—how it is packaged, how it is mixed, and the rates at which it is sown. Read about lawn seed on pages 91–99.

The time of year you seed is important. Cool-season grasses such as the bluegrasses and fescues, which are most common throughout the northern United States, are best sown from late summer to early fall. Allow 4 to 6 weeks before the first frost so the grass will be well established before cold weather begins. Follow these steps for a successful lawn from seed:

1. *Rake and level the seedbed carefully.* Use a steel rake for final grading and removing stones. In large areas, a piece of chain-link fence or wooden drag can be especially helpful in leveling. Take your time on this step—it will prevent future scalping from lawn mowers and future water puddles. Later on, it will be difficult to correct the grade.

2. *Sow the seed.* You can use the same equipment to sow grass seed as to

The steps in planting a lawn, from left to right, are: raking the seed bed, sowing the seed, raking the seeds in lightly, rolling the seeded lawn, rolling an added mulch with a peat applicator, and watering.

spread fertilizer, if the spreaders are calibrated to distribute seed at recommended rates. As long as you don't drastically overseed or underseed, the results will be the same. Lawn seed can also be sown by hand.

Regardless of the seeding method, divide the seed into two equal lots. Seed the second lot at right angles to the first, covering the entire lawn area in each pass. When using wheeled spreaders, it may be necessary to touch up edges by hand.

3. *Rake the seed in lightly; then roll.* To ensure good contact between seed and soil, lightly rake the entire area. Be sure not to rake too roughly—this may redistribute the seed or ruin the final grade. Hard raking also can bury grass seed too deeply. A depth of ⅛ inch to ¼ inch (depending on seed size) is usually considered good for seeding.

4. *Add mulch.* If you mulch the area where grass seed has been sown, the moister soil that results will hasten germination and also protect young seedlings. On slopes, mulching can be useful in preventing soil erosion during watering.

Many materials can be used as mulches. The photo shows a thin layer of peat moss being applied with a peat applicator (available at local rental yards). In areas that have abundant rainfall or strong winds, use a heavier mulch. Although wind is often a problem with lightweight mulches, various types of netting are available to solve this problem.

Leave the mulch covering thin enough to expose some of the soil of the seedbed. Never completely cover the area. If a light mulch such as peat is used, follow it up with a rolling. Rollers are usually available on loan from nurseries, or at rental yards. Rollers should be one-fourth to one-half full of water to provide the necessary weight.

5. *Water thoroughly.* A newly seeded lawn that won't grow properly is likely to have been improperly watered. For even germination, the very top layer of soil (always the first to dry out) must stay constantly moist. A new lawn needs a thorough soaking after sowing, and then as many as three to four light sprinklings by hand each day until the young grass is established. How long establishment takes depends on the variety of grass, the time it takes to germinate, its rate of growth, and daily weather. Remember that more frequent watering will be required in hot or windy conditions.

Water with a fine spray- or mist-type nozzle to minimize disturbing soil or washing seed away. Prevent standing water.

Stringing the area with brightly colored flags will warn neighbors and children (but not necessarily dogs) to stay off.

Once established, a lawn like this one, started from sprigs, is relatively easy to maintain.

Starting from vegetative forms. In the most southerly or easterly transition zones of the North, many of the warm-season grasses are available only in vegetative forms—sprigs, plugs, or sod. (See page 35 for information on starting a lawn with vegetative forms.) Bermuda grass, St. Augustine grass, and hybrid Bermuda grass are available as sprigs. However, common Bermuda and centipede grass are often planted from seed. Sow warm-season grasses in late spring or early summer.

Cool-season grasses can be sown in spring, and warm-season grasses can be sown in late summer, but planting at these times of the year results in young grass germinating in weather that is less than ideal for active growth. Cool-season grasses may go dormant in warm weather. Warm-season grasses go dormant when it turns cool. Weeds may not follow this schedule and can take over before your new lawn is established. Never sow in the heat of summer—watering at that time will become almost a full-time job.

Watering

Probably more questions are asked about watering than any other aspect of lawn care, and rightly so. Water is a basic requirement for growing grass, without which your lawn would not survive. Watering your lawn would be a simple matter if there were set rules on exactly how much water to apply and how often. Your lawn's water requirements will vary according to the type of soil you have and the temperatures and climate of your area. Wind velocity, humidity, and the frequency of rainfall will also determine how often you will need to water, as well as the prescribed maintenance practices for the type of turf being used. But even with all these variables, some general rules do seem to emerge. Your own experiences and growing knowledge of local conditions will enable you to establish your own rules.

How often should you water a lawn? The answer is simply "when it needs it." A lawn has to be watered when the soil begins to dry out, before the grass actually wilts. At that stage, areas of the lawn will begin to change color, picking up a blue-green or smoky tinge. An even more evident signal is a loss of resilience—footprints will make a long-lasting imprint instead of bouncing right back. Soil-moisture testers and coring tubes are other ways to check for adequate moisture. There are two types of moisture testers— mechanical and electrical. The mechanical type, called a tensiometer, has a porous tip and a water-filled tube. Water in the tube is pulled out by dry soil. The suction created is measured on the gauge. Once installed, tensiometers are left in place. The electrical type operates on the principle that wet soil conducts electricity better than dry soil. A coring tube takes a plug of your lawn and the underlying soil. It allows you to see and feel the moisture level of your lawn's soil.

How long your lawn can go between waterings also depends on how you water. Roots grow toward moisture, so if you constantly wet only the top few inches of soil, the roots will stay near the surface rather than grow any deeper. Eventually, the limited size of the root system will force you into watering more often. That means trouble, because frequent watering keeps the surface wet, which is ideal for weeds and diseases. If roots go deep into the soil, they can draw on a larger water supply, and the lawn can go much longer between waterings. Thus, less frequent but more thorough saturation is the best way to water.

Soil conditions can also affect how often you need to water. For example, 12 inches of loam soil will hold about 1½ inches of water; a sandy soil will hold about half that much; and a clay soil will hold twice as much. Lawns in sandy soil will need water more often than those in a rich loam. Lawns in a clay soil will need water less often, and it will have to be applied at slower rates to avoid wasteful runoff.

Different types of grasses have different water requirements, which in turn affect watering frequency. Grasses are listed according to their drought tolerance on page 90. Local weather patterns are also important. Seasonal rain can play an integral part in a watering program. When it's hot and windy, obviously more frequent watering is required.

In case of drought. In areas of the Midwest and Northeast fortunate enough to have ample summer rain, only supplementary watering may be needed. Other areas need more attention. The New York State Extension Service has this to say about summer watering of cool-season grasses: "If your lawn will not survive an ordinary drought without watering, it probably needs re-building. You will avoid numerous problems and save money and effort if you can learn to accept brown turf in occasional dry summers."

Cool-season grasses such as bluegrass or fescues usually go dormant in the hottest part of the summer, returning to full vigor in cooler fall weather. Nonetheless, many people do want to keep their lawns green in summer, as shown by the increasing numbers of underground irrigation systems being installed. If you want to keep your cool-season grass green in summer, and if you have started a watering program in the spring, continue throughout the summer. If the lawn does go dormant, let it stay that way. Too many fluctuations between dormancy and active growth can weaken a lawn.

Parts of the western United States also have abundant summer rain, in which case irrigation may only need to be supplementary there as well. The Pacific Northwest has such a climate. But other western areas are subject to dry summers and occasional drought.

Parts of the South that have sufficient rain need only occasional watering. Around New Orleans, for instance, some areas receive so much water that drainage is the big problem. In northern parts of the South, cool-season grasses such as Kentucky bluegrass or fescue usually go dormant in the hottest months of summer, but then return to normal growth in the fall. In the drier parts of the South, such as sections of west Texas, periods of drought are common.

Here are some guidelines about watering in case of drought.

1. Do not apply fertilizer to lawns when drought conditions exist.
2. Mow your grass higher and less often. However, don't let it grow a third more than its recommended mowing height.
3. Reduce weed competition.
4. Irrigate to root-zone depth (about 6 to 8 inches), and only when your lawn shows the need. Avoid runoff.

These are not normal lawn-care practices. Under a system of survival irrigation, the lawn may develop a spotty, thinned appearance. Another alternative, although drastic, is to let the lawn die out altogether, and to replant with more drought-tolerant turf when suitable weather returns.

On pages 104–131 are local weather characteristics for all regions or states. They should be helpful in setting up your specific watering program. Rain gauges are also useful. By knowing how much rain has fallen, you can tell how much supplemental water is needed. Don't be misled by light drizzles that supply very little moisture to the soil. However, watering right after a light shower may be an effective way of reducing water use.

How much is enough? To keep roots growing deeply, the soil should be moistened to a depth of about 6 to 8 inches. This should take between 1 and 2 inches of water over the lawn surface. Depending on the weather and the soil type, the average lawn will use this amount of water in about one week. To find out whether the water has gone down that deep, wait 12 hours and check with a soil sampler. Or simply poke a screwdriver into the ground—if it penetrates about 6 inches without much resistance, the lawn is usually wet enough.

Apply water as uniformly as possible, and no faster than the soil can absorb it. Avoid applying so much at one time that wasteful runoff results. If it does, divide your watering into timed intervals. Sprinkle until the soil can't take any more, then stop for 20 or 30 minutes to allow for absorption. Continue until the desired amount has been applied.

What time of day should you water? There are many answers to this question, and not all of them are right. Some people suggest that afternoon watering causes sun scald of the grass blades. This has proven to be false. Others suggest that moisture left on a lawn overnight from a late afternoon or evening watering promotes disease. In both cases, these statements need to be qualified.

First of all, there are several disadvantages to afternoon watering. At that time, evaporation caused by the wind and sun is at a maximum. Also, less of the water applied is actually made available to the lawn. Wind can disrupt sprinkler patterns, causing poor coverage. Local water consumption is usually highest in the afternoon, which can result in low water pressure. Keep in mind, too, that drought symptoms are more evident in the afternoons and evenings. These symptoms can be induced by the higher temperatures and winds typical of that time of day, but are not always an indication of water stress. Often the grass will regain its color as temperatures and winds subside.

Whether or not afternoon or evening watering promotes disease is still debated among experts, but it shouldn't cause any uncertainty in your watering program. Dew makes most lawns wet at night naturally. Proper fertilizing, regular dethatching, and mowing at recommended heights will do more to prevent disease than watering at the "wrong" time of day will promote it. If you feel that a wet lawn at night is increasing disease problems, water in the early morning rather than evening. This will save water and your grass will not be wet at night.

Early morning, then, is an ideal time to water, but the answer to the question "when" is still: *water when your lawn needs it.*

But for a new lawn. . . . There is a different set of rules for watering a newly seeded or sodded lawn. Sprinkling is at least an everyday requirement. Watering is needed even more frequently in order for seed to germinate or for sod roots to knit to new soil. (See page 23 for a discussion of new-lawn watering.)

Portable sprinklers. You have to understand your lawn's requirements and signals. And you must also be very familiar with your sprinkling equipment. The rates at which the water is applied and the pattern of water distribution will vary whether you choose a reliable portable sprinkler, or an automatic underground system. Automatic systems, if properly designed and installed, are usually more precise and predictable. If you choose portable sprinklers, look over the many types with a skeptical eye and a thought for uniform coverage and minimum water waste.

Because there are many types of portable sprinklers, there are many patterns of water distribution. Even sprinklers of the same type can have completely different patterns. A very conscientious waterer who doesn't know this can end up with overwatered and underwatered sections of lawn. This produces uneven green and brown areas and unnecessary weeds and disease. It always helps to understand sprinkler patterns and water distribution, as well as knowing about soil and climate conditions.

Revolving Sprinkler

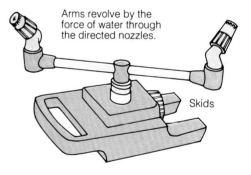

Arms revolve by the force of water through the directed nozzles.

Skids

Oscillating Sprinkler

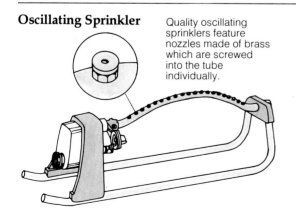

Quality oscillating sprinklers feature nozzles made of brass which are screwed into the tube individually.

Impulse Sprinkler

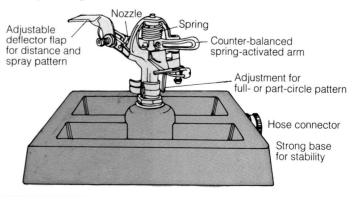

Nozzle

Adjustable deflector flap for distance and spray pattern

Spring

Counter-balanced spring-activated arm

Adjustment for full- or part-circle pattern

Hose connector

Strong base for stability

Plastic containers spread evenly around the lawn are good for checking a sprinkler's pattern and rate of distribution. Above: A stationary fan-type sprinkler. Right: An oscillating-arm sprinkler designed to apply water over a large area.

Measuring sprinkler distribution. There is an easy way to measure sprinkler-water distribution. Set up a pattern of small, identical-size containers on a section of the lawn. The pattern may change for different types of sprinklers, but start with a straight line of containers. Extend them at set intervals, from close to the sprinkler head to just outside the reach of the water. Turn the sprinkler on at normal pressure for a set time and then record the amount of water deposited in each container. This will give you a good idea of the sprinkler pattern, as well as the amount of water distributed.

Realizing that a lawn needs about an inch or so of water per week, you can easily tell how long a sprinkler should be run and to what degree the pattern should be overlapped for efficient watering.

Of 15 of the major types of sprinklers whose patterns of water distribution were measured using the testing method described previously, the most inefficient was the stationary-fan type. Rates of water accumulating in the containers varied from 8 inches an hour in one spot, to 2 inches an hour just 4 feet away, to almost nothing very close to the sprinkler head. There did not seem to be any predictable pattern that could lead to proper overlapping and efficient watering. However, this does not mean that the fan-type sprinkler is useless. As long as the water distribution is known, this type can be valuable for spot watering or as a supplement to other types of sprinklers.

Many believe that the popular oscillating-arm sprinkler deposits maximum amounts of water near the sprinkler, and decreasing quantities toward the periphery as the arm moves furthest from vertical. This is true of older models, but a newer model from one manufacturer stalls momentarily when the arm is least vertical, thus depositing more water near the periphery of the pattern to even out the distribution. This demonstrates the need to test each individual sprinkler.

This whirling-head sprinkler applys water in overlapping patterns. Occasional hand watering may be required to assure even coverage.

The whirling-head type deposited the largest amount of water close to the sprinkler, and decreasing amounts at greater distances from the source of the spray. When this type of sprinkler is used without overlapping, water distribution is uneven. With a 50 percent overlap, its efficiency is increased and the sprinkler becomes quite useful.

With a little experimentation as well as an observant eye, you can easily set up a watering pattern with a portable sprinkler.

Pay attention to your lawn. Your lawn will teach you how to treat it if you pay close attention. Certain areas of the lawn will consistently signal water need before others. It may be an area on a slight slope facing south with maximum sun that always dries out first. Or it may be an area exposed to more wind than others. These spots are clues, and they will mark the time to begin watering. Hand watering isolated dry areas can sometimes extend waterings a day or two.

Watering efficiently. In addition to watering deeply and less frequently, other cultural practices will increase your watering efficiency. Two major problems that affect proper water penetration are thatch and compacted soil. If they are bad enough, either one can actually repel water, causing wasteful runoff. Regular dethatching and aeration (as described on pages 56–59) increase water penetration, provide air in the root zone, and aid in nutrient absorption. Following recommended mowing heights or mowing even higher in hot summer months will also conserve water.

Proper fertilization is another important factor in efficient watering. Poor fertilization invites competition from water-hungry weeds, and reduces the wear-and-tear capacity of the lawn. On the other hand, overfertilization promotes the lawn's vigorous, water-hungry growth, which can cause thatch to develop.

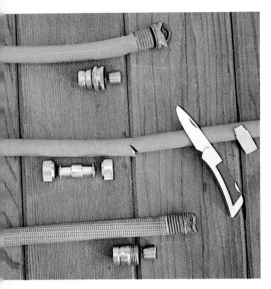

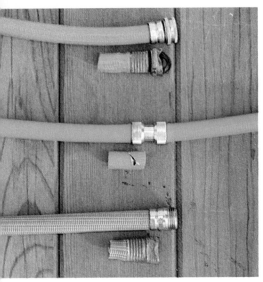

Fixing a leaky or broken hose is easy and inexpensive. The top photo shows some of the more common hose problems. Above, the same hoses are shown repaired.

A hose you can depend on. Most gardeners realize that a hose can be their best friend or their worst enemy. Improper use or a poor-quality hose can do more harm than good. Does your hose have leaky connections? Is it impossible to roll up? Is it too short?

If you answered yes to any one of these questions, you probably need to make minor repairs or purchase a new hose. Repair is easy and inexpensive. On the other hand, although a high-quality hose is more expensive, it will provide excellent service for a long time.

A well-made hose will be flexible in any weather. This is usually the case with high-grade rubber and laminated filament hoses. It is seldom true of inexpensive plastic models. The hose you buy should be long enough to reach all areas of your yard, and have a large enough diameter to supply sufficient quantities of water. The larger the diameter of the hose, the more water it can deliver. Home-garden-variety hoses are available in ¾ inch, ⅝ inch, and ½ inch diameters. The ⅝ inch is a usual choice for a medium-size lawn area. If your hose needs repair, a wide variety of hose repair equipment is available, from clamp-on to screw-on kits. The brass screw-on type is one favorite.

If you have ever damaged plants when dragging the hose around, consider putting heavy wooden stakes at the corners or in key areas of the garden. They will keep the hose out of planted areas as you move from one area to another.

Underground Irrigation

The interest in underground irrigation systems seems to increase every year. The advantages over portable sprinklers are many, but the most obvious is the convenience of not having to constantly move sprinklers. In the majority of cases, underground systems are also more efficient. Sprinkler heads apply predictable amounts of water over an exact area, eliminating the worst feature of portable sprinklers—uneven water distribution. An underground system, combined with an automatic timer, can even water while you're away from home. A poorly designed or poorly installed underground system will be as bad as or worse than a portable sprinkler.

The one disadvantage of an underground system is the initial cost. But materials have become cheaper as well as easier to install. Galvanized steel and copper pipe have gradually given way to lightweight PVC (polyvinyl chloride) plastic pipe and flexible polyethylene pipe. The heavy wrenches required to fit metal pieces together have been replaced by easy-to-use glue. Manufacturers have spent time and money to produce simplified directions for homeowners who wish to do the work themselves.

A typical underground installation. Rather than giving detailed information on installing an underground system, here is a typical underground installation. After all, materials differ greatly among manufacturers, and each specific site has too many variables. The example offered here indicates where the problems might arise, how they can be solved, and the different types of equipment that can fit ideally into specific situations.

Be careful in choosing the manufacturer as well as the supplier. Consult neighbors who have underground systems and talk to irrigation specialists, nurserymen, or your County Extension Agent to get help in selecting a trade name that will best suit your needs. Then you can either write the manufacturer, or obtain the available installation aids and catalogs from a local distributor.

Most manufacturers will provide completely illustrated, easy-to-follow instructions that are useful not only if you want to do the entire job yourself but also if you prefer to contract the job out to an irrigation specialist.

Plan ahead. Once you have decided to put in an underground irrigation system, you need to decide how much (if any) of the work you are going to do yourself. Companies specializing in irrigation can install a system in no more than a few days, and often within hours. Do-it-yourself installation may take several weekends. If the sprinklers are to be installed prior to planting a new lawn, the clutter of equipment may mean nothing. In an established lawn, however, installation may be bothersome or even damaging. Cost is also a consideration. If you are handy with tools and have the time, it is much cheaper to do it yourself.

However you decide, remember the importance of choosing reliable specialists to assist you.

Begin to design your sprinkler system by drawing a layout on graph paper (10 grids to an inch works well); you will also need a soft lead pencil, a dime-store compass, and a measuring tape. Planning it out on paper will help you install a better system, will make it easier to order materials and get advice from your garden center, irrigation specialist, or hardware dealer, and will serve as a record of where the pipelines are laid.

Make your plan complete. A good plan is actually a bird's-eye view of your property drawn to scale (1 inch equaling 20 feet is good for the average homeowner). This scale should allow you to fit all important details on an 8½- by 11-inch piece of paper. The plan should show all construction and landscape features that could affect the design and installation of the sprinkler system. This includes shrubs and trees, paved areas, and fencing, as well as less apparent objects such as mailboxes, raised planters, and buried drainage or power lines. It may also be helpful to note prevailing wind direction, sun and shade areas, steep slopes, and high and low spots in your landscape.

Draw the plan for both the front and back yards, even if you plan to install the system in only one area. You may want a similar system in another area at a later date. If you want to include sprinklers for trees and shrubs, indicate on the plan any water-sensitive or especially thirsty plants.

Gallons per minute. One of the most important aspects of building a successful sprinkler system is determining the available water in gallons per minute (gpm). The best way to find available gpm is to use a gauge. A gpm gauge automatically compensates for friction loss, pipe corrosion, and similar variables. Most sprinkler suppliers will lend you this gauge upon request.

Even without this gauge, you can still deduce available gpm. First, check the water-meter size. This should be stamped on the meter itself; if it isn't, ask your local water company. Common meter sizes are ⅝ inch, ¾ inch, and 1 inch. Next, determine your static water pressure with a gauge measured in pounds per square inch (psi). These gauges are much more commonly available than the gpm gauge. When figuring static pressure, use an outside faucet connected to the service line, and have all water inside the house turned off. Last, find out the size of the service line from your meter to the house.

Types of pipe. Ease of handling, assembly, durability, good flow characteristics, cost, and availability are reasons why PVC pipe and solvent-welded fittings are excellent for sprinkler installations. Schedule 40 PVC is normally sold in 20-foot lengths. Use the heavy-duty schedule 40 for all pressure-holding lines. To save money and materials, use class 200 or class 315 pipe for all lateral lines that will never be required to hold constant pressure.

Flexible polyethylene pipe is also acceptable and very easy to use in sprinkler lines, but it may not be able to handle the pressure between the water meter and control valves. The advantage of the flexible pipe is that you're not restricted to straight lines. Polypipe comes in 100-foot or 200-foot rolls and can be cut with a knife. Fittings are inserted into the pipe and held in place with stainless steel clamps that are tightened with a screwdriver or wrench.

Pipe and Valve Sizes

Valve or pipe size	Maximum GPM flow	
	PVC pipe	Polyethylene pipe
¾"	14	9
1"	25	15
1¼"	40	30

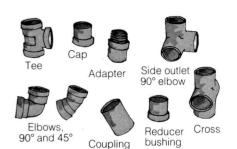

Tee   Cap   Adapter   Side outlet 90° elbow

Elbows, 90° and 45°   Coupling   Reducer bushing   Cross

Working with PVC

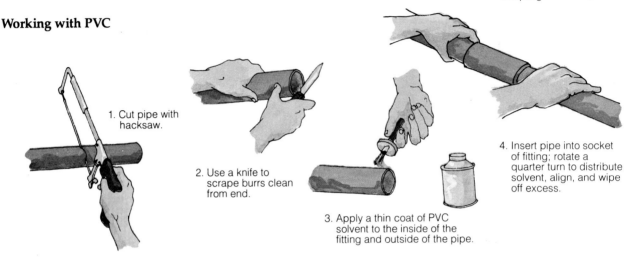

1. Cut pipe with hacksaw.

2. Use a knife to scrape burrs clean from end.

3. Apply a thin coat of PVC solvent to the inside of the fitting and outside of the pipe.

4. Insert pipe into socket of fitting; rotate a quarter turn to distribute solvent, align, and wipe off excess.

Sprinkler heads. There is a wide variety of sprinkler heads for every conceivable application, but most residential lawns and gardens can be best served by using adjustable, pop-up lawn sprinkler heads with full, half-circle, and quarter-circle watering patterns. When not in use, the head rests flush to the ground, out of the way of mower and foot traffic. Each sprinkler head is designed to discharge a specific number of gallons per minute over a given radius, and each head requires a certain water pressure in order to achieve its designed throw.

When adjusting the arc of a sprinkler head, check the specifications to see that this does not drastically affect the rate at which the water is applied to the lawn (precipitation rate). This could change your watering strategy.

Square-pattern and low-precipitation-rate heads also are available. Square patterns are useful in narrow areas such as side yards and parking strips. Use low-precipitation heads in areas where runoff is a problem because of a sloping grade or clay soil.

There are also impulse sprinklers, which can be useful in large areas. However, they can be rather difficult to use efficiently in smaller lawns. In center areas of a lawn, especially if wind is a problem, consider pop-up sprinklers with rotary action, which disperse water in large drops rather than a spray.

Include sprinklers in your plan. Set your compass to match the radius of the sprinkler heads according to the scale of your plan. Lightly draw in quarter circles wherever a 90-degree angle is shown within the area to be sprinkled. Next, draw the half-head circles normally located adjacent to paved areas, buildings, and property lines.

Finally, fill in center areas with full-circle symbols. A variety of spray diameters are available. Many installers find one or more different diameter spray heads to be most convenient for fitting a sprinkler spray to irregular-shaped areas. Overspray can be a problem.

Here are a few good rules to follow:

1. Overlap the outer third of a sprinkler head's spray radius; more if wind is a problem.
2. Cut back the radius of your circles to accommodate design, but do not attempt to stretch it.
3. Design your system so that water is applied from the outside perimeter inward toward the center.
4. Experiment with various full- and part-circle head combinations and spacing patterns until coverage is complete, with sufficient overlap and no potential dry spots.
5. Water lawns and planted areas separately, unless the sprinkler heads are designed to deliver optimum amounts of water to the plants.

Control valves. Your irrigation system will have to be divided into a number of separate circuits that operate one at a time. There probably will not be enough available water pressure to water the entire lawn at once. Each circuit will have a separate control valve. Together, all the control valves compose the manifold, which should be placed in a convenient location (usually, next to a doorway and out of reach of the sprinkler spray). One manifold each will be needed for both the front and back yard. Draw the manifold on your plan. Try to conceal the manifold with some sort of cover or box (the plumbing is seldom attractive). An anti-siphon valve will prevent backflow of water into the house supply. These valves sometimes are required by local ordinances, and are always a good idea.

Use the three figures obtained earlier (water-meter size, static-water pressure, and size of service line) to determine the gpm available to any one circuit. Group the sprinklers into circuits, making sure that the total gpm discharged does not exceed what you've just determined is available. It's all right to have less, but try to keep each circuit about the same. Do not mix different types of sprinkler heads (e.g., impulse, spray, and shrub bubblers) in one circuit. Take your time planning your different circuits. It may take two or three tries to get it right.

Whenever possible, group sprinkler heads according to the requirements of an area. In other words, water sloping areas with low-precipitation heads, and water windy areas with heads that apply larger drops of water.

Valve and pipe size. Draw the piping in from the valves to the sprinklers. Avoid going under sidewalks and driveways if possible. Split the flow whenever you can so that you can use smaller-size (cheaper) pipe. Pipe size determines the maximum number of gpm that can flow through. Use the chart on page 32 to determine pipe and valve size. For example, if a circuit requires 16 gpm, use available 1-inch PVC. However, if the flow down the line is reduced to 8 gpm, the size can be reduced to ¾ inch.

Pipe size from the control valve to the supply line should be the size of the largest valve in the system. If the distance between supply line and valves is over 100 feet, go one size larger.

Change in water pressure. Two factors can influence the water pressure available to operate a sprinkler head: (1) friction, which is caused when water moves through the pipe, and (2) a change in elevation between the water source and the sprinkler head.

Pressure loss due to friction depends on the length and size of the pipe and the amount of water traveling through. It is cumulative and can be determined in psi per 100 feet of pipe. Increasing the pipe size will increase flow and decrease friction (see chart).

If your irrigation system runs up a slope, almost half a pound (.433, to be exact) per square inch of pressure will be lost for every foot of rise. Conversely, if it runs down a slope, the pressure will increase this same amount for every foot of fall.

Loss Due to Friction PVC Pipe
(pressure drop psi per 100 ft. of pipe)

Flow GPM	Pipe size ½"	¾"	1"	1¼"
1	.21	.06	.02	
2	.76	.22	.06	
3	1.16	.46	.14	.04
4	2.74	.79	.23	.08
5	4.14	1.19	.35	.10
10		4.29	1.27	.37
15			2.68	.78
20				1.33

Consult an expert. At this point you should be ready to begin installation of your underground irrigation system. In order to avoid costly problems, it is a good idea to have your plan checked by a specialist before you begin. The retail dealer who supplies your equipment may offer help, in which case you may have it checked free of charge. Otherwise, it will be money well spent to engage the services of an independent installer.

Installation information. Installation specifics will vary among manufacturers. This information should be spelled out in detail in printed material that is available from dealers, distributors, or the manufacturer. Here are the basic steps:

1. *Install the valve system.* Assemble the valve assembly with PVC adapters in advance. Then cut in the tee for the sprinkler main. Dig a trench to the valves. Install and flush the valves. Be sure to check for leaks.
2. *Stake the layout of the system.* Use stakes and string to mark sprinkler heads and pipe trench locations.
3. *Dig trenches.* Use a flat-edged spade to dig V-shape trenches (5 inches wide at the top and 6 to 8 inches deep).
4. *Assemble PVC pipe.* Solvent-weld PVC pipe and fittings. Wait 12 hours. Then insert plastic risers; flush out pipe lines; install sprinkler heads.
5. *Test for coverage.* Turn on each valve and be sure the entire area to be watered is covered properly. Then lower the pop-up heads to the proper level.
6. *Backfill trenches.* Fill the trenches a little higher than the final soil line. Soak the soil to allow for settling. Finally, check the final leveling.

Precautions for cold-winter climates. In areas where the soil freezes in winter, drain valves must be installed at the lowest point in each circuit, as well as between the control valves and the first gate valve near the water meter. (The latter will most likely be in the basement.) Use a level to avoid any water pockets in the system.

The drain valves in each circuit should be aimed down on a slight tilt, covered with a short piece of pipe, surrounded with gravel, and covered with visqueen plastic. Never put a drain valve in a fitting before the fitting is attached to the pipe; PVC solvent may clog the valve.

Riser height and backfill. Before connecting the sprinkler heads, use a ruler to determine the proper length of the riser. This length will depend on: Whether the lawn is old or new; whether a new lawn is seed or sod; its eventual mowing height; and the height reached by the nozzle of a pop-up sprinkler. If the risers are too long, the sprinkler head may be damaged by mowers; if they are too short, they may become clogged with soil. Make them longer if sod will be installed, shorter if you are starting a lawn from seed.

Several types of risers are available to make this easier. A cutaway riser has sections of thread in short increments along its entire length. Small ½-inch pieces are easily cut away one or two at a time until the proper height is reached. Flexible risers require proper height adjustment, but if by accident the sprinkler head is kicked or hit by a mower, they flex rather than break. Repairing underground damage to PVC can be troublesome.

Test your system first, then replace the soil in the trenches and water it thoroughly to settle it in. Repeat as necessary until the trenched area is level with the surrounding soil. This will avoid high and low spots.

Automatic timers. For complete automation in lawn watering, you may want to install an electric timer and automatic valves on your system. Most manufacturers also supply timers. Put the timer where it will be protected from sun and rain and near an electrical outlet—a garage is ideal. The positioning of the timer may influence the location of your control valves.

Vegetative Forms—Sprigs and Plugs

With the exception of zoysia grass (and in some areas along the eastern seaboard, Bermuda grass), planting a lawn by sprigs or plugs is limited to southern and southwestern parts of the United States, where warm-season grasses predominate. Because most of the warm-season grasses spread horizontally by aboveground stolons (runners) or underground rhizomes, sections of the plants can be evenly spaced over an area. In time they will cover the entire area, forming a beautiful lawn. This planting method is not practiced with most cool-season grasses.

With some grasses (for example, hybrid Bermuda grass), planting vegetatively with sprigs, plugs, or sod is the only possible way because they do not produce viable seed.

The first step for any of these methods is to prepare the soil properly, according to the instructions beginning on page 16.

Sprigs. A sprig is an individual stem, or piece of grass stem. If it has at least one node or joint it has the potential of developing into a grass plant and spreading. Sprigging is simply planting individual sprigs at spaced intervals. A suitable sprig should have roots, or at least two to four nodes from which roots can develop. Bermuda, zoysia, and bent grass are commonly planted by this method.

You can buy sprigs by the bushel, or you can buy sod and pull it apart into separate sprigs. Sprigs bought by the bushel will probably be shipped to you from the point of origin in bags or boxes. Shipping usually takes place within 24 hours after shredding.

The soil should be ready to plant when the sprigs arrive. Keep the sprigs cool and moist until planting time, which should be as soon as possible. As little as five minutes of sunlight can damage sprigs in plastic bags. Even when stored properly, sprigs will decay rapidly.

There are several ways to plant sprigs. One method is to cut 2- to 3-inch-deep furrows in the seedbed, placing the sprigs in the furrows up to 12 inches apart (depending on how fast you want coverage to occur). The furrows can be dug with a hoe and spaced from 4 to 12 inches; again, this depends on the rate of coverage you want. Close spacing results in more rapid coverage, but involves more material and labor.

If you use the furrow method, place the runners up against one side of the furrow so that any tufts of foliage are aboveground and the light-colored runner is belowground. Firm the soil around it and level the area as well as possible. A light rolling will help firm soil around runners and aid in the leveling.

It's best to begin working with slightly moist soil, but this often causes more problems than it's worth. In any case, *don't let the sprigs dry out.* Water sections as you plant them, and keep the soil moist until the runners are established.

Another method of planting sprigs is to place the runners on the soil at desired intervals and lightly press them in with a notched stick.

A third and faster method is called stolonizing, broadcast sprigging, or shredding. The sprigs are broadcast over the area like a mulch, either cut into the soil with a sprigging disc or covered with a mulch or soil and rolled. Peat moss, ground bark, or sawdust work well as mulches—a cover of about ¼ inch is satisfactory.

Plugs. Plugging is exactly what it sounds like—small circles or squares of sod are plugged into the soil at regular intervals. Square plugs are cut from sod with a shovel or knife, while round plugs are cut with a special steel plugger similar to a bulb planter. The plugs are placed in corresponding-size holes spaced 6 to 12 inches apart in the lawn area. The plugs are then tamped (or rolled) and watered. Although plugs do not dry out as fast as sprigs,

These sprigs or pieces of individual grass stems are planted at regular intervals. They root and spread to form a lawn.

Planting Methods for Warm-Season Grasses

Grass	Method
Bahia	Seed
Bermuda Common	Sprigs, Plugs, Sod, Seed
All others	Sprigs, Plugs, Sod
Carpet	Sprigs, Plugs, Sod, Seed
Centipede	Sprigs, Plugs, Sod, Seed
St. Augustine	Sprigs, Plugs, Sod
Zoysia Z. japonica	Sprigs, Plugs, Sod
All others	Sprigs, Plugs, Sod

A square yard of sod provides: 2,000 to 3,000 Bermuda or zoysia sprigs; 500 to 1,000 St. Augustine or centipede grass sprigs; 324 two-inch plugs; 84 four-inch plugs; approximately one bushel of sprigs. Row planting requires about 2 to 6 bushels per 1,000 square feet. Broadcast planting requires anywhere from 3 to 10 bushels.

keeping the surrounding soil moist is still very important. Coverage from plugs will occur more slowly than from sprigs, but less plant material is damaged or lost.

St. Augustine grass and centipede grass are usually cut into plugs 3 to 4 inches in diameter and planted on 1-foot centers. Bermuda and zoysia grass plugs are usually 2 inches in diameter and planted on 6- or 12-inch centers. It is spacing that determines how much time it will take to achieve complete coverage.

When plugging or sprigging, it is usually necessary to top dress with soil or organic matter after the initial establishment to level the lawn. Irrigation and rain can cause the soil to wash out between sprigs or plugs, yielding an uneven and bumpy lawn.

The best time to plant plugs and sprigs is just prior to the warming days of spring. The onset of warm weather will provide optimum growing conditions for warm-season grasses.

Sod Lawns

Sod is turf that is grown commercially, cut into strips, and lifted intact with a thin layer of soil held together by the rhizomes, the roots, or netting. Installing a sod lawn is much like laying a carpet. The objective is to reestablish the grass roots in well-prepared soil.

In the southern and southwestern United States and even coastal areas of the North, plugging or sprigging is the common way to install a lawn. Bermuda grass is available as sprigs, sod, or seed; St. Augustine grass from stolons, 2-inch sod plugs, or sod; zoysia grass from sprigs or 2-inch sod plugs; centipede grass from seed, sprigs, or 2-inch sod plugs.

Compared with establishing a lawn by seed, sprigging, or plugging, laying sod gives much quicker results. A sod lawn can be functional in as little as 2 weeks, although mowing and traffic on it should be kept to a minimum until its roots are properly knitted with the soil. This can be checked by lifting corners. Under proper conditions, sprigging of Bermuda grass may cover in 8 to 10 weeks. Plugging of St. Augustine grass can take 3 months to cover, and a seed lawn requires 14 to 21 days for germination, followed by a 6- to 10-week establishment period before daily use.

While timing is critical for a seeded lawn, a sod lawn (weather permitting) can be installed almost any time of year. Ideal times are late summer and early fall for cool-season grasses, and late spring and early summer for warm-season grasses. Cool-season lawns can also be installed in early spring.

Sod can be installed in areas where a seed lawn may be difficult to establish due to traffic, or on a slope where erosion can be a problem. The one drawback of sod is the initial cost and the labor involved, which can be substantial compared to a seed lawn. But this is the price tag of instant results.

Choose high-quality sod. Sod of cool-season grasses is generally available in the same varieties or blends of varieties as in seed mixes. Mixtures usually include both shade-tolerant and sun-loving grass types. Select a high-quality, healthy turf of a grass that adapts well to your area and site.

Sod usually comes in rolled or folded strips from 6 to 9 feet long and 2 feet wide. It should be moist but not too wet, and definitely not too dry. If the sod is high quality, it will be uniformly green. Don't buy any sod with poor color or yellowing.

The thickness of different varieties of sod may vary, but generally it should be about ¾ to 1 inch thick. If the sod is too thick it will root slowly or poorly; if it is too thin it will dry out too fast. It should not fall apart easily when handled.

Some states have a sod-certification program to ensure that the sod is

Below: A cutting machine lifts strips of turf at a sod farm.

Bottom: Make sure the sod you buy is freshly harvested.

labeled correctly and is relatively free of insects, weeds, and disease. If certified sod is not available, make sure that the sod you buy originates from a reputable sod farm. Your County Extension Agent or local nurseryman should be helpful. In addition, many nurseries sell and install sod.

Prepare the soil. Even though you are laying actively growing grass with good soil already attached to it, you still have to take steps to prepare the soil properly.

Prepare the soil as you would for a seed lawn (see pages 16–23). Make the final grade about an inch lower so that the sod will fit flush against sidewalks, driveways, and sprinklers. If the soil test indicates the necessity, add lime or sulfur.

Take time to make sure that the soil is as level as possible, using a drag leveler if necessary. Once the sod is laid it is difficult to level. If large quantities of amendments have been added to parts or all of the future lawn area, wet the soil thoroughly to settle it; then allow it to dry, and regrade.

Spread fertilizer and moisten the soil. If the proper amounts of fertilizer have been worked into the soil during site preparation, you don't usually have to fertilize again for six weeks, or whenever the lawn starts showing the need. If fertilizer has not yet been added, rake in a high-phosphorus fertilizer to a depth of 2 or 3 inches.

Lay the sod on damp soil. Muddy soil causes footprints and uneven spots. Dry soil will lead to drying and eventual weakening of the sod. If the soil is

Top: For a sod lawn, you will need to prepare the soil as you would for seeding. Make sure it's as flat as possible.

Left: It's important that enough fertilizer is spread and raked into the soil before laying the sod.

dry, plan to wet it a day or so prior to delivery of the sod so it has adequate time to become simply damp.

After delivery. Sod is usually delivered on pallets to the site where it is to be installed. Once the sod arrives, install it as soon as possible. Do not leave it rolled and stacked on pallets more than one day in hot weather. If the weather is cool, sod can remain rolled for two to three days. Store it in a cool, shaded area.

Do not allow the soil on the outer rolls to dry out. Occasionally give the rolls a light sprinkling, but be sure not to oversaturate them or they will be hard to handle.

Laying the sod. The easiest way to begin laying sod is to start with a straight edge, such as a sidewalk or driveway. If you have an irregular-shape lawn, draw a straight line through it or string a line across it, and start laying sod to either side. Handle the sod carefully to avoid tearing it.

The rolls of sod are heavy—each strip can weigh as much as 40 pounds. Therefore it's a good idea to have two or three helpers ready to unload the rolls from the truck.

To roll out the sod, place the loose end of the rolled sod tightly against the previously laid strip and unroll it carefully. Stagger the ends of sod pieces much as a bricklayer staggers the ends of bricks.

Here's a good tip: When rolling out sod strips, stand or kneel on a board or piece of plywood to distribute your weight. Otherwise, you are likely to end up with pockets and uneven spots.

To avoid unnecessary drying, keep the edges of the sod as close together as possible without overlapping. Firm the edges together with your fingers, but do not try to stretch the sod.

If gaps cannot be avoided, fill them with good soil or organic matter and pay close attention to them while watering; they will be the first areas to dry out. Do not attempt to fill small gaps (less than 3 or 4 inches square) with sod; these small pieces of grass usually dry out and die.

Along curved edges or odd-shape areas, custom fit sod by trimming with a sharp knife or garden spade. It's best to begin with a straight edge and work toward irregular areas.

After all the sod has been laid, roll it with a water-filled roller to ensure good contact between sod roots and the underlying soil. It is best to roll perpendicular to the length of the strips. If the weather is warm, you may have to roll the sod in sections, as it is laid.

Rolling will also have a leveling effect, but it is better to start with a level sod bed rather than compacting the soil with repeated rolling.

On a hot day, it's a good idea to lightly sprinkle the strips as soon as they are laid.

Installing sod on a slope. When laying sod on a slope, start from the lowest point and move uphill. Always lay the sod so that it runs perpendicular to the slope, and stagger the joints to avoid excess erosion during irrigation or rain.

Pegging or staking sod strips may be desirable on steeper slopes. Three pegs 6 to 8 inches long will usually hold each sod piece in place. Place one peg near each corner and one in the center. Drive the pegs through the sod near the top edge of the strip, vertically rather than perpendicular to the slope.

Top: A sod delivery.
Middle: Laying the sod.
Above: Cutting pieces to fit.

Watering newly laid sod. Proper watering is the single most important step in the establishment of a sod lawn. After the sod is in place, you may have to water it every day for up to two weeks until the roots have sufficiently knitted with the underlying soil. If a large area is being sodded, it's better to work in sections. Lay the sod in one area, roll and water, then move on to another area. This is much less risky, especially if the weather is warm.

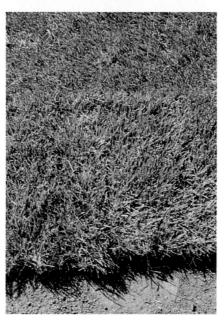

Top: Rolling out the sod strips.
Center left: Placing the edges tightly one against the other as shown center right.

Below: Rolling the new sod lawn with a water-filled roller.
Bottom: Watering the new lawn.

After watering, lift a corner of the sod to be sure that the soil underneath is moist. An inch of water over the area is usually sufficient to wet soil and sod. Keep the soil moist at all times but not so wet that it is saturated.

The edges of the sod strips and borders along paths and driveways will be the first to dry out and the last to knit with the soil. Once the sod begins to knit with the soil, you can begin to settle into a normal watering schedule (see pages 24–34).

Avoid foot traffic; it can slow or damage the establishment of a sod lawn. If this is a problem, cordon the area with stakes, string, and bright flags.

Mowing and aeration. When to do the first mowing depends on what species you plant. Mow newly sodded areas as soon as the grass is 2½ to 3 inches high. Clip frequently enough to prevent removal of more than one-third of the growth at one mowing. (See pages 40–46 for more on mowing.)

Aerating a newly laid sod lawn two or three months after installation will help in the formation of a strong, well-rooted turf. Some lawn growers aerate even sooner. Moisture, air, and fertilizer can then more easily pass through the turf into the root zone where they are needed.

LAWN MAINTENANCE

A healthy, well-groomed lawn can be achieved by following these tips. Good nutrients and good tools, and when to use them, are discussed.

Growing the "perfect" lawn—and the corresponding amount of work required—may not interest you. In fact, the extent of care you give your lawn is completely up to you. You are the owner of the lawn, after all—not the other way around. But if you *want* a meticulously kept lawn, this chapter will tell you how to do it.

How Much Maintenance Does Your Lawn Really Need?

When it comes right down to it, any lawn looks better than having no lawn at all. Take a walk through your neighborhood and observe some of the lawns that look appealing. Notice at the same time how the lawn complements the house. Look closely. Is it weed free? Are there bad spots? We doubt that you'll find many perfect lawns, but lawns don't have to be perfect—only appealing and functional.

The degree of lawn maintenance depends a good deal on convenience and the amount of time you have to spend on lawn care. *When* you fertilize, mow, or take care of weeds probably depends on when you have the time. These tasks do not have to detract from the pleasure you get from your lawn. Who can say whether the "lawn connoisseur" or the "Saturday morning mower" gets more enjoyment?

Keeping Balance in Mind

Although on paper the various aspects of taking care of a lawn can be broken down conveniently into chapters and subchapters, actual lawn care is not so precise. A lawn that is properly watered and fertilized will have fewer problems with weeds and disease. On the other hand, it will also have to be mowed more often. Regular mowing is a good method of weed control.

No matter what your maintenance approach, the key to success is a balanced program of lawn care. If you mow less, water and fertilize less. If you enjoy getting outdoors and watering, balance the extra watering with extra fertilizing.

By understanding all the needs of your lawn, you will achieve the lawn you want. And you will see that lawn care can be workably simple and enjoyable.

Mowing

Despite jokes to the contrary, most people don't really mind mowing their lawns. Mowing is a good way to stretch muscles and get out among the neighbors. It also provides a most wonderful by-product—the smell and feel of a freshly cut lawn.

Many people who want an attractive lawn don't realize the importance of mowing. A lawn mowed at the right time and to the proper height resists invasions of weeds, insects, and disease, and looks lusher and healthier. Mowing infrequently often results in the removal of too much grass at one

time, and will eventually produce a lawn with a thin, spotty, or burned-out appearance.

But how often should you mow? How frequently to mow your lawn depends primarily on three things: (1) the type of grass; (2) how often and how much you water and fertilize; and most important, (3) the time of year. Here is the best rule of thumb: Mow when the grass grows to one-fourth to one-third taller than its recommended mowing height, as shown in the chart on page 43. In other words, if your lawn's mowing height is 2 inches, mow when it's about 3 inches high, thus removing one-third of the height of the grass blade. Of course, this may not fit your natural, once-a-week habit or allow for variations. In some cases, it means frequent mowing. For instance, well-fertilized improved Bermuda grass may need mowing every two or three days in midsummer.

There is a stiff penalty for not following this rule. By letting grass grow too high and then cutting away half or more at once, you expose stems that have been shaded and are not adapted to strong sunlight. Grass leaves may be burned by the sun and turn brown. Mowing too high results in deterioration of green leaf tissue at lower levels. More importantly, roots are severely shocked by a heavy mowing and may need several weeks to recover. Research has shown a direct relationship between the height of the cut and the depth of roots. Roots of grasses that are properly mowed at correct heights will grow deeper. Deep roots are an important advantage and make lawn care significantly easier.

Recently tested growth regulators have displayed the ability to slow lawn grass growth for 5 to 8 weeks. When these chemicals are used, lawns are mowed only half as often.

However, they are not currently being marketed for home use because of several difficulties: The regulators work best only on single-grass lawns; slowed growth may favor weeds and disease; weather, stage of growth, fertility status, and time of application all affect the results; and improper application can damage the lawn.

For now, these growth regulators are best limited to professional use for difficult or impossible mowing situations—for example, along fences, along walls, or on steep, unmowable slopes.

The time of year greatly affects how often you should mow. The cool-season grasses of the northern states slow down or become dormant in hot summer weather. Mowing at this time will be infrequent—once every two or three weeks. During the cool months of spring and fall, most lawns will be growing at a maximum rate and require mowing at least every week.

How much water and fertilizer you apply affects the growth rate of lawns and, consequently, the frequency of mowing. Obviously, lawns maintained at high levels of growth-stimulating fertilizer will require more frequent mowing. For example, golf course greens are usually mowed several times per week, sometimes daily. Increased labor is one price of the luxuriant lawn.

And to what height? How high or low to mow depends primarily on what kind of grass you have. Check the chart on page 43 for the recommended mowing heights of the major lawn grasses. A little theory will help you understand the height rules.

Generally, grasses grow either horizontally or upright. For instance, Bermuda grass and bent grass spread widely with lateral-growing stems called stolons. Because these stolons parallel the ground as well as the cut of the mower, normally they are not mowed off. Unless grasses like these are kept mowed low (preferably with a heavy, reel-type mower), in time they will build up large amounts of thatch.

Think of it this way: A certain amount of leaf surface is necessary to keep the grass plant healthy and growing. If that leaf surface is spread out low,

This mower is equipped with a bag to catch the clippings. See page 43 for the advantages and disadvantages of leaving clippings on the lawn.

over a wide area, the lawn can be mowed close to the ground without reducing the necessary leaf surface.

Vertically growing grasses cannot be mowed excessively low, since there isn't enough leaf surface area to support the plant. Tall fescue, St. Augustine, bahia, and common Kentucky bluegrass fit into this category. Below a certain height (1½ or 2 inches from the ground), there is too little remaining leaf surface to maintain a good turf.

Mowing too low is probably more detrimental to Kentucky bluegrass lawns than any other single practice. This is especially true in transitional areas where adaptation is marginal. When it is cut high, Kentucky bluegrass is much more disease resistant and can successfully compete with weeds and insects. The tall growth also shades the soil, keeping temperatures lower for cool-loving roots.

Exceptions are some of the new varieties of bluegrass, which are essentially dwarfs. They are more compact and have more leaf surface in less area (see page 139). 'Fylking' and 'Nugget' are two varieties in this category. These dwarfs will tolerate much lower mowing (as low as ¾ inch) than common Kentucky bluegrass.

The best practice is to increase the height of cut as temperatures increase in summer and to reduce it in the fall as temperatures drop. Along the coast, dichondra does well when cut at ½ inch, but in hotter inland areas the height should be raised to 1 to 1½ inches. Cut common Bermuda grass short in spring—less than 1 inch. Then, as it grows fast in summer, allow it to reach as high as 1½ inches before cutting it back again in the fall. Where shade is a problem, mow another ½ inch higher. This increases the light-trapping power for photosynthesis of the lawn.

Washboard effect. Turfgrass areas that are regularly cut with a power mower may develop wavelike ridges running at right angles to the direction of mowing. Alternating the direction of cut will help correct these ridges.

Clippings: to remove or not to remove? Some experts say that clippings should always be removed; others say it isn't necessary. How can you tell who's right?

The latest research has shown that clippings of cool-season grasses left on the lawn do not cause or contribute to thatch; rather, it's the woody, slow-to-decompose stems, rhizomes, and stolons below the grass blades. Clippings of the warm-season zoysia grass help form thatch buildup because they are stiffer and slower to break down. How much the clippings of other warm-season grasses contribute to thatch is still an open question.

Clippings return nutrients to the lawn. Just how much it's hard to measure, but some estimates suggest that as much as one-third of a lawn's nitrogen requirement can be supplied by decaying grass clippings.

There are two reasons why it's a good idea not to leave clippings on your lawn. First, they can be unsightly. Clippings are removed from many a high-quality, carefully maintained lawn for just this reason. Second, if your lawn is not mowed frequently enough, when it *is* cut, too much grass will be cut off at one time. Instead of sifting down and decomposing, the clippings can mat on top and suffocate the grass underneath.

At whatever time of year your lawn is growing vigorously, you will probably have to remove clippings. However, with very large lawns—for example, parks and golf courses—removal of clippings becomes impractical.

Lawn clippings as a mulch. If you use lawn clippings as a compost or mulch in the vegetable garden, take care that the lawn clippings are free of 2,4-D and other broadleaf weed killers. 2,4-D affects plants in various ways—for example, continuous mulching of tomatoes with treated clippings has resulted in distorted plants. Let clippings treated with 2,4-D settle back into the lawn, or discard them.

Mowing Heights

Grass	(inches) Height
Bahia grass	2-3
Bent grass	¼-1
Bermuda grass	
Common	½-1½
Hybrid	½-1
Bluegrass	
Common	2-3
Improved (varies by variety)	¾-1½
Buffalo grass	1-3
Carpet grass	1-2
Centipede grass	1-2
Dichondra	½-1½
Fescue	
Chewing	1-2
Red	2-3
Tall	3-4
Annual rye	1½-2
Perennial rye	1-2½
St. Augustine grass	1-2½
Zoysia grass	½-1½

Sharpening a Rotary Mower Blade

As you move the file across the blade, use a down motion. Keep the bevel at the same angle.

Balancing the Blade

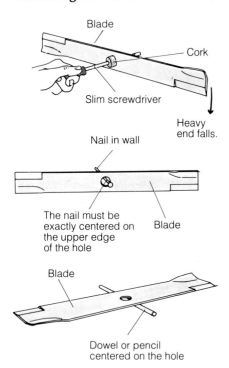

Blade

Cork

Slim screwdriver

Heavy end falls.

Nail in wall

The nail must be exactly centered on the upper edge of the hole

Blade

Blade

Dowel or pencil centered on the hole

One way to check the blade for balance after sharpening is to drill a hole through the exact center of a cork and put it in the blade hole. Put a thin screwdriver through hole in the cork and hold it horizontally to see if the blade stays level. Another way is to put the blade on a carefully centered nail. If one side tilts, remove more metal from that side.

What about brand-new lawns? Newly seeded lawns are more delicate than established ones. That's why you have to be more careful mowing them. By the time of the first mowing, the soil is still very soft, and the grass plants usually are not deeply rooted. On the other hand, mowing young lawns, especially those planted vegetatively, encourages spreading, thus promoting a thicker lawn. Basically, use common sense and apply the same principles of proper mowing of any lawn.

You'll probably want to let the new grass grow a little beyond the normal recommended cutting height. Even then, however, mow it very lightly, removing less than a third of the total height. If you can, use a mower that's not too heavy, especially if the soil is still soft. A lightweight rotary or a sharp push-reel mower is best.

If the soil remains too soft or if the new grass is too loosely knit to mow without damage, wait—let the lawn keep growing. Then cut it gradually until it is down to the proper height (reduce the height by ½ to ¾ inch every second mowing until the desired height is reached).

General tips on lawn mowing

Don't cut wet grass. It can cause uneven mowing. And not only are the clippings messy but they also can mat and suffocate the grass.

Pick up stones and sticks before mowing.

Alternate mowing patterns. Mowing in the same direction every time tends to compact the soil and causes wear patterns.

For an attractive "checkered" finish, mow your lawn twice, with the direction of the second mowing at right angles to the first.

Don't push your mower too quickly. Reel mowers sometimes cause a ribbed pattern, leaving the lawn with a washboard look. This occurs when the mower is moved forward too fast for the height of cut. In other words, it's possible to push a mower faster than the blades can make regular cuts.

Check blade height with a ruler extended from the cutting edge to a flat surface such as a sidewalk or driveway.

Beware of making sharp turns with a mower—they can cause uneven cutting. Make wide turns or use sidewalks and driveways, but be aware of rocks or debris on pavement areas.

Watch out for scalping. If the ground is uneven from settling of the soil in some areas, scalping may result as you go over the high spots.

Use reel mowers for fine lawns. They cut the grass cleanly with a scissor-like action, and follow surface contours smoothly. They perform poorly on tall grasses and lawns with high, wiry seed heads.

Keep the blades of rotary mowers sharp—they are easy to sharpen at home. Only a small portion at the end of the blade actually cuts the grass. Sharpen the edge with a file or grindstone, making sure to even out any rough spots. Check the balance before remounting.

You can also use flail (also known as hammer knife) and sickle bar mowers. These are less common types of mowers. Flail mowers use floppy T-shaped blades revolving on a horizontal shaft to cut grass. They are useful in maintaining rough areas such as vacant lots and the sides of highways. Sickle bar mowers are used for cutting very high grass and weeds. Farmers use this sort of mower to cut hay, field oats, and other grains.

Mowing steep inclines requires safety measures, but experts disagree about the safest way to mow them. Some say across; others say up and down the slope. Use common sense, and be conscious of the danger a power mower represents. Check its stability and be aware that a slipping mower can injure both you and your lawn.

Give trees in a lawn special protection from mower damage. See page 87.

Kinds of lawn mowers. There are many varieties and styles of lawn mowers—indeed, the number increases each year. It pays to shop around to find the mower that fits your needs.

The two most common basic mowers are the reel and the rotary. Within each basic type are variations of gas or electric power, walking or riding, push or self-propelled. Some have bagging attachments, or catchers.

Before buying a lawn mower, look it over carefully. Consider its maneuverability. Make sure the grass catcher is easy to put on and take off. Check to see how easy the blades are to adjust. Ask about the safety features. These points will help you choose the right mower.

Mowers can be very specialized. Some are designed to cut high weeds, others are engineered to produce the carpetlike nap of a putting green. There are also unusual types, such as the one that rides on a cushion of air, and another that cuts with spinning monofilament line.

Reel or rotary. The choice for most people is usually either a rotary mower or a reel. The rotary is by far the most popular. It is generally lower priced, more versatile, and easier to handle and maintain than the reel type.

However, rotary mowers require greater caution in use. They need larger motors with more horsepower; they can never cut as cleanly as a sharp, properly adjusted reel; and few can mow lower than 1 inch.

Reel mowers are available in manual (push) models, or powered with gasoline or electric engines. They cut with a scissor action, which produces the cleanest cut. They conform better to land contours than do rotaries, but are impractical on rough, uneven ground or tall-growing grass. Since they can be adjusted to cut very low, they are the preferred type mower for lawns of Bermuda or bent grass, for example.

Power reel mowers discharge clippings from the rear (rear-throw) or the front (front-throw). The rear-throw type is widely available and somewhat less expensive. It was most popular before the rotary became the common choice.

Front-throw reel mowers are used primarily by professional landscape gardeners. They usually are well made and can stand constant use. The weight and power of these mowers makes them perfect for the low-mowing requirements of tough Bermuda or zoysia grass lawns. Height is also easier to adjust—usually it can be done with just a lever. Some can be adjusted low enough to cut right at the soil line.

Riding mowers. You will probably need a riding mower if your lawn is measured in units or multiples of acres. But they are not toys; don't let children play with them. Riding mowers cut with the same action as their smaller counterparts, both rotary and reel. Rotaries are the most common.

If your lawn is large enough to warrant a riding mower, it's probably a wise investment.

Taking care of your mower. Proper maintenance of your lawn mower will lengthen its lifetime as well as eliminate many time-consuming problems. The manufacturer's maintenance manual for your mower is the best guide. Basically, keep the blades sharp (this is very important) and be sure the motor oil is at the proper level. Clean the mower after use with a soft spray of water. Forceful cleaning with water or air can push dirt into delicate bearings. Do not spray water onto a hot engine.

Keep gaskets and fittings tight; oil or gas dripping onto the lawn will kill the grass.

If you're storing the mower for winter, clean it and drain the gas tank. In spring, change the oil, clean the spark plug, and refill the gas tank.

Keeping safe. Power lawn mowing equipment is so common that it's easy to take it for granted. But power mowers alone are responsible for thousands of accidents each year. If you follow the guidelines below and those of the mower manufacturer, you won't become an injury statistic.

Don't disconnect manufacturer's safety features, and always keep in mind the possible dangers.

Make a habit of turning off the power and disconnecting the spark plug before thinking about reaching into the clogged grass. Many fingers have been lost unclogging discharge chutes of rotary mowers.

Basically There Are Two Types of Mowers...but with Several Variations

Power rotary mowers (there are no hand-operated rotaries) are popular because they are easy to maneuver. They are also easy to adjust for higher cutting and can be used to mow weeds. But they can't go very low and are likely to scalp bumps when set low. They require more power than reel mowers.

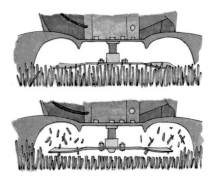

Rotary mowers cut like a spinning scythe. They stand rougher use than reel types. The blades are easy to sharpen, but if they get out of balance the whole mower shakes.

Reel-type mowers give a cleaner, more tailored cut than rotaries, but cannot be operated on high weeds. They do mow lower, making them essential for grasses such as improved Bermuda and bent grass. Standard models have four or five blades; models with more blades cost more but give a finer cut.

Reel mowers cut with a scissorlike action of spinning blades against a bed knife. They are available in rear and front throw models. Keep the blades sharp—patronize your local mower shop.

Don't try to mow where the terrain is too steep or uneven. Many accidents have also occurred on slippery, steep slopes.

Walk over a lawn area before mowing and look for rocks, toys, sprinkler heads, and other possible obstructions.

Don't allow children to mow until they are strong and mature enough to handle the job.

Fertilizing Your Lawn

All gardeners know that a lawn needs water, but a less well-known fact is that grass must eat as well as drink. Lawn grasses live in a basically unnatural environment. They are crowded together and compete with one another, as well as with neighboring trees and shrubs, for water and nutrients. They are mowed regularly, and their clippings often are removed.

Because of this competition and the unnatural demands placed on lawns, they must be fertilized. Just as a balanced diet works best for people and animals, the same is true of lawns—they need fertilizer for sustenance. If it is fertilized properly, the lawn will maintain good color, density, and vigor,

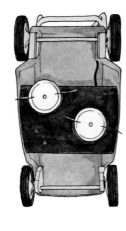

Electric nylon mowers cut grass with nearly the same efficiency as steel-blade mowers, and are of course much more safe. Two counter-rotating discs powered by separate electric motors spin monofilament line to mow and trim.

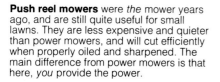

Push reel mowers were *the* mower years ago, and are still quite useful for small lawns. They are less expensive and quieter than power mowers, and will cut efficiently when properly oiled and sharpened. The main difference from power mowers is that here, *you* provide the power.

Riding mowers and gang mowers (above) are best for lawn areas that are simply too large or time-consuming to mow with a conventional reel or rotary. Gang mowers are often used to cut grass at parks and golf course fairways.

and will not easily succumb to insects, weeds, or diseases. If it is under-fertilized, the lawn is not only less attractive but also is considerably more susceptible to environmental stress and damage.

Nutrient requirements. There are 16 different mineral elements that are essential to the growth of all plants. Some are very common, such as oxygen from air and hydrogen from water. Others, such as zinc and boron, are needed only in the minute amounts usually found naturally in most soils.

Nitrogen. This is by far the most important element a lawn needs. Nitrogen promotes rapid growth and gives lawns a healthy color. It is also the element most often in short supply. Watering flushes it from the soil and the growing plant needs a plentiful and continuous supply. Without sufficient nitrogen, growth stops and the lawn becomes pale and yellowish.

Phosphorus. This is the second most important element needed for healthy growth of lawn grasses. Phosphorus is required to produce strong root growth. It stimulates early root formation, which is particularly essential to the proper development of new plantings. Because it is not readily flushed from the soil by watering and is needed by grass only in small quantities, most balanced lawn fertilizers contain only a low percentage.

Potassium. This is the third critical element. Like nitrogen, it is flushed out by water, but at a much slower rate. It is very important to the hardiness and disease resistance of lawn grasses, and helps promote wearability. Potassium is needed in about the same quantity as nitrogen. However, since soil minerals supply a considerable amount, not as much is added to fertilizers.

Calcium, sulfur, and magnesium. These minerals are also needed in relatively large amounts. Calcium is either present in adequate quantities in the soil or is added through periodic applications of lime. Dolomite (or dolomitic limestone) supplies magnesium as well as calcium. Most sulfur reaches a lawn through the air, water, or organic matter.

Micronutrients. These elements are needed in small amounts. If your lawn does not green-up with an application of nitrogen, the problem may be a shortage of iron. This is particularly true in areas where soil pH is high. (Yellowing can also be caused by sulfur deficiency, overwatering, manganese deficiency in sandy soils, and a pH of less than 5.) A soil test may help solve persistent, seemingly soil-related problems such as these.

Fertilizer types. A visit to your local garden store will show that there is an abundance of lawn fertilizers. You'll see labels proclaiming "fast-acting," "slow-release," "organic," and so on. But if they all contain the same basic minerals (which they do), what are the differences? The following description of these products should explain them.

Organic. In this context, "organic" refers only to those fertilizers derived from plant or animal matter.

The variety of organic fertilizers is endless. There are manures of all kinds—municipal sewage sludge, blood meals, and seed meals. They all have advantages and disadvantages. In some areas, they may be inexpensive and easy to obtain, in others not. Most have distinctly beneficial soil-building properties (these are covered in more detail on pages 16–20).

Because the action of organics is slow, it is difficult to make a mistake and overfertilize. This is the major difference between organic fertilizers and synthetic fertilizers—nutrients are released slowly. (Blood meal is an exception. It is a fast-release organic—almost as fast as mineral fertilizers.)

Organics are bulkier, heavier, and more difficult to handle. Since they have a low percentage of nitrogen, it is necessary to apply a much greater quantity at one time. (They also may smell unpleasant.)

The main disadvantage of organic fertilizers is that the timing of nutrient release is not predictable. This is because soil microbes must digest the material to make the nutrients it contains available to the lawn. Because microbes are most active when the soil is warmest, much of the organic fertilizer's nutrient is made available during warm weather—which is not the best time for a lawn to receive a heavy fertilization.

Soluble synthetic. This is the most common type of fertilizer used on lawns today. It too has advantages and disadvantages.

The big advantage of this type of fertilizer is predictability. Because its characteristics are known precisely, you know exactly the effect it will have on the lawn. For many types of lawns, this is important. Soluble synthetics are available to the lawn before the soil has thoroughly warmed in summer, they are cheaper than organic fertilizers, and they are easier to handle. Also, less material need be applied, since the percentage of nitrogen is usually high.

The gardener who uses this type may have more work to do. More applications are necessary because the effects are short term. If your lawn requires 8 pounds of actual nitrogen a year, almost that many separate applications will be necessary.

Further, there is the possibility of "fertilizer burn" if the fertilizer is overapplied, if the lawn is wet when you spread the fertilizer, or if the fertilizer is not thoroughly watered in after application.

The exceptions are some "weed and feed" products which are formulated with soluble fertilizers and are designed for use on wet grass (when temperatures are moderate—under 85°F.).

Slow release. To some extent, this type of fertilizer combines the characteristics of the organics and soluble synthetics. Usually it has a high percentage of nitrogen, so handling large quantities of material is not necessary. But the possibility of fertilizer burn is greatly reduced, since the nitrogen does not become available to the plant all at once.

There are a variety of types, but most are labeled on a fertilizer bag under the heading "W.I.N.," meaning water insoluble nitrogen. Many of the commonly available lawn fertilizers are actually a combination of soluble nitrogen and water insoluble nitrogen.

Slow-release fertilizers are favored by many lawn growers because they make possible heavier applications of nitrogen; therefore, fewer applications are necessary. However, they don't provide a quick green-up. They don't give the degree of control of greening response of soluble synthetics, but do give slightly more control than with organic fertilizers.

Determining the W.I.N. percentage. In order to determine the actual percentage of water insoluble nitrogen (W.I.N.), it's necessary to do a little arithmetic. For example, if you have a 25-3-7 fertilizer with 7.6 percent W.I.N., multiply the 7.6 by 100, equalling 760. Divide the 760 by the total percentage of nitrogen shown on the bag. In this case, 760 divided by 25 equals 30.4. Thus 30.4 percent of the nitrogen is W.I.N.

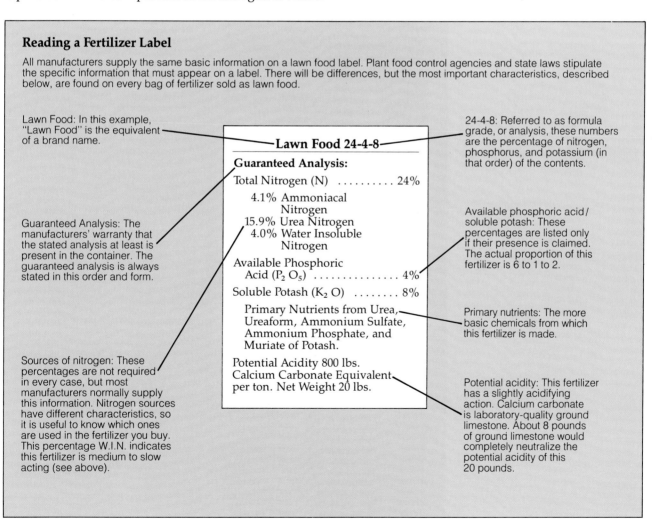

Reading a Fertilizer Label

All manufacturers supply the same basic information on a lawn food label. Plant food control agencies and state laws stipulate the specific information that must appear on a label. There will be differences, but the most important characteristics, described below, are found on every bag of fertilizer sold as lawn food.

Lawn Food: In this example, "Lawn Food" is the equivalent of a brand name.

Guaranteed Analysis: The manufacturers' warranty that the stated analysis at least is present in the container. The guaranteed analysis is always stated in this order and form.

Sources of nitrogen: These percentages are not required in every case, but most manufacturers normally supply this information. Nitrogen sources have different characteristics, so it is useful to know which ones are used in the fertilizer you buy. This percentage W.I.N. indicates this fertilizer is medium to slow acting (see above).

---Lawn Food 24-4-8---

Guaranteed Analysis:

Total Nitrogen (N) 24%

    4.1% Ammoniacal
        Nitrogen
  15.9% Urea Nitrogen
    4.0% Water Insoluble
        Nitrogen

Available Phosphoric
  Acid ($P_2 O_5$) 4%

Soluble Potash ($K_2 O$) 8%

  Primary Nutrients from Urea,
  Ureaform, Ammonium Sulfate,
  Ammonium Phosphate, and
  Muriate of Potash.

Potential Acidity 800 lbs.
Calcium Carbonate Equivalent
per ton. Net Weight 20 lbs.

24-4-8: Referred to as formula grade, or analysis, these numbers are the percentage of nitrogen, phosphorus, and potassium (in that order) of the contents.

Available phosphoric acid/soluble potash: These percentages are listed only if their presence is claimed. The actual proportion of this fertilizer is 6 to 1 to 2.

Primary nutrients: The more basic chemicals from which this fertilizer is made.

Potential acidity: This fertilizer has a slightly acidifying action. Calcium carbonate is laboratory-quality ground limestone. About 8 pounds of ground limestone would completely neutralize the potential acidity of this 20 pounds.

Lawn experts have determined that fertilizers with less than 15 percent W.I.N. are basically fast acting. Fertilizers with between 15 and 30 percent are medium; any that are more than 30 percent insoluble are slow-release. A slow-release fertilizer is less likely to burn the lawn after application and is less subject to being flushed from the soil by water.

A complete fertilizer is best. A complete fertilizer is one that contains all three of the primary nutrients: nitrogen (N), phosphorus (P), and potassium (K). Every state requires that the percentages of these three elements be prominently displayed on every bag of fertilizer. Always, the first number is nitrogen, the second phosphorus, and the third potassium. An example is 24-4-8. These numbers state the percentages of nutrients in the bag compared to the total contents of the bag.

As a general guide, a 3 to 1 to 2 ratio of nutrients has proven to be good for home lawn fertilization. However, factors such as local climate, soil conditions, and the form of nitrogen in the fertilizer can influence what is best in various localities.

A 3 to 1 to 2 fertilizer could have a formula of 21-7-14. It is not critical for a fertilizer to be exactly this ratio, but something close to it is recommended. For instance, a higher nitrogen ratio of 6 to 1 to 2 (formula 24-4-8) is common.

Generally, this ratio of nutrients is properly applied by using the products of a lawn food manufacturer according to the directions on the label. There are general-purpose types as well as those designed for specific grasses.

These ratios are based on the demand of the growing lawn for these nutrients. Usually, a lawn needs three to five times as much nitrogen as phosphorus, and two times as much potassium as phosphorus. (Although nitrogen and potassium are needed by the plant in similar amounts, some nitrogen is flushed from the soil by water and is lost.)

Nitrogen Requirements

Pounds of nitrogen per year	Warm-season	Cool-season
1 to 3	Carpet grass Centipede grass	Hard fescue
2 to 4	—	Red fescue Chewings fescue Kentucky bluegrass (common)
4 to 6	Bahia grass St. Augustine grass Zoysia grass	Tall fescue Annual rye Colonial bent grass Perennial rye
6 to 12	Bermuda grasses Dichondra	Kentucky bluegrass (improved) Creeping bent grass

These rates how the range for grasses with a long growing season. Lower rates would apply to northern and eastern areas with short seasons.

Actual nitrogen. "Actual" nitrogen is simply a convenient way to say how much fertilizer a lawn should receive, without figuring the specific type or formula of lawn fertilizer you might use. For example, a 100-pound bag of 24-4-8 (24 percent nitrogen) contains 24 pounds of actual nitrogen. A 20-pound bag of 24-4-8 contains 4.8 pounds of actual nitrogen (20 pounds multiplied by .24 equals 4.8 pounds).

If you want to apply 1 pound of actual nitrogen over 1,000 square feet of lawn using this 24-4-8 fertilizer, you would use 4.17 pounds.

The directions on the bag will usually tell you how much to use. Most labeled instructions follow the basic guideline of recommending application rates that supply approximately 1 pound of actual nitrogen per 1,000 square feet. There are exceptions: Fertilizers with high percentages of W.I.N. or slow-release forms of nitrogen are often applied at higher rates.

Fertilizer and pesticide combinations. In recent years, many combinations of pesticides and fertilizers have become available. Common types contain herbicides for broadleaf weed control or pre-emergence herbicides for crabgrass control. There are also products that include other pesticides for insect and disease control.

These products do have definite advantages. Considerable time, labor, and equipment are saved if two jobs can be accomplished in one. Less total material is handled and less storage space is required. In addition, the cost of the combined material may be less than the cost of the individual ingredients purchased separately. Most important, the pesticide can often be applied more evenly and closer to the recommended rate than if it were sprayed on the lawn.

The disadvantage of these products is the difficulty in making applications at the proper time, since the best time to fertilize is not always the best time to control insects or weeds. Be certain the growth cycles of the insects and weeds coincide with applications of combination products for best results. A fertilizer combined with a pesticide is most useful if you understand its advantages and limitations.

When should you fertilize? In spring, gardeners rarely need to be reminded to feed their lawns. Spring fertilizing helps a lawn get a head start on pests, weeds, and the summer heat that's soon to come.

By midsummer, heat and light intensity slow down the growth of the cool-season grasses. They usually remain green but are essentially dormant. As a rule, do not feed cool-season grasses in midsummer, although there are a few exceptions.

Apply liquid fertilizers with a hand-held, hose-end sprayer, taking care to spray evenly.

The most important time to fertilize cool-season grasses is in fall. Fall fertilization keeps the grass growing green and longer into cold weather. The lawn is stimulated to become more dense. Since not much top growth takes place in fall, fall feeding also gives the lawn a chance to store food that will get it off to a fast start the next spring.

Growth of the warm-season grasses peaks in midsummer, then tapers off in fall, continuing at a slower pace until frost. The first sign of spring green comes when the soil is still cold. This is the time when lawn food with quick-acting forms of nitrogen pays off, by making grass fully green sooner.

Warm-season grasses can also benefit from fall fertilization, with two exceptions: If winter weeds are a problem, their growth will be further stimulated by the feeding. A heavy fertilization may also promote a flush of succulent growth that, in some areas, leaves the grass more susceptible to cold injury. Otherwise, fall fertilization will keep grass green and growing longer in the fall and promote earlier spring green-up.

Lime. In areas of the country with heavy rainfall, soils tend to be acid. Grasses grow poorly in highly acid soils because of nutrient imbalance and toxicity. Acid soil is corrected by adding lime. The only sure way to know when your lawn needs lime is by means of a soil test. However, if liming is commonly done in your area, your soil undoubtedly needs lime too.

Spreading fertilizer evenly by hand takes practice. The underhand swing, shown here, gives the best coverage.

Soil acidity is measured by its pH. On a scale of 14, pH 7 is neutral, above 7 is alkaline, and below 7 is acid. If your soil pH is below 5.5, lime is necessary. A soil pH between 5.5 and 7.5 is good for most grasses, and 6.0 to 7 is ideal. (Centipede grass is an important exception: It prefers more acid soil. Add lime if pH is below 4.5, enough to raise the pH to 6.)

The easiest and best form of lime for lawns is ground limestone. Your soil test will provide recommended rates. Lime is best applied with a mechanical spreader.

Applying fertilizer. The five basic methods of applying fertilizer are shown in the photographs on these pages.

Liquid fertilizers are applied by hand-held or hose-attached sprayers.

If your lawn is small, a drop spreader can be very useful. Overlap the application slightly so that no strips are left unfed.

Turn the side-arm crank to operate a broadcast spreader. The fertilizer flies out from a whirling wheel.

For large lawns, a push-type broadcast spreader is ideal. Measure the "throw" to avoid uneven applications.

Their basic faults are difficulty in applying the fertilizer evenly, frequent need to refill dispensers, and the amount of time it takes to apply adequate amounts. Read the directions carefully on both the liquid fertilizer and the sprayer. Rates are set up according to ratios of liquid fertilizer and water added to the sprayer. Also make sure that all parts of the sprayer are attached and operational.

You can broadcast dry fertilizer by hand, but it requires a talented touch to do a good job. This method often results in uneven streaking in the lawn. Use it only in very small areas, or if there is no other alternative.

A drop spreader is a very common way to apply a dry fertilizer. It requires more passes than a broadcast spreader, and is most useful on a medium-size lawn. When using a drop spreader, overlap the wheels enough so that no strips are left underfed. However, don't double feed any sections, or you'll have uneven greening in the lawn, or, worse yet, fertilizer burn.

A broadcast spreader is probably the easiest way to apply a dry fertilizer. There are two types—hand-held and push-wheel models. Each throws the fertilizer pellets over a wide area via a whirling wheel. Because they require fewer passes to completely cover the lawn, they are easier to use, especially on large lawns. Make sure you measure the throw width so you know how far to space your passes. This can be easily determined by running the spreader over dark-colored pavement for a short distance. (Note: Some overlap is necessary for uniform coverage.)

Spreader settings. Push-type drop and broadcast spreaders usually have adjustable settings, which correspond to application rates on fertilizer bags. Although fairly accurate when the spreaders are new, they should be calibrated (the actual application rate tested) at least once a year. Instructions for doing this are on page 142 of this book. Hand-held broadcast spreaders can be calibrated the same way.

Drop-type fertilizer spreaders are also used to spread seed. Calibration is again necessary to make sure you apply appropriate quantities of seed.

Application. The best technique for applying lawn food is to cover the ends of the lawn first, then go back and forth the long way. To avoid double applications, make sure to shut off the spreader as you approach the end strips. Keep the spreader closed while you are turning around, backing up, or stopped. For even and thorough coverage, walk at normal speed and keep the spreader level.

If you do happen to spill or drop some extra dry-fertilizer in one area, scrape or vacuum it up. Then flood the area with water to avoid fertilizer burn.

After fertilizing, brush or wash out the spreader immediately after use to avoid corrosion. Dry it thoroughly before storing.

Grooming

Edging a lawn with a border of wood, stone, or concrete makes maintenance less of a chore. Because your mower can ride over the edging, you don't have to do as much hand trimming. This edging will keep a lawn looking its best and keep troublesome creeping grasses from climbing into flower borders. You can lay 1 × 4s or 2 × 4s on edge, line bricks in a row, or pour a band of concrete.

Lawn colorants. When colorants first were introduced, there were cries of protest. However, many of those objections no longer apply. Quality colorants will not rub off, walk off, or wash off. They have become fadeproof, nontoxic, and long wearing. Make the first application immediately following the first killing frost, but first prepare the turf: Mow the grass to 1 inch or less; then mow at right angles to the first pass to provide as even a turf as possible. Remove all clippings, litter, and debris before applying colorant. Mix the colorant according to the directions on the label. That ratio will vary,

Turf grass planted in concrete paving blocks is one alternative to the concrete driveway. The weight of the car is supported by the blocks.

depending on the intensity of color you desire. Normally, 1 gallon of colorant will cover 4,000 square feet of turf. Apply the colorant twice, making the second application at right angles to the first to ensure uniformity of color.

Paving-block lawns. When concrete paving blocks are combined with turf grass, a new kind of multi-use lawn results. Paving blocks are available from many manufacturers, and can be used in driveways, parking areas, or pathways. They look like oversized checkerboards, with alternating squares of supportive blocks and planting holes. Standard concrete building blocks also can be used.

It's easy to plant a lawn with paving blocks. If the area must support heavy weight (e.g., a driveway), prepare a solid base for the blocks. Place the paving blocks in position side by side and fill the holes with a quality soil. Then plant seed or sod plugs, the same as for any new lawn.

This type of lawn has many advantages. It is naturally more attractive than bare soil or an artificial surface, it is cooler, and it produces less glare. During the rainy season, water runoff is less, due to the lawn's greater absorption qualities. Different grass types produce different effects. A vertically growing grass such as tall fescue will obscure the blocks completely. A horizontal grass such as Bermuda will stay low, allowing some of the paving block to remain exposed, thus providing a textured pattern.

The cost of a paving-block lawn varies with the particular situation. Generally, however, it costs the same as or even less than poured concrete.

Spring Clean-up

For a spring clean-up and quick green-up of cool-season grasses, follow these steps:

1. If an ice covering has been coating the lawn for a long time, break it. Do not walk on frosted turf.
2. Clean the lawn of winter debris. Use a rake for clean-up.
3. Spread seed at a rate of 3 pounds per 1,000 square feet for bare spots, a quarter of that for thin areas.
4. Follow the seeding with an application of siduron (Tupersan) for crabgrass control. Read the label. This application will not injure the seed you have just planted, whereas other crabgrass controls prevent germination of *all* grass seeds.

RENOVATING A LAWN

*An old lawn can have new life.
Follow these renovation techniques,
using seed or sod, and working with
your climate.*

If your lawn is lackluster or generally unresponsive to routine cultural practices, such as mowing, fertilization, watering, and weed control, it is probably time to renovate. Renovating allows you to renew your lawn without having to completely rebuild it.

Renovation may involve renting heavy equipment from a rental yard (see page 57). There are many lawn service companies that specialize in these kinds of services. In any case, renovation is a chance to improve the overall quality of your lawn.

Thatch

If you need to renovate your lawn because of thatch buildup, you have a lot of company. Lawns with heavy thatch feel spongy as a result of a thick layer of slowly decomposing stems, roots, and debris. A thin (¼- to ½-inch) layer of thatch may actually be beneficial because it buffers soil temperature and increases the lawn's resilience, thereby reducing the compaction of soil that can result from heavy use.

In many areas of the West and South, dethatching is an annual practice. It is a good way to make a seedbed for overseeding dormant Bermuda grass. If you decide to dethatch, do it at the time of year most favorable to the germination and quick establishment of the overseeding grass. Otherwise, weeds will be quick to fill any bare spots.

If thatch is thick enough, it can actually be water repellent. You may think you are applying enough water, but actually the water never reaches the soil. Grass roots that grow in the thatch layer instead of in the soil naturally are less drought resistant, since the moisture in the thatch evaporates much faster. Insects and diseases find thatch a particularly suitable living environment. Since water cannot penetrate, neither can pest-control materials. Finally, the variable thickness and density of thatch means that mowers will inevitably scalp the soil.

Why does thatch accumulate? Lawns composed of spreading-type grasses are the quickest to accumulate thatch. Notorious thatch builders include warm-season grasses such as Bermuda and zoysia grass. In temperate climates, the bent grasses and 'Merion' Kentucky bluegrasses are the worst.

Removing thatch. Soil penetrants, or wetting agents, don't reduce thatch, just its symptoms. They counteract thatch's water repellent character, but the effect is short-lived and definitely not a cure. Bacterial agents that supposedly break down thatch have also proven ineffective.

There are attachments for rotary mowers that may help remove thatch. A thatch hand rake that has knifelike blades instead of the usual hard steel teeth can be used. As a last resort, a sod cutter can remove especially thick thatch if it has built up to impossible levels (but this applies only to grasses that have underground runners). Adjust the sod cutter to cut just above the

soil level instead of below. Fixed, flail, and spring-tooth mowers are also available for dethatching.

According to the University of California, "A vertical power mower is the most effective piece of equipment for thatch control, especially on large lawns where hand removal is impractical. A vertical mower has a series of revolving vertical knives, which cut through the thatch and bring it to the lawn surface so that you can remove it."

Warm-season grasses vary in their recuperative powers after dethatching. To compensate for this, some vertical mowers have adjustable blade spacing. Make only one pass on a slow-to-recover grass if you cannot adjust the blades properly.

If you can adjust the blades, Bermuda and zoysia grass can stand heavy thinning. Space the blades of the mower about an inch apart. Centipede grass should be thinned less severely. Space the blades 1½ to 2 inches apart. Bahia and St. Augustine grass should be thinned the least—space blades 3 inches apart. They also are the slowest to recover and should not be vertical-mowed lower than 1 inch from the ground. For other grasses, adjust the depth of penetration of the blade so that the blade will completely penetrate through the thatch layer and into the soil under the thatch. It is difficult to adjust blades on a vertical mower, and on a rented mower such adjustment is probably impossible. If you cannot properly adjust the blades, make only one pass on a slow-to-recover grass.

Southern grasses respond differently to dethatching by vertical mowing. The Texas Agricultural Extension Service bulletin MP-1180 says:

"Bermuda grass and bluegrass respond favorably to vertical mowing, but care should be taken with nonrhizomatous turfgrasses such as St. Augustine grass. If the St. Augustine grass is not well-rooted, serious thinning can occur as a result of vertical mowing. Equipment blades should be spaced 1½ to 2 inches apart and should not penetrate too deeply into St. Augustine grass turf. Vertical mowing can best be accomplished in early spring, just prior to the initiation of new growth. Fall vertical mowing of Bermuda grass may cause an increase in clover, annual bluegrass, and other winter weeds. Likewise, early summer dethatching of Kentucky bluegrass may increase the infestation of crabgrass."

When to dethatch. The best time to dethatch is just before the lawn's most vigorous growth of the season. For warm-season grasses, dethatch when warm weather begins in late spring. Cool-season grasses grow best in spring and fall. The prime time to dethatch is in the fall; the second-best time is early spring.

Aeration. Roots need air as well as water and nutrients in order to grow. Lawns, especially those that receive heavy use, can develop compacted, air-deficient soil. Compacted soil also restricts the absorption of water as well as air. A footpath worn into a lawn is compaction. To correct the many problems of compacted soil, lawn professionals have developed specialized tools and techniques.

Correcting compacted soil is described by a variety of terms, including "hole punching," "coring," and "aerating." All are based on the same principle: Hollow metal tubes ¼ to ¾ inch in diameter are pushed into the soil, by foot or machine, to a depth of 3 to 4 inches, sometimes deeper. The soil should be *moist* when this is done—not too wet and not too dry. Note the photograph of the aerator on page 59.

Patching

Patching involves removing the weedy, dead, or damaged section of the lawn and reseeding or replacing it with a piece of sod. It is always done with the same variety of grass as the established lawn. Many nurseries normally stock a small amount of sod just for this purpose.

This manual-model aerator works well on small lawns. It helps to correct compacted soil and allows air, water, and fertilizer to reach the roots.

Repairing a damaged section of lawn is very simple with a piece of sod cut to fit.

Dig out the damaged area and loosen the soil underneath. If spilled gasoline or herbicide is the cause of the dead spot, remove several inches of the soil and replace it. Bring the underlying soil to proper grade and cut a piece of sod to fit.

Of course, you can patch with seed, too. The process is the same as with any new seeding. Regardless of the method, remember to keep the patch well watered for several weeks.

Overseeding in Winter

The only disadvantage of the warm-season grasses is that they are dormant in winter. Scientists say that it is caused by the grasses' response to a combination of low temperatures and winter sunlight. Whatever the cause, most owners prefer their lawns to be green all year long. To get this result, lawns can either be painted green (see page 52) or overseeded.

Grasses suitable for overseeding. Annual rye grass is suitable for overseeding dormant Bermuda grass. The seed is inexpensive and widely available. Use it heavily: about 10 pounds per 1,000 square feet.

Turf-type perennial rye grass is excellent for overseeding. The color is a dark green and the growth rate is slower than that of annual rye grass, which means less frequent mowing.

The fine fescues are also good for overseeding. Use them alone or in combination with the rye grasses.

To overseed successfully, it's best to mow closely, dethatch, and (if possible) aerate. These steps help ensure that the seed will make close contact with the soil. Or, alternatively, mow close to the soil with a heavy, reel-type mower. Seed, and finish with a top dressing of peat moss or similar organic material. Don't forget to water frequently until the new grass is firmly rooted into the soil.

The following spring, encourage the growth of the permanent lawn grass at the expense of the winter cover. Just before the late spring flush of growth, vertical mow again, or mow closely and fertilize. This will be enough of a shock to the winter cover and enough of a boost for the main lawn grass to reestablish the warm-season lawn.

A trip to a rental yard produced this photograph of lawn equipment for rent. Clockwise from upper-left corner: **a** A sickle or bar mower is perfect for an empty lot that's overgrown with weeds. **b** A high-wheel rotary mower cuts higher than most rotaries—about 4 inches—and is much easier to maneuver over rough terrain. **c** A sod cutter can be useful in two ways: to strip off old turf, or to remove thatch. **d** Riding mowers are perfect for big, relatively smooth lawns. The type pictured has a rotary mower mounted midsection. **e** As soil becomes compacted, the amount of air space in the soil is reduced. Lawn aerators are used to remove cores of soil. This provides air in the grass-root zone. **f** A vertical mower goes by at least two other names: dethatcher and lawn comb. This piece of equipment cuts perpendicular to the surface of the lawn, slicing deep into thatch. After one pass it's easy to rake up the thatch debris. **g** Two types of edgers are pictured—power and manual. Hand edgers are fine for most trimming needs. Power types are an advantage for large lawns. **h** These two lawn rollers may look similar, but they have completely different uses. The barrel type is filled with water to reduce the fluffiness of freshly rototilled soil, and to provide good contact between seed or sod and the soil. (Use it half or less than half full.) The other roller is used to spread bulky organic topdressing materials such as peat moss, manure, or composted bark. **i** In addition to vertical mowers and riding mowers, most rental yards will have a variety of common lawn mower types. You can rent a heavy reel mower for the one or two times you need to cut the lawn extra-low for thatch removal.

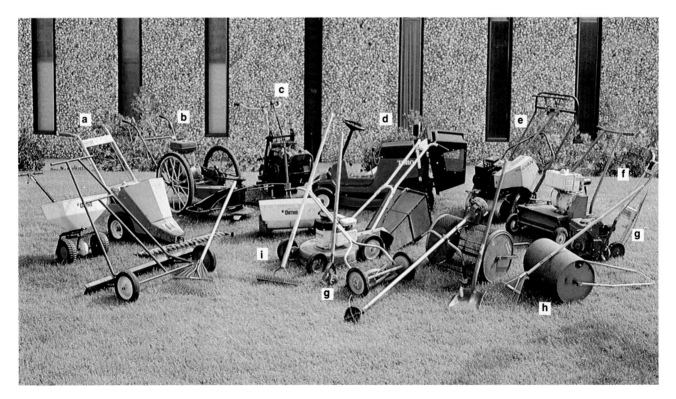

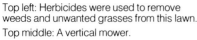

Top left: Herbicides were used to remove weeds and unwanted grasses from this lawn.

Top middle: A vertical mower.

Top right: Grooves in soil left by vertical mower.

Below: A hand rake should be used to remove debris after vertical mowing.

How to Renovate

You can renovate a lawn with seed or with sod. Sod grows faster but is more expensive; seed gives you the full growing experience as well as lower cost.

If your soil has recently been tested, you don't need another soil test. If it hasn't, however, it's worthwhile to know just what type of soil conditions you have. See pages 104–130 for a list of soil-testing agencies.

1. *Remove weeds and undesirable grasses.* Use herbicides such as 2,4-D if your lawn is infested with broadleaf weeds. Always read labels carefully when using herbicides. Be sure materials are safe to use around trees and shrubs. Never use pre-emergent weed controls (unless they are specifically recommended) prior to reseeding. Make sure that any chemical used leaves no residue that may harm young grasses.

   The lawn in the photo at left contained Bermuda grass as well as various broadleaf weeds. The entire lawn was purposely killed with glyphosate.

2. *Vertically cut the existing lawn with a vertical mower.* In order for there to be contact between seed and soil, as much thatch as possible must be removed. Vertical mowers remove thatch like mechanical rakes, slicing vertically into the soil with knives or tines. Notice in the photo the grooves that the vertical mower leaves in the soil. Use the vertical mower on a lawn that's damp, never dry or soaking wet. For best results, go over the lawn twice, in opposite directions.

   Low mowing and vigorous raking with a steel rake may be sufficient to remove thatch from small lawns. However, it is a tedious process and much less efficient than a vertical mower. Dethatching attachments are also available for rotary mowers, but these are still not as thorough as the vertical mower.

3. *Rake up debris.* Thoroughly rake up any loose debris left by vertical mowing. (There can be quite a lot.) This guarantees the all-important contact between seed and soil. Discard the debris if chemicals were used previously. Otherwise, the dead grass and thatch removed by vertical mowing make an excellent addition to the compost pile or a mulch for the vegetable garden.

4. *Aerate the soil.* Aerators remove small cores of soil from the lawn, which allows air, water, and nutrients to pass freely to the roots. Aeration is best done on a damp lawn. Remove the soil cores by raking, or shred with a rotary mower, and use them to level any uneven spots.

The lawn in the photo had several low spots that made mowing difficult. If there are high and low spots in the new seedbed, fill in the low spots with a good topsoil or peat moss and sand, and level with a rake. You may have to flatten high spots with a steel rake. If crushed soil cores left over from aeration are used for leveling, you may need to blend them with additional organic matter.

5. *Add lime; fertilize; sow seed.* If liming is needed, this is the time to do it. It's also the time to apply a complete balanced fertilizer.

   If a good percentage of desirable grasses is present, you may only have to fertilize and water heavily rather than reseed. If you do seed or use vegetative methods to reestablish your lawn, be sure to follow a good watering program.

   Right after planting is a critical time in the reestablishment of healthy turf. You may need to water several times a day in hot weather in order to keep the seed, sprigs, or stolons moist until they become established.

6. *Keep up the maintenance program.* Once your lawn is fully renovated, your job isn't really finished. In order to keep problems from reoccurring and to keep the lawn looking its best, you need to follow an efficient program of fertilization, watering, mowing, and dethatching.

Top left: An aerator.

Top middle: Cores of soil removed by aerator.

Top right: Applying lime, fertilizer, or seed the easy way, with a broadcast spreader.

Below: The end result—a renovated lawn.

Dandelions are now considered a problem
by many lawn growers. This restored
colonial garden in Williamsburg, Virginia,
harkens back to days before chemical
controls existed.

LAWN PROBLEMS

Learning to identify weeds, insects, pests, and diseases is the first step to effective control.

Getting a new lawn off to a good start with proper cultivation and planting can prevent some problems. Still, weeds, insects, and diseases can show up in any lawn, and it's good to know how to identify and treat them as early as possible.

Weeds

Weeds are simply plants that are in the wrong place. The finest lawn grass plant is a weed in the vegetable garden; dandelions are cultivated in some of the best vegetable gardens. Most lawn weeds are easy to eliminate. Mowing at the right height, fertilizing adequately, and following good watering practices will go a long way toward maintaining a weed-free lawn. If your lawn is healthy, it will not be troubled much by weeds. But the following information on weeds may help start you out with a healthy, weed-free lawn.

What *are* weeds? Here are some definitions that may help you understand weed terminology.

Annual. A plant that lives only one year.

Perennial. A plant that lives for many years.

Herbicide. A chemical used to kill plants.

Pre-emergent. A term used to describe herbicides that are effective against germinating seeds—*before* the plant emerges through the soil surface.

Post-emergent. A term used to describe herbicides that are effective *after* a plant breaks through the soil surface.

Contact herbicide. This kills plant parts that are covered by the spray. Only the aboveground parts are affected.

Systemic herbicide. This is absorbed by the plant to circulate inside it, killing all parts, including the roots.

How do weeds get into the lawn? Millions of weed seeds are in most soils. They wait, dormant, until brought to the soil surface or until the lawn grass dies, when light and moisture start them growing. Some seeds can remain alive in the soil for many years. That is why it's helpful to treat for weeds before you plant.

Controlling lawn weeds. It's best to eliminate as many weeds as you can *before* planting your lawn—that way you will have fewer to eliminate later on. One of the best methods of weed elimination is to simply keep the soil bare and moist for three or four months. Then either till, or spray with a contact herbicide every three weeks, as the weed seeds germinate. If you don't want to leave your soil bare for so long, you might try fumigation or a pre-emergent herbicide instead.

Fumigation is another pre-planting weed treatment. It also usually involves time—you must wait at least three weeks between fumigating and planting. (Check the label directions.) Vapam makes a gas that kills many weed seeds and other soil organisms. It works very well, but is both

Bent and fescue grasses give a stately, sculptural look to this residential landscape.

expensive and difficult to apply. Also, it may harm nearby tree or shrub roots if they extend into the treated area. Methyl bromide is another soil fumigant that works well and is fast (two to three days), but it is the most dangerous one to use—so much so that it is not recommended for home lawns, unless used by a professional. In fact, a special permit usually is required. The only other pre-planting weed control method is the use of a pre-emergence herbicide. Some types (for example, Tupersan) will discriminate between the weed and the lawn grass seed.

Weed killers. There are two types of weeds: broadleaf and narrowleaf. Broadleaf weeds have more obvious, showy flowers. Their leaves have a network of small veins originating from a principal point or vein that divides the leaf in half. Dandelion and Carolina geranium are typical broadleaf weeds.

Narrowleaf weeds are undesirable grasses. They usually have hollow stems and long, narrow leaf blades with parallel veins. Dallis grass and crabgrass are common narrowleaf weeds. Other, less common weed types are the sedges. These look similar to grasses but have triangular stems.

These weed types are significantly different, and an herbicide that kills one type may not even affect others. Pay strict attention to label instructions. Many weed killers or pest controls are effective only within certain temperature ranges and stages of plant maturity. Be very careful when applying any chemical products. Don't spray on windy days, and keep children away when you do spray.

Weed killers are either pre-emergent or post-emergent. The post-emergent types are further categorized as either contact or systemic. In the following list chemical names are listed first; trade names follow in parentheses.

Pre-emergent weed killers.
Benefin (Balan). Controls annual grasses in most lawns. Don't use on bent grass. It will prevent all seeds from germinating for up to 8 weeks.

Bensulide (Betasan). Another control for annual grasses and certain broadleaf weeds. Do not reseed for 4 months after application.

DCPA (Dacthal). Especially effective on germinating grasses and seed of certain broadleaf species, including chickweed and purslane. Don't use on new lawns and don't reseed for 10 to 12 weeks after using.

Siduron (Tupersan). Effectively controls weedy grasses such as crabgrass, foxtail, and barnyard grass. It has the unique quality of not interfering with the germination of cool-season grasses such as Kentucky bluegrass.

Post-emergent weed killers.
Cacodylic acid (Contax, Phytar-560). Kills only upon contact. Very effective, although repeat treatments are necessary before it will kill tough perennials such as Bermuda grass. Kills all green-growing leaf tissue; does not move within plants to roots. It is often used to clear lawns of existing growth prior to renovation.

2,4-D. Widely available in many forms and products. It is essentially a growth-influencing hormone that singles out and kills the broadleaf weeds in the lawn without damaging most lawn grasses.

MCPP (Mecoprop). Related and very similar to 2,4-D but safer to use on new lawns or sensitive grasses such as bent grass or St. Augustine grass.

Dicamba (Banvel). Particularly effective against clover, beggarweed, chickweed, knotweed, and red sorrel. It is a hormone-type weed killer like 2,4-D, but it is taken up through roots as well as through leaves. *Be very careful using it around trees and shrubs or in areas where roots underlie the area to be treated.*

Dalapon (Dowpon). Effective against all grasses. Usually used for spot treatment of undesired clumps of Bermuda grass or tall fescue. Used in the West to eliminate Bermuda grass from dichondra lawns. Use carefully— excessive doses can damage dichondra.

DSMA, MSMA, MAMA (available in many combinations under several trade names). Used to control grassy weeds such as crabgrass and foxtail. They kill mostly by foliage activity. Effective against hard-to-kill nutsedges.

Glyphosate (Roundup). Nonselective and systemic, it will kill both grasses and broadleaf weeds. It is the best herbicide for control of Bermuda grass, and is also useful against other perennial grassy weeds.

Commonly Found Weeds
The following weeds are those most likely to crop up in your lawn.

Annual bluegrass or *Poa annua.*
Type: Narrowleaf. Annual.
Season of fast growth: Prefers the cool weather of spring and fall. Tends to die out in summer.
Pre-emergence control: DCPA, bensulide, and benefin. Apply in early August. Several applications may be necessary.
Post-emergence control: None.

Bermuda grass, devil grass.
Type: Narrowleaf. Perennial.
Season of fast growth: Summer. Grows fast when temperatures are high.
Pre-emergence control: None.
Post-emergence control: Dalapon is one of the best. The newer glyphosate will also control Bermuda grass, but it must be used with care since it is a non-specific herbicide.
Comments: Where Bermuda grass is well adapted to the climate, you can deliberately plant it as your lawn, but if you don't you can also discover it growing there as a weed.

Bur clover.
Type: Broadleaf. Perennial.
Season of fast growth: Spring and fall.
Pre-emergence control: None.
Post-emergence control: Use dicamba or mecoprop (MCPP) in spring or fall.

Annual bluegrass, or *Poa annua.*

Bermuda grass, devil grass.

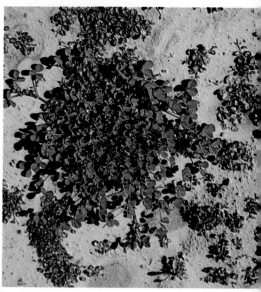
Bur clover.

Above: Crab grass. Above right: Dallis grass.

Dandelion.

Dock.

Crabgrass.

Type: Narrowleaf. Annual.

Season of fast growth: A summer weed. Begins in early spring and grows fast until seed heads form in later summer to fall.

Pre-emergence control: Products containing DCPA, benefin, bensulide, and siduron. Apply weed killer in spring before seedlings appear. Check "Regional Grasses," pages 99–131, and "Lawn Care Calendar," pages 102–103.

Post-emergence control: DSMA, MSMA, MAMA. Apply when weeds are small and much easier to control. One or more repeat treatments at 7- to 10-day intervals may be necessary.

Dallis grass.

Type: Narrowleaf. Perennial.

Season of fast growth: Dallis grass is a summer weed, but it will grow year-round in mild climates.

Pre-emergence control: None.

Post-emergence control: Use DSMA, MAMA, or MSMA every 10 days or as the label directs as a spot spray. Check label before using on St. Augustine, centipede, or bahia grass.

Comments: Thrives in low, wet areas. Try to drain the soil first for control. Bahia grass is a close relative and sometimes infests Bermuda grass lawns, but it can be controlled with a similar treatment.

Dandelion.

Type: Broadleaf. Perennial.

Season of fast growth: Spring and fall.

Pre-emergence control: None.

Post-emergence control: Sprays containing 2,4-D or mecoprop are very effective. Apply during spring or fall when growth is active, but before yellow flowers appear. Spray or treat on a windless day when temperatures are above 60°F. but below 80°F.

Comments: Improved turf varieties resist dandelion invasion well.

Dock.

Type: Broadleaf. Perennial.

Season of fast growth: Spring and fall.

Pre-emergence control: None.

Post-emergence control: Use 2,4-D, mecoprop, or dicamba in midspring or midfall. Spot spray with glyphosate.

English daisy.

Type: Broadleaf. Perennial.

Season of fast growth: Cool weather of spring and fall. Grows all season if protected from drought and high heat.

Pre-emergence control: None.

Post-emergence control: A difficult-to-control weed; 2,4-D and mecoprop will give fair control. Apply in late spring.

Henbit.

Type: Broadleaf. Annual.

Season of fast growth: Spring and fall.

Pre-emergence control: None.

Post-emergence control: Use 2,4-D or mecoprop in fall or spring. Two applications may be required.

Comments: This weed is from the mint family; it has a four-sided stem. It shows up in late winter or early spring.

Knotweed.

Type: Broadleaf. Annual.

Season of fast growth: Early spring through early fall.

Pre-emergence control: None.

Post-emergence control: Mecoprop or dicamba is the favored treatment any time throughout season of most active growth, beginning in early spring.

Comments: A common weed in hard, compacted soils. Thorough aeration may help.

Mallow, cheeseweed.

Type: Broadleaf. Annual.

Season of fast growth: Has a long growing season. Gets started in early spring and survives through fall. A difficult weed to control.

Pre-emergence control: None.

Post-emergence control: Use 2,4-D, mecoprop, or dicamba midspring to late spring.

Mouse-ear chickweed.

Type: Broadleaf. Perennial.

Season of fast growth: Cool weather of spring or fall.

Pre-emergence control: None.

Post-emergence control: Mecoprop. Apply in fall or in early spring when temperatures are between 60° and 70°F.

Above left: English daisy. Above: Henbit.

Knotweed.

Mallow, cheeseweed.

Mouse-ear chickweed.

Oxalis.

Plantain.

Below: Purslane.
Below right: Quackgrass.

Oxalis.
Type: Broadleaf. Perennial.
Season of fast growth: Spring and late summer to fall.
Pre-emergence control: None.
Post-emergence control: Products containing 2,4-D and dicamba may be used. Apply in spring or fall on a day when the wind is still and air temperatures will remain above 60°F. but below 80°F. In many areas, late summer to fall treatment is most effective. Not easy to kill; usually requires several treatments.

Plantain.
Type: Broadleaf. Perennial.
Season of fast growth: A cool-season weed.
Pre-emergence control: None.
Post-emergence control: 2,4-D or mecoprop is very effective if applied in spring or fall before formation of flower spikes. Mature plants can be sprayed with glyphosate.
Comments: Forms rosettes with prominently veined leaves.

Purslane.
Type: Broadleaf. Annual.
Season of fast growth: Summer.
Pre-emergence control: DCPA applied early spring to midspring.
Post-emergence control: Use 2,4-D midsummer to late summer.

Quackgrass.
Type: Narrowleaf. Perennial.
Season of fast growth: Spring and fall.
Pre-emergence control: None.
Post-emergence control: No selective control. Spot-treat with dalapon or glyphosate.
Comments: Underground stems are vigorous; even digging out by hand is rarely successful.

Spotted spurge.
Type: Broadleaf. Annual.
Season of fast growth: Most aggressive growth is from late spring through early fall. A summer weed.
Pre-emergence control: Use DCPA or siduron in early spring before germination, then again in midsummer.

Post-emergence control: Products containing 2,4-D and dicamba may be used.

Comments: Possible minor damage to turf grasses from summer treatments.

Tall fescue.

Type: Narrowleaf. Perennial.

Season of fast growth: A perennial, but it grows fastest in spring and fall.

Pre-emergence control: None.

Post-emergence control: Spot-treat only. Use either repeated sprays with a contact herbicide or dalapon. Glyphosate applied any time the weed is actively growing will also give good control.

Comments: Frequently confused with crabgrass. Can be dug out by hand.

Thistle.

Type: Broadleaf. Perennial.

Season of fast growth: Strongest growth occurs during the cool weather of fall and spring.

Pre-emergence control: None.

Post-emergence control: 2,4-D is effective. Spray in fall. Two applications may be necessary. Spot treatment with glyphosate is another approach.

Comments: There are several different types, commonly found in northern regions. Leaf forms frequently vary. Roots may spread underground horizontally.

Veronica, speedwell.

Type: Broadleaf. Annual.

Season of fast growth: Spring and fall.

Pre-emergence control: None.

Post-emergence control: 2,4-D is effective. Spray in fall. Two applications may be necessary.

Comments: Dense patches of veronica become established below mowing height. A tough weed to kill. Several slightly varying species can be found. Flowers are light blue, and seed pods are heart-shaped.

White clover.

Type: Broadleaf. Perennial.

Season of fast growth: Cool seasons of fall and spring. Profuse flowering in early summer.

Pre-emergence control: None.

Spotted spurge.

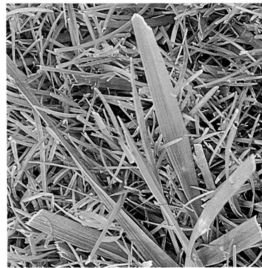

Tall fescue.

Below left: Veronica, speedwell.
Below: Thistle.

White clover.

Wild onion, wild garlic.

Post-emergence control: Mecoprop or dicamba in spring or fall. Choose a warm, windless day.

Wild onion, wild garlic.
Type: Broadleaf. Perennial.
Season of fast growth: Spring to midsummer.
Pre-emergence control: None.
Post-emergence control: 2,4-D or dicamba. May need several treatments. Herbicide-impregnated bars are more effective. Best used in late fall when weeds are still small; once mature, they are difficult to control.
Comments: Wild onion differs from wild garlic in two ways: (1) wild onions do not produce the underground bulbs common to wild garlic, and (2) garlic has a hollow leaf, onion does not.

Dichondra

To control weeds in dichondra lawns, use dalapon. It gets rid of Bermuda grass, young stages of annual bluegrass, and crabgrass. Follow these steps:

1. Apply dalapon to mature dichondra, never to newly seeded or newly transplanted areas.
2. If the lawn has not been fertilized, apply fertilizer and water thoroughly five to seven days before applying weed killer.
3. Apply in spring and summer when weed grasses are young and green.
4. Apply to leaf portions of weed grasses, using a fine mist spray. Use a minimum of water—just enough to wet foliage, like fog or dew.
5. Avoid soaking the soil—watering can cause unsatisfactory results. Instead, use a sprayer with an insecticide nozzle to produce a fine mist.

Insects and Pests

Could insects be the cause of that patch of dead grass next to the driveway, or that dead spot under the oak tree? The most difficult and important part of any lawn problem is diagnosing the cause.

A typical lawn contains hundreds of kinds of insects and similar creatures. Some are so tiny that they're hardly visible; others are quite large. Most do little damage to the lawn itself. Other insects (e.g., fleas and ticks) are troublesome to people but not lawns. Only a few serious lawn pests (e.g., sod webworm, the grubs of various beetles, and chinch bugs) can destroy a lawn within a short time, and then only if conditions are right for their development.

How can you tell if the problem is caused by insects or a disease (or something else, such as gasoline or a dog)? And if it is caused by insects, how can the damage be stopped?

Discovering the cause of damage. The easiest, most reliable way to find out what's damaging your lawn is to look at it closely. Get down on your hands and knees; chances are you will be able to see the pest in action. Some appear only at night, or only in a shady spot, or only in a sunny corner. Specific habits and characteristics of the most common lawn pests are noted on the following pages.

Just because you may discover insects in your lawn does not necessarily mean you have to spray. If there is a problem, try to link the symptom to the pest. For example, look for the green, pelletlike droppings left by the sod webworm. Remember, too, that damage is hardly visible until the pest population has built up to a considerable extent.

Many insects are troublesome only to certain kinds of grass. For instance, chinch bugs are by far most damaging to St. Augustine grass. Wireworms rarely attack any grasses other than bahia or centipede. As much as possible, choose a grass that's not bothered by insects, or at least doesn't have a number-one enemy.

If your lawn is healthy and well-maintained, it will be much less subject to serious insect damage. It is also more able to recover quickly if problems do occur.

Identifying the culprit. Lawn-damaging insects can be conveniently grouped according to where they are most active (above or below the ground) and the type of damage they do. Control methods are different for each group.

Live above the soil surface and suck plant juices—chinch bugs, leafhoppers, spider mites, and similar pests.
To control:

1. Mow the lawn.
2. Remove clippings.
3. Water heavily.
4. Wait until grass blades are dry, then apply insecticide according to label directions. Do not water for two days.

Live at the soil surface and feed on leaves—sod webworms, cutworms, army-worms, and fiery skipper larvae.
To control:

1. Mow the lawn.
2. Remove clippings.
3. Water heavily.
4. Wait until grass blades are dry, then apply insecticide according to label directions. Best applied in late afternoon when insects are active.
5. Do not water for two days.
6. Fertilize to aid in recovery of the lawn, if the season is appropriate.

Live below the soil surface and feed on roots—grubs, wireworms, ground pearls.
To control:

1. Mow the lawn.
2. Remove clippings.
3. Apply recommended insecticide according to label directions. Water heavily immediately after spraying, but not so much that the insecticide washes away.
4. Fertilize to aid in recovery of the lawn if the season is appropriate.

Chemical control. Insecticides are not the only answer to lawn-pest problems. But if and when you decide they are necessary, first learn which is which and what does what. Many forms of insecticides are available. If used properly, they are relatively harmless.

Here are some brief descriptions of insecticides commonly used by homeowners to control lawn pests. For the sake of simplification, we have listed the most frequently used trade or chemical name.

Aspon. This is a good control for chinch bugs and sod webworm. It works fast and is effective up to two months. Water the lawn before spraying, then withhold water for two or three days to permit the chemical to do its job. Keep off the lawn until the chemical has been washed into the soil.

Baygon. Similar to Sevin (see below). Frequently used in baits. Controls chinch bugs, earwigs, leafhoppers.

Carbaryl. Also known as Sevin. This chemical has been around a long time and is available in a wide variety of forms from many manufacturers. It has several uses for home-lawn insect control.

Chlorpyrifos. This is more commonly known by its trade name, Dursban. It remains effective for four to six weeks.

Diazinon. Like carbaryl, this is widely available in many forms. One of

Hose-End Sprayer

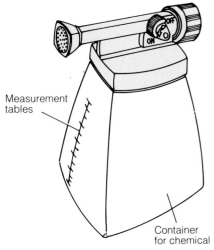

Measurement tables

Container for chemical

Some models have adjustable nozzles for fine or directional spray.

Compression Sprayers

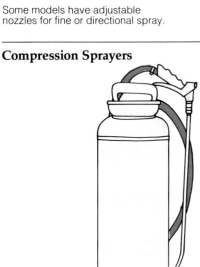

Sprayers are made of metal or plastic and come in sizes from 1 to 4 gallons.

the best for grub control. Protects against several lawn pests up to four to six weeks.

Mesurol. This is a very effective killer of slugs and snails. Lightly water the area before spreading the bait.

Metaldehyde. Look for this ingredient in slug and snail baits. Use it where snails hide, such as around ground covers. Both snails and slugs hide in cool, moist areas during the day and come out at night. They especially like new lawns and dichondra.

Methoxyclor. A common ingredient in many spray mixes. Generally, it is very useful and has about a two-month residual.

Milky spore disease. (Biological control.) This is a natural disease of Japanese beetle grubs. It has no effect on other kinds of grubs or any other insects. It is established in soils over a period of years where Japanese beetles are present. It is slow to establish and control is not total, but it will keep the beetles in check.

Bacillus thuringensis. (Biological control.) Similar to milky spore disease in that it is very specific. It will kill only caterpillars (butterfly and moth larvae). Very useful in many situations, although it is not widely used on lawns.

Of course, the best information on these and other pest control products is on the product label. Read the label in the nursery or garden shop before buying and then again, carefully, before using.

Cautions. Read the label every time you spray or dust, and pay attention to cautions and warnings. Mix sprays on a solid, level surface to lessen spillage. Avoid spilling pesticides on the skin or clothing; wash exposed areas thoroughly with soap and water. Do not eat or smoke while spraying. Keep all chemicals out of reach of children—store them in a locked cabinet or high on a shelf. Set aside a special set of mixing tools, measuring spoons, and graduated measuring cups to use only for measuring and mixing sprays. Be sure to keep all chemicals in their original, labeled containers. Store lawn fertilizers combined with weed killers separately from garden fertilizers to prevent accidental misuse.

Backpack Pump Sprayer

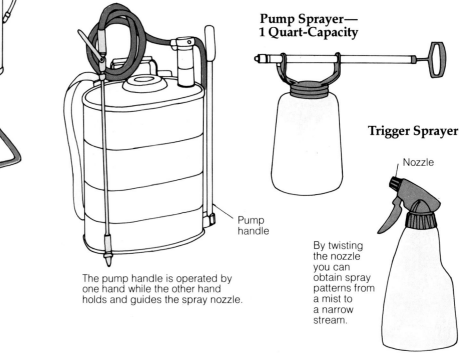

Pump Sprayer— 1 Quart-Capacity

Trigger Sprayer

Nozzle

Pump handle

The pump handle is operated by one hand while the other hand holds and guides the spray nozzle.

By twisting the nozzle you can obtain spray patterns from a mist to a narrow stream.

Armyworms, Cutworms, and Fiery Skipper

Symptoms: These three moth larvae chew off the grass blades above the soil surface. The damage they cause is very similar to sod webworm. Armyworms cause round, bare areas in lawns. If there are many of them, the grass will be eaten to the soil level. Cutworms also feed on the grass leaves, cutting them off near the surface. Fiery skippers are usually a minor problem, but can be serious pests of bent grass and Bermuda grass lawns, especially hybrid Bermuda. They can also be a problem on bluegrass lawns in some areas.

Descriptions: Skippers are easy to distinguish from other pests. They're about an inch long and brownish yellow, with very distinct dark brown heads and thin necks. Cutworms are plump, smooth, and almost always curled when you find them. They're usually brown to nearly black, but some are spotted and some are striped. Armyworms are yellowish white and have an upsidedown "Y" on their head.

Control: Products that contain diazinon, Dursban, or Sevin are all useful.

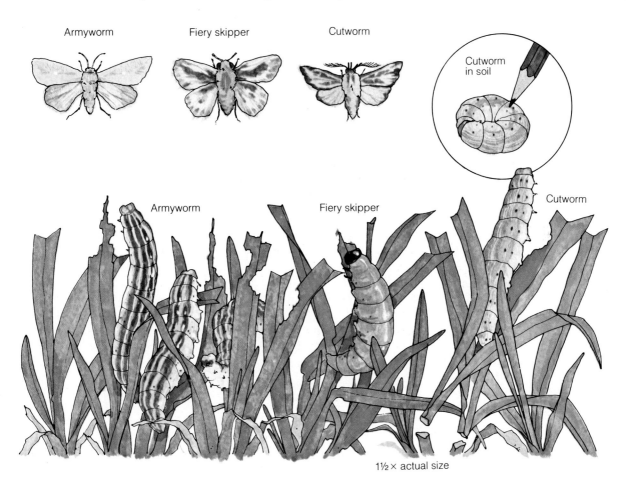

Armyworm   Fiery skipper   Cutworm

Cutworm in soil

Armyworm   Fiery skipper   Cutworm

1½ × actual size

50× actual size

Clover Mite

Symptom: You may first become aware of these pests when they move inside your house looking for a warm place to spend winter. They live primarily on clover and similar plants in the lawn.

Description: Tiny green to red-brown spiders that live and feed on the undersurface of grass blades. Sometimes their webbing is visible.

Control: Usually kept in check by other insects, predators or insecticide treatments for other pests. If treatment is necessary, use diazinon or Kelthane, a miticide, as the label directs.

Sod Webworm

Symptom: In late spring, look for small dead patches 1 to 2 inches in diameter in the healthy growing grass. By midsummer, these may be large dead patches. The most severe damage usually occurs in July and August. Sod webworms chew grass blades off just above the thatch line and pull the blades into a silken tunnel to eat them. Eventually, the small patches will coalesce, forming large, irregular dead patches.

Description: The adult form of the webworm is a buff-colored moth with a wing span of about 1 inch. They fly in a jerky, zigzag pattern, just a few feet above the lawn. The moths don't damage the lawn but they drop eggs into the grass that, upon hatching, develop into very hungry caterpillars.

Adult as seen at rest.

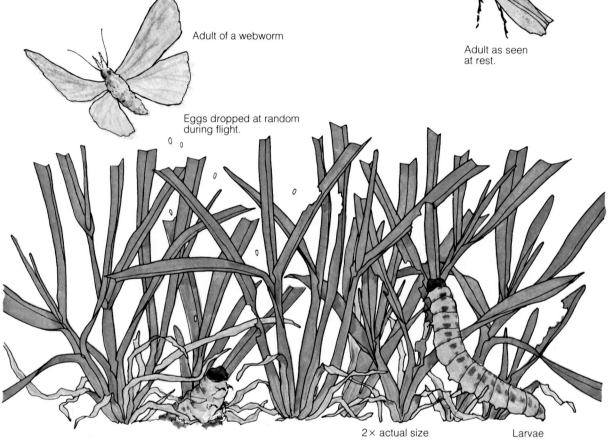

Adult of a webworm

Eggs dropped at random during flight.

2× actual size   Larvae

Sod webworms feed at night. Look for them by carefully breaking apart the damaged areas with your fingers. Other evidence is their green-tan excrement, little pellets about the size of a pin head. Also, flocks of birds feeding on the lawn may indicate large populations of sod webworm. When sod webworms are suspected, they can be forced to the surface of the grass by drenching 1 square foot area with 1 gallon of soapy water.

(Use ¼ cup of laundry or household detergent per gallon.)

Control: Aspon, diazinon, Dursban, Sevin, Baygon.

Japanese beetle

Pupa **Eggs**

Young grubs feeding in soil. Apply insecticide at this stage, usually late July.

Maturing grubs move deeper into soil during winter.

Adult grubs return to surface in spring to feed and pupate.

1½ × actual size

Checking for grubs.

Grubs

Symptoms: Distinct brown patches, usually irregular in shape. Since the grubs eat grass roots, the dead grass pulls loose easily. If the dead patch of grass rolls back easily like a section of carpet, you can be pretty sure it is caused by belowground grubs. They are most damaging in late spring or early fall. If you see more than two C-shaped grubs in a square-foot area, the patch should be treated. As with sod webworm, another sign of grubs is unusual numbers of birds or moles around the lawn. They know the grubs are there and are looking to make a dinner of them.

Description: Grubs are the larvae of many kinds of beetles. They are whitish or grayish in color, with brown heads and dark hind parts. The adult beetles appear in late spring or summer and feed on shade trees or garden shrubs.

Control: If your lawn is already infested with grubs, keep in mind that they are insulated by a layer of grass leaves and soil. The insecticide must get to this depth in the soil by repeated heavy waterings. Use products that contain diazinon or Dursban.

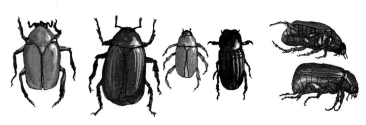

June beetle May beetle Masked chafer *Ataenius spretulus* European chafer (top) *Phyllophaga crinita*

Actual size

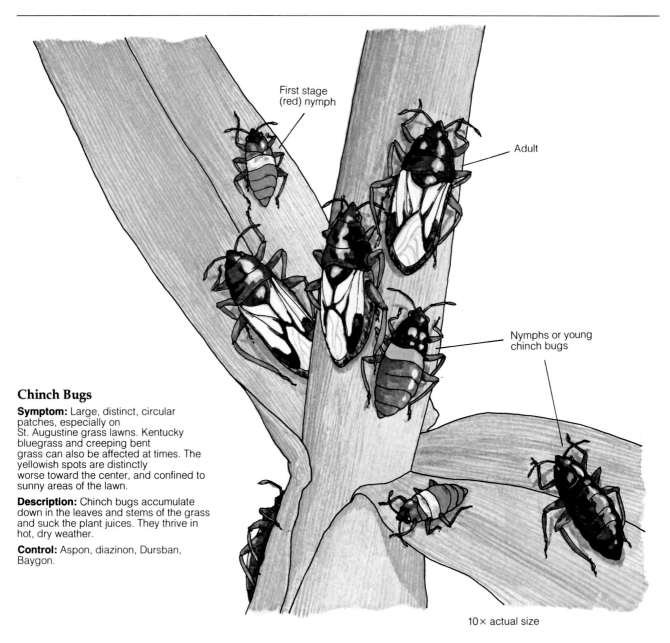

First stage
(red) nymph

Adult

Nymphs or young
chinch bugs

Chinch Bugs

Symptom: Large, distinct, circular patches, especially on St. Augustine grass lawns. Kentucky bluegrass and creeping bent grass can also be affected at times. The yellowish spots are distinctly worse toward the center, and confined to sunny areas of the lawn.

Description: Chinch bugs accumulate down in the leaves and stems of the grass and suck the plant juices. They thrive in hot, dry weather.

Control: Aspon, diazinon, Dursban, Baygon.

10× actual size

To check for chinch bugs, work a bottomless metal can into the affected area and fill with warm water. Most will not be in dead or green areas, but where the grass is just beginning to turn yellow. When abundant, they will float to the surface within a few minutes.

2½ × actual size

Billbug

Symptom: A small and distinct circular pattern becomes yellowish or brown. Adult billbugs feed on stems, while grubs of billbugs feed on roots. Most damage is caused in late summer. Grass stems within the dead areas lift easily out of the soil.

Description: Different species of billbugs prefer different types of grass. In the southernmost regions, Bermuda and zoysia grass are commonly attacked, while in the northern regions, Kentucky bluegrass is preferred.

Control: Use an insecticide such as diazinon or Baygon in midsummer if you find more than one billbug grub per square foot.

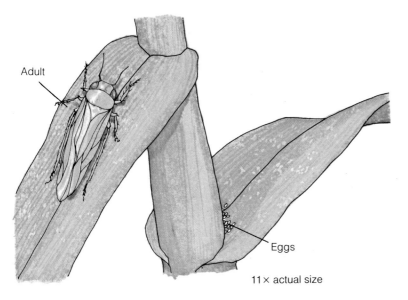

11 × actual size

Leafhopper

Symptom: These tiny insects are nearly always present to some degree on the surface of lawns. When severe, they can wipe out a newly seeded lawn and cause a mature lawn to look bleached and unhealthy.

Description: They are tiny, even when full grown. Their color is usually green, but may be yellow or grey. If your lawn has a lot of them, each step through the grass will kick a swarm.

Control: Insecticide treatments are usually not necessary, they may be more of a nuisance to you than to the lawn. Diazinon will effectively control them if necessary.

Actual size

Slugs and Snails

Symptoms: Their silvery trails in the morning are a giveaway. Be on the lookout for them if you have a border of ivy or similar ground cover. In many cases, they'll eat away a strip of grass or dichondra bordering such a ground cover.

Description: These are pretty well-known creatures. They hide in cool and shady spots during the day and feed at night.

Control: Use baits containing metaldehyde or mesurol.

2½ × actual size

Mole Cricket

Symptom: Irregular streaks of brown and wilted grass. Most common on bahia grass, Bermuda, St. Augustine and sometimes centipede and zoysia grass. The dead grass will pull up easily. You can find the tunnels with your fingers.

Description: Mole crickets are about 1½ to 2 inches long and brown or greyish brown. They look similar to a common cricket, except their head is large and notable. Their front legs, which they use for digging, are especially large. They feed on the turf roots and, by tunneling, cause nearby roots to dry out.

Control: Baits for mole cricket containing Baygon are most common. Apply the bait the evening before a warm night and water the lawn first. Or use diazinon, in spring, about a week after seeing the first signs of mole cricket activity.

Nuisance Pests

1½ ×

Brown dog tick
This pest is most common to lawns that are near wooded areas. Ticks will be most active in spring and early summer. *Don't* try to get them off with a hot match. Diazinon, Dursban or Sevin are good lawn sprays.

2½ ×

Ants
Ants are a problem in lawns because of the nest mounds they make, not because they feed directly on, or otherwise harm the grass. Diazinon granules, Dursban, or diazinon sprays will control them for up to two months.

5 ×

Gnats
A type of tiny fly, gnats are similar to mosquitos in many ways; most need water to lay eggs. They can be annoying when they swarm around the lawn. The best treatment is a fogging spray.

1½ ×

Earwigs
These hard, dark reddish brown insects hide in dark places during the day. Their pincers aren't nearly as dangerous as they look; they're only useful against other earwigs. Baits containing Baygon, scattered in the evening, are very effective, or spray with diazinon, Dursban, or Sevin.

50 ×

Chiggers
Chiggers are not insects. They are actually tiny spiders or mites. Their eggs are laid in the soil. After hatching, the larvae crawl up onto the grass or weeds waiting for an animal to brush by. Repellents containing diethyltoluamide are effective as well as sprays of diazinon.

4 ×

Fleas
These are certainly well-known pests to dog or cat owners. They may fall off a pet and wait in the lawn for another host animal. The insecticides diazinon, malathion, and Sevin are good controls.

Occasional Pests

Some of the insects and other pests included in this group can, in specific situations, cause extensive damage. But they are not nearly so common as sod webworm, grubs, and chinch bugs. Several are problems only in relatively confined regions. Others, such as wireworms, sowbugs, pillbugs, millipedes, and centipedes are widespread but rarely cause serious damage.

3× actual size

Actual size

Aphids
Frequently found in lawns. Recently, their damage has been on the increase. In areas of heavy infestation, treat with diazinon.

Pearl scale
A serious problem of hybrid Bermuda grass lawns in the Southwest. Starting in mid-May, spot-treat with diazinon every 7 to 14 days through the month of June.

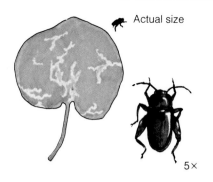

Actual size

5×

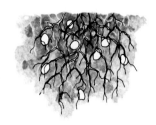

Dichondra flea beetle

These tiny beetles look harmless enough, but they can quickly decimate a dichondra lawn. They're easily visible against white shoes or a piece of paper. In southern California, they first appear as early as April. Be ready for them by the first of June elsewhere. Control with diazinon, Dursban.

Ground pearl

These tiny "pearls" are attached to the roots of Bermuda grass and centipede grass. About ⅛ inch in diameter, they damage the grass by feeding on the roots. No chemical control is presently used.

Periodical cicada

These are large insects that live deep in the soil for several years. When they leave the ground, a large number of holes are made. The adults damage nearby shrubs and trees rather than the lawn.

1⅓× actual size

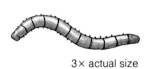

3× actual size

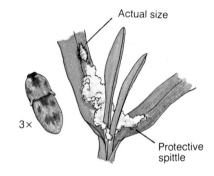

Actual size

3×

Protective spittle

Sowbugs and pillbugs

These bugs are very similar in appearance and behavior, but pillbugs are the ones that can roll themselves into a ball. Usually they eat decaying organic matter. They are easily controlled by removing their cool, moist hiding places, such as leaves and organic debris.

Wireworms

These larva of click beetles feed on lawn roots. They're brown, about 1 inch long. Only when present in excessive numbers will they damage lawns. Look for them as you would for grubs—in the root zone of the dead sections of grass. Control with diazinon.

Spittlebug

They're rarely responsible for much damage but are a common inhabitant of lawns. They hide under a material that looks just like spittle (hence the name). If necessary, they can be controlled by either Sevin or diazinon.

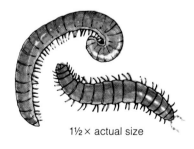

1½× actual size

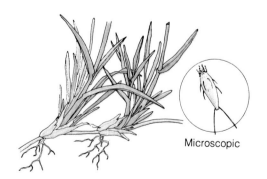

Microscopic

Millipedes and centipedes

Rarely damaging to lawns, these segmented wormlike creatures are often found in or near them. Like sowbugs, they like cool, moist hiding spots. If there are too many in your yards, a good clean-up of trash or wood will control them.

Bermuda mite

These are microscopic pests known best by the damage they cause. Bermuda grass lawns attacked have shortened space between leaves. These infested areas become clumps that interrupt the lawn's texture and gradually yellow and die. You can sometimes see them by shaking infested grass over white paper. Thatch removal is helpful in controlling this problem. Diazinon can also be used.

Lawn Diseases

It is often difficult to diagnose lawn problems, especially if considerable time has elapsed between the cause of the damage and the diagnosis. Often the problem will be attributed to an insect or disease, when actually the climate, environmental conditions, or cultural practices are the cause. Mowing height, competition from tree roots, chlorosis, soil compaction, improper watering, and herbicide damage are some of the many factors that either cause the symptoms or are related to the development of the disease.

In the South chinch bugs are the most damaging insect pest. Sod webworms, armyworms, and mole crickets may also damage St. Augustine grass. See pages 71–77.

Brown patch and grey leaf spot are the two most serious diseases. Occasionally, dollar spot, *Helminthosporium* leaf spot, and rust are problems. Nematodes may be a problem if growth is poor and other treatments, such as fertilizing, bring no response. See pages 80–85.

Taking proper care of your lawn. Proper maintenance will reduce lawn problems, especially when it comes to lawn disease. Most of the diseases that attack typical home lawns are due to improper management. Thatch is one of the most common causes of disease in the home lawn. Thatch restricts the movement of air, water, and fertilizers into the soil, and generally weakens the lawn, therefore making it much more disease prone.

When and how much you fertilize also affects disease development. An overfertilized or underfertilized lawn is more susceptible to disease. Timing also is critical. For example, if you give a cool-season lawn heavy doses of growth-stimulating fertilizer in late spring and summer (periods of naturally slow growth), it becomes increasingly susceptible to leaf spot and *Fusarium* blight. It's important to follow a fertilizer program that conforms to the growth cycle of your particular lawn grass. The lawn experts say, "*Let* the grass grow, don't *make* it grow."

Watering practices can also affect disease susceptibility. Lawns that are watered deeply but infrequently usually have fewer disease problems. Constantly wet grass in poorly drained soil promotes disease.

Lawn diseases are easier to prevent than to cure. Follow these steps to prevent diseases from becoming established in your lawn:

1. Plant a grass type and variety that is adapted to your climate.
2. Mow at the proper height.
3. Fertilize at recommended rates and on a schedule that fits the growth cycle of your cool- or warm-season grass.
4. Water deeply and infrequently, and only when the lawn needs it.

When a serious disease does attack your lawn despite your best efforts, you need to use a chemical control.

Fungicides. Turf diseases are far more prevalent in moist areas than in dry ones. It takes moisture to activate fungus spores.

As experts at the University of Arizona say: "We who live in deserts have built-in disease protection, for nearly all diseases of grasses are fungal types, which must have wet, humid conditions to infect and spread. During most of the year then, the dryness of our desert weather minimizes lawn diseases except for brief rain periods or irrigating improperly. Warm wet grass, for more than a few hours at a time, is an incubator of fungus disease infestations. The inclination of many to sprinkle lawns too often or during the nights is asking for it, particularly during our 'monsoon' when the wetness is even more prolonged by rains and humid air."

Make a distinction between prevention and cure in fungicide action. Disease damage can't be cured. However, if your lawn is already afflicted, don't despair. You can choose from over a dozen chemicals that are commonly sprayed on lawns by homeowners to prevent and control disease. These chemicals are categorized as either "systemic" or "nonsystemic."

Because systemic fungicides work from inside the plant, they are usually the most effective. However, they are very specific and will control only certain diseases.

Nonsystemic fungicides work from outside the plant. They are best used before a disease starts. For example, if you know from past experience that a certain disease will attack your lawn in two weeks or so, start spraying the appropriate fungicide now. This will prevent the disease.

Look at the chart for a breakdown on the uses of the various fungicides. Use the succeeding pages to help identify and control any diseases that occur in your lawn. For the sake of simplification, chemical names rather than trade names are used to describe controls in the disease descriptions.

Treating the cause. If a trouble spot develops, first find the cause. Then treat *it* rather than the symptom. For example:

Dry spot. A dry spot that appears repeatedly in the lawn may be due to a lack of organic matter or improper grading. Also, if the soil above bedrock is insufficiently deep, or if there is buried concrete or debris, drying will occur.

Moss. If you have a problem with moss, there are temporary cures; but for a permanent solution, look for the cause. Moss is usually the result of improper drainage and too much shade, not of soil acidity. Other contributing factors include poor air-circulation and insufficient light, which slow the evaporation of water from the soil.

You can use chemical controls—powdered copper sulfate at 3 tablespoons per 1,000 square feet. Also, fertilizers containing ferrous and ferric ammonium sulfate will control moss. However, this amount of ammonium sulfate may furnish too much nitrogen for cool-season grasses if it is applied in late spring.

Common Fungicides

Common Name/ Trade Name	Uses
anilazine/ **Dyrene**	Dollar spot and melting out, rust, snow mold. Nonsystemic.
benomyl/ **Benlate Tersan 1991 Cleary 3336**	Brown patch, dollar spot, *Fusarium* patch, *Fusarium* blight, powdery mildew, and stripe smut. Has systemic action.
captan/ **Orthocide**	Melting out, damping off, and stripe smut. Nonsystemic, contact only.
chlorothalonil/ **Daconil 2787 Bravo**	Brown patch, dollar spot, *Fusarium* patch, melting out, and red thread. Nonsystemic fungicide.
chloroneb/ **Tersan SP Demosan**	*Pythium* blight, grey snow mold, Nonsystemic.
cycloheximide/ **Acti-dione**	Brown patch, dollar spot, leaf spot, melting out, powdery mildew, snow mold. Nonsystemic.
diazoben/**Dexon**	Damping off, *pythium* (grease spot). Nonsystemic.
ethazol/**Koban Truban**	*Pythium*. Nonsystemic.
folpet/**Phaltan**	Melting out. Nonsystemic, contact only.
mancozeb/ **Dithane M-45 Fore**	Red thread, rust, and melting out. Nonsystemic.
maneb/**Dithane M-22**	Rust. Nonsystemic.
oxycarboxin/ **Plantvax**	Rust. Nonsystemic.
PCNB/**Terraclor**	Brown patch. Melting out. Slight systemic activity.
thiabendazole/ **Mertect 140F.**	Brown patch, dollar spot, *Fusarium* patch, snow mold. Nonsystemic.
thiophanate methyl/**Topsin Spot Clean Fungo-50**	Brownpatch, dollar spot, *Fusarium* blight, *Fusarium* patch, stripe smut. Systemic.
thiram/ **Tersan 75**	Should be combined with other fungicide.

Disease Trouble-shooting

Looking closely	Cause
Fungus growth can be seen on the blade:	
Black, long streaks of powdery spores	**Stripe smut**
White and powdery	**Powdery mildew**
Red or orange, like a powder	**Rust**
Grey and easily rubbed off	**Slime mold**
Visible spots on leaves, actual fungus is not visible (just the results of fungus infection):	
Reddish brown to blue-black and circular or oval	**Leaf spot (melting out)**
Straw-colored bands with a reddish brown border	**Dollar spot**

Looking at the whole lawn	Cause
The diseased area is circular:	
Present in late winter or early spring	**Snow mold**
Present in spring, summer, or fall	
1 inch to 4 feet or more in diameter	
Mushrooms just inside or outside the circle	**Fairy ring**
No mushrooms	**Brown patch**
1 to 8 inches in diameter	
Small, with many throughout the lawn	**Dollar spot**
Only in full sun and with green centers (frog-eye)	***Fusarium* blight**
In low areas and often in streaks	**Pythium**
Yellow in center	
Grass at edge more vigorous than surrounding lawn	**Dog urine**
The dieased area is irregular in shape:	
New lawn seedlings wilt and die	**Damping-off**
Mature lawn affected, spots on leaves	**Melting-out (leaf spot)**
Mature lawn affected, thin, no spots on leaves	**Nematodes**

Note: Due to space limitations, not all lawn diseases will be in this chart; this is only a helpful guide.

Mushrooms. After prolonged periods of wet weather, mushrooms may come up in the lawn. This often indicates the presence of construction debris or old tree roots and stumps that are decaying below the surface. It may be years after construction before the mushrooms appear. There is no effective chemical control for these fungi, and they cause no damage to the turf. However, if you feel they are unsightly or poisonous, remove them with the lawn mower or a bamboo rake.

Moles. A single mole can range over several acres, digging several thousand feet of tunnels. The structure of the surface tunnels and the temporary way in which they are used makes mole control difficult. Poisonous gases introduced into these tunnels to kill the moles are ineffective because they will quickly diffuse through the thin sod covering overhead. Since moles are primarily insectivorous, it is difficult to poison them. The most practical control is to trap the animal (which can be very time-consuming) or to remove their food supply so that they migrate elsewhere. Until their primary food source of grubs and earthworms is eliminated, moles will continue to move in to feed. If you have moles, the best solution is to treat for grubs.

Mushrooms in the soil usually means decaying debris below the soil surface. See text at right for treatment information.

Melting Out, Leaf Spot

April to November

Description: Melting out refers to a number of leaf spot diseases favoring Kentucky bluegrass, fescue, and Bermuda grass. The most obvious sympton of the disease is elongated circular spots on the leaves. These spots have a brown or straw-colored center with black to purplish borders.

Favorable climatic conditions: Cool, (50° to 70°F.) moist conditions are most favorable; first appears in the shade. Most severe in closely mowed lawns.

Susceptible grasses: 'Park' and 'Delta' Kentucky bluegrass are very susceptible.

Resistant varieties: 'Merion' and 'Adelphi' Kentucky bluegrass. Many of the newer improved bluegrass varieties also have good resistance.

Cultural control: Reduce shade. Improve aeration and water drainage. Mow at recommended height.

Chemical control: Anilazine, captan, chlorothalonil, cycloheximide, folpet, and mancozeb.

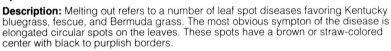

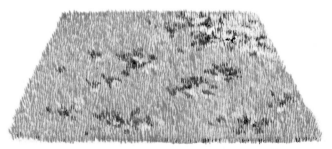

Corticium Red Thread, Pink Patch

September to November

Description: This disease is most common to the Pacific Northwest, although it occasionally occurs in the northeast. The first symptoms are very small patches of dead grass. Under wet conditions, the fungus is visible as bright pink threads.

Favorable climatic conditions: Besides moist air, low levels of nitrogen favor the disease's development. When grass growth slows way down the disease becomes most prevalent.

Susceptible grasses: Red fescue, rye grass, Kentucky bluegrass, and sometimes bent grass.

Tolerant grasses: Many improved Kentucky bluegrass varieties.

Cultural control: Increased nitrogen.

Chemical control: Chlorothalonil, mancozeb.

Ophiobolus Patch

May to June, August to September

Description: Found only in the cool, moist, coastal regions of the Pacific Northwest. It first appears as small brown spots that will enlarge quickly with a favorable climate.

Favorable climatic conditions: Acid soils and maritime climate.

Susceptible grasses: Bent grass is most commonly damaged, but Kentucky bluegrass and rye grass may also be bothered.

Resistant grasses: Fescues.

Cultural control: Best cultural control has been found with slightly acid soil. Apply 2 pounds of sulphur per 1,000 square feet when problem becomes severe.

Chemical control: Many recommend an acid-forming fertilizer, such as ammonium sulphate.

Fusarium Patch

September to May

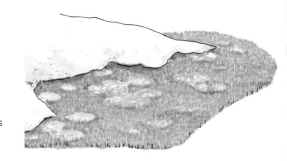

Description: This disease is called pink snow mold if it develops under snow or at the margins of a melting snow bank. It causes circular patches 1 to 8 inches in diameter. Tiny white or pink masses are sometimes seen on dead leaves. Fungal threads, also white or pink, can be seen in early morning.

Favorable climatic conditions: Cool (40° to 60°F.) temperatures and moisture.

Susceptible grasses: Rye grass, fescue, zoysia grass, and colonial and creeping bent grass.

Resistant grasses: Improved Kentucky bluegrass.

Cultural control: Reduce shade, if any. Improve soil aeration and drainage. Avoid excess nitrogen fertilization in the fall.

Chemical control: Benomyl, chlorothalonil, mancozeb, thiabendazole.

Fusarium Blight

May to October

Description: The disease begins as scattered light green patches ½ to 8 inches in diameter, that turn dull tan to reddish-brown. The most diagnostic of these larger diseased patches in the lawn is the "frog-eye" pattern. This is an apparently healthy green patch of grass partially or completely surrounded by a ring of dead grass.

Favorable climatic conditions: Hot, dry, and windy weather is especially favorable. It occurs most commonly in areas that have suffered water stress.

Susceptible grasses: Of the Kentucky bluegrasses, 'Arboretum', 'Fylking', 'Park', and 'Dennstar'.

Resistant varieties: 'Glade', 'Parade', 'Sydsport', 'Columbia', 'Adelphi', and Kentucky bluegrass.

Cultural control: Avoid heavy fertilization and follow correct watering and mowing practices. Light frequent watering will help during drought.

Chemical control: Benomyl and thiophanate have been most useful but control is difficult. Water the night before and thoroughly drench fungicide into turf.

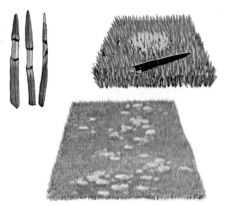

Dollar Spot

May to November

Description: A common fungus disease that attacks several different types of grass, but is most severe on Bermuda and bent grass. It kills in small spots from 3 inches to 12 inches in diameter, but the spots may coalesce into large areas. Diseased spots are usually bleached from tan to straw-colored.

Favorable climatic conditions: Moderate temperatures, excess moisture, and heavy thatch all contribute to this disease. Underfertilized lawns are more prone.

Susceptible grasses: Bent grass, Kentucky bluegrass, Bermuda grass, rye grass, and fescues.

Resistant varieties: Some of the new, improved Kentucky bluegrasses.

Cultural control: Increase nitrogen, keep thatch at a minimum, water deeply when necessary.

Chemical control: Anilazine, benomyl, chlorothalonil, thiabendazole.

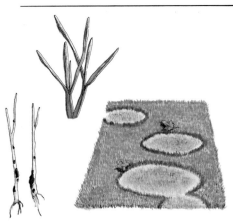

Brown Patch

July to August

Description: Recognize it by the large irregular, circular areas, which can be up to several feet in diameter. The patches usually have a brownish to grey discoloration, with a water-soaked appearance around the edges of the patch. Normally, only the leaves and stems are attacked.

Favorable climatic conditions: High temperatures (75° to 95°F.), excessive thatch, high humidity, lush growth from overfertilization, and excessive moisture are perfect for this disease.

Susceptible grasses: A serious disease in the South on centipede and St. Augustine grass. It also attacks bent grass, Bermuda grass, dichondra, rye grass, fescue and zoysia grass.

Resistant grasses: Improved Kentucky bluegrass.

Cultural control: Avoid heavy nitrogen fertilization, reduce shading, and water deeply when necessary.

Chemical control: Benomyl, thiophonate, chlorothalonil.

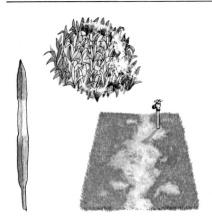

Pythium, Grease Spot or Cottony Blight

July and August

Description: Generally a problem on newly established lawns, but will occur on any lawn if conditions are favorable. The diseased area may be a few inches to several feet in diameter. It frequently occurs in small, circular spots about 2 inches across on closely cut lawns. Look for it in early morning while dew is still on the grass, or during humid weather. The diseased areas are surrounded by blackened blades covered with a white or grey fungus. Dry weather will stop the disease.

Favorable climatic conditions: High temperatures and excess moisture.

Susceptible grasses: Rye grass, tall fescue, bent grass, Bermuda grass, and bluegrass.

Resistant varieties: None.

Cultural control: Avoid excessive watering during warm weather, don't overfertilize. Seed late in the fall.

Chemical control: Use a fungicide such as diazoben, mancozeb, koban or thiram at first sign of the disease.

Damping Off

Seedling lawns

Description: New seedlings fail to fill in properly. If possible, look closely and you can see young seedlings have emerged from the soil, but collapsed. This disease is caused by a number of different fungal organisms.

Favorable climatic conditions: Overwatering after seeding especially if soil is heavy and days are overcast. No problem if starting from sprigs or stolons.

Susceptible grasses: Any seeded grass.

Resistant varieties: None.

Cultural control: Make sure pH is nearly neutral. Do not overwater; and provide good drainage.

Chemical control: Use seeds treated with captan or thiram or spray captan or thiram at first sign of trouble.

Powdery Mildew

July to November

Description: First symptoms are light patches of dusty, white to light gray growth on grass blades. Lowest leaves may become completely covered. Generally not too serious a problem, but can be severe. Most common in shady areas.

Favorable climatic conditions: Slow or nonexistent air circulation and shade are the most common causes.

Susceptible grasses: Kentucky bluegrass (especially 'Merion'), zoysia and Bermuda grass.

Resistant varieties: 'Glade', 'Nugget', and 'Birka' Kentucky bluegrass; 'Fortress', red fescue.

Cultural control: Reduce shade, if possible. Don't overwater. Avoid overfertilization.

Chemical control: Benomyl, cycloheximide.

Rust

July to November

Description: This disease is appropriately named. The affected lawn will have a rust-colored cast noticeable from a distance. Close-up, the dustlike rust spores are in circular or long groups on grass leaves. The rust rarely causes severe damage to home lawns but are very serious where grasses are grown for seed.

Favorable climatic conditions: Moderately warm, moist weather. Dew that lasts on the lawn for 10 to 12 hours is enough to promote germination of the fungus spores. Any stress conditions that restrict growth of the lawn grass favor the development of rust.

Susceptible grasses: Most all commonly grown grasses can be affected by rust. Kentucky bluegrass and the rye grasses are most frequently damaged.

Resistant grasses: Fine fescues.

Cultural control: Keep the lawn growing rapidly by fertilizing with nitrogen and frequent watering. Then mow frequently, every four or five days.

Chemical control: Maneb, anilazine, and oxycarboxin are moderately effective.

Stripe Smut

April to November

Description: Diseased plants are usually pale green and stunted. Long black stripes of spores are visible on the leaf blades. Affected leaves curl, die, and become shredded by the advancing disease.

Favorable climatic conditions: Moderate temperatures of spring and fall. Hot and dry weather will often halt the disease.

Susceptible grasses: Kentucky bluegrass and bent grass are commonly attacked.

Resistant grasses: 'A-34', 'Adelphi', and 'Sydsport' are some of the many Kentucky bluegrasses that are resistant.

Cultural control: Keep thatch to a minimum and avoid overwatering.

Chemical control: Two systemics, benomyl and thiophanate, will provide some control. Best applied in late fall.

Typhula Blight, Gray Snow Mold

Any time with snow

Description: First appears as vaguely straw or tan-colored circular areas, a few inches to a few feet in diameter. The dead grass may actually be covered at some point with a grayish fungal growth. It occurs primarily in the northern United States and Canada, not reaching as far south as pink snow mold.

Favorable climatic conditions: A deep snow cover that is slow to melt.

Susceptible grasses: Most all the cool-season grasses.

Resistant grasses: None.

Cultural control: Be sure the lawn is not succulent or lush (overfertilized with nitrogen) before the first snowfall. Also, avoid excessive use of lime. Keep thatch layer to a minimum.

Chemical control: Apply anilazine or thiram in the fall before the first snowfall is forecast. Snow mold (pink and gray) is often only found in areas where snow lies for a long time, such as against a house or garage. These areas may be all that will need treatment.

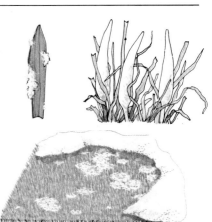

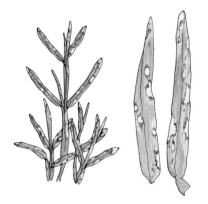

Gray Leaf Spot of St. Augustine Grass
June through August

Description: Commonly attacks St. Augustine grass, especially recently sprigged or plugged lawns. Mostly on the leaves but some symptoms on the stems too. The spots on the leaves are round and ash-to-brown in color. They are surrounded by a dark margin. The most serious effect of the disease is this scorching or dying back of the leaves. Seldom will it kill an entire lawn.

Favorable climatic conditions: Warm, rainy periods of summer.

Susceptible grasses: St. Augustine grass.

Resistant varieties: 'Roselawn' has shown some resistance.

Cultural control: Do not overfertilize with nitrogen and water as infrequently as the lawn will tolerate. When you do water, however, be sure the moisture penetrates to at least 5 inches. Prune shade trees if possible, to increase light and air circulation.

Chemical control: Chlorothalonil, anilazine, mancozeb, maneb, captan.

St. Augustine Grass Decline (SAD)
Anytime

Description: This is a virus disease that causes a mottling of the leaf blade, overall yellowing, and a general decline in the lawn's vigor. A St. Augustine grass lawn attacked by SAD will generally be invaded by Bermuda grass and weeds which are not affected.

Favorable climatic conditions: Known to occur only in Texas and Louisiana.

Susceptible grasses: Only St. Augustine grass.

Resistant varieties. At present, 'Floratam' St. Augustine grass.

Cultural control: If your lawn is infected, the only control is to plant plugs of 'Floratam' into the middle of the infested areas. It will eventually replace the diseased grass.

Chemical control: None.

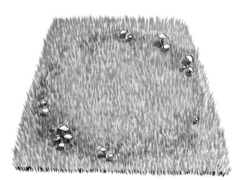

Fairy Ring
April to November

Description: Appears as a ring of dark green grass surrounding areas of dead or light-colored grass. The rings can be produced by the growth of any one of over 50 different kinds of fungus. The dying grass in the ring is caused by lack of water penetration.

Favorable climatic conditions: Fairy rings will develop in soils that contain undecomposed woody organic matter, such as dead tree roots or old construction materials. Primarily a problem in acid soils.

Susceptible grasses: All.

Resistant grasses. None.

Cultural control: Try to keep the lawn growing by applying adequate nitrogen fertilizer to hide the problem. Aerate the ring to improve water penetration. Keep areas wet for about two weeks, and mow frequently.

Chemical control: It's best to try to live with it. Complete eradication with a soil fumigant is difficult.

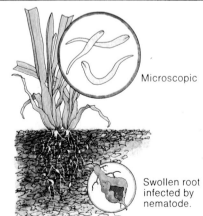

Nematodes

Description: Nematodes are very common in the soil. These small worms are so small you need a microscope to see them, but scientists say they are the most common form of life on earth. There are thousands of different kinds, but only a few damage plants.

Symptoms: The grass will be generally unthrifty, thin, yellowish, and drought susceptible in summer. It will not respond to other treatments such as aeration, fertilization, or watering. Upon inspection of the roots, they will be stubby, shallow, and possibly show swelling or galls. Complete diagnosis requires a microscope.

Control: Keep the grass as healthy as possible. If the presence of damaging nematodes is confirmed by a professional, consult with an experienced pest control operator or your County Extension Agent.

Microscopic

Swollen root infected by nematode.

Scalping and Dull-Mower Injury

Lawn scalping occurs whenever too much of the grass plant is cut off at one time. Reducing the height of the lawn by more than one-third creates a severe shock, but the results may not be immediately visible. When the mower blades dip down, suddenly removing most of the green part and the leaf blade of the lawn, the effects are obvious and should not be confused with insect or disease damage.

If your mower blades are dull, the lawn will have a greyish cast a day or so after mowing. This happens when the leaf tips have been shredded instead of cut, thus turning brown. This is especially noticeable when the weather is dry. Besides being unsightly, shredded tips are an easy entry point for many disease organisms.

Chemical Burn

Many lawns are damaged by spilled fertilizer, herbicide, gasoline, or by dog urination. These types of injuries are characterized by distinct and abrupt patches of dead grass. The damage of dog urination is slightly more confusing. It is characterized by bright green grass surrounding a patch of dead grass. The solution to these problems is to thoroughly drench the soil with water. If this doesn't work, you'll have to replace the soil under the dead spot and repatch the damaged area. (See page 56 for patching instructions.)

Summer Drying Out

Drying out affects all grasses and can do considerable damage. It's easy to see but often mistaken for insect or disease damage. It could be caused by compacted soil in one area, or by the sprinklers just missing a spot.

The first indication of insufficient water is when part of the lawn changes color from bright green to dull green. Then, if your footprints don't spring back in a reasonable length of time, water stress is confirmed.

If you have a cool-season grass, raise the cutting height at least ½ inch and water deeply. Check the soil moisture occasionally with a soil probe or moisture meter. If one area begins to show signs of drought, use a portable sprinkler or a hand held hose to soak the area. See the section on watering, pages 24–34.

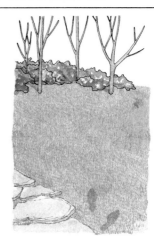

Nitrogen or Iron Deficiency

Nitrogen is the nutrient needed by lawns in the greatest quantity. The actual amount will vary with the type of grass, but most need some lawn fertilizer every year. If you haven't been applying fertilizer, your lawn will probably be slightly yellow and not growing as well as it could.

If you have fertilized adequately and the lawn is still yellow and slow growing, the problem could be a lack of iron or improper pH. Some grasses, centipede grass for instance, are especially sensitive to a lack of iron. A typical lawn fertilizer applied on a lawn that needs iron may actually increase the yellowish look. Apply iron either as a liquid spray or as a supplemental, granular, dry lawn application, which is available in combination with nitrogen and sulfur.

You can grow grass in the shade, in many situations—if you plant appropriate varieties and maintain them properly. See text for more information.

Lawns in the Shade

Many people think of establishing and caring for a good-quality lawn in the shade as a real headache, but it needn't be. Many beautiful lawns are grown in the shade of spreading trees. Understanding the relationship between the tree and the grass underneath is one requirement for a successful shady lawn.

There are many types of shade—light, half, dappled, full, and heavy. Few grasses will grow in full or heavy shade. Although it's difficult to figure out exactly what percentage of the sunlight passing through a tree a lawn needs to sustain it, the estimated figure is 50 percent.

Helping the grass without hurting the tree. The grass growing under your tree competes with the tree for water, nutrients, and—most important—light. If the shade is heavy enough, and the lawn receives no care, the tree will almost always win. The grass will become thin and spotty or gradually die out altogether.

Your job is to supply the requirements of the grass without harming the tree. Of course, if the tree is not a functional part of the landscape, you may decide to remove it altogether.

A shade-tolerant grass is a mandatory requirement. On page 90 grasses are listed according to their ability to grow in shade. Even within species, certain varieties are more shade tolerant than others. (See the variety charts on pages 138–141.)

Where the turf is already established, you may want to do small-scale renovation and reseed with a better-adapted grass. Some gardeners reseed every year with turf-type rye to keep fresh new grass under trees.

Which grass should you plant? If you have recently planted a young tree, shade probably isn't a current problem—but it may be in the future. If you are at the stage of considering planting trees in your lawn, plan ahead. Choose trees that cast filtered shade, and do not overplant. Several lawn trees are listed below.

If a suitable grass is already growing under your trees, good maintenance practices will help it stay healthy. However, there are some slight modifications of normal practices that will help even more.

Mow the lawn higher, at the highest cut suggested on page 43. More blade length means more light-trapping ability. If fertilization is called for, consider soil injections for the tree instead of applying fertilizer directly on the lawn. Overfertilization is a major problem of grass in the shade.

Watering deeply (but not overwatering) is especially important when trees are growing in the lawn. Shallow watering causes surface rooting, which in turn causes mowing problems and causes the tree roots to rob the lawn of its nutrients.

If surface roots are already a problem, most trees can stand some root pruning without being greatly harmed.

Protective clean-up. Grasses that grow in shade are more tender than those that grow in full sun, so pay close attention to insect and disease problems.

Fallen leaves and heavy grass-clippings can smother growing grass and increase damage from pests. This is particularly true in shaded areas.

Some leaves blow away easily, and some leaves are big and stay on your lawn. Some trees drop their leaves in a short time; others seem to drop forever. Regardless of when and how leaves fall, rake them up and add them to the compost pile. They will decay faster if they're shredded. Leaves do not act like a blanket to keep the grass warm—they actually smother the lawn, especially when it's wet, depriving the grass of light.

Dealing with excessive shade. The most obvious (sometimes the simplest) solution to a shade problem is to prune the tree. Proper thinning can remove as much as 40 percent of a tree's leaf surface without drastically changing the tree's appearance. In fact, pruning usually enhances it.

It is possible to have too many trees. Removing a few can be helpful not only for the lawn, but for the trees that remain. You might also consider planting ground covers, rather than grass, around trees. There are other alternatives, as well—for example, an attractive stone or bark mulch.

Trees in the Lawn

Trees are damaged when lawn mowers bump the trunk—any wound in the bark is an invitation to insects and disease. You can protect young trees by placing three wooden stakes about a foot from the trunk.

Grass growing against the trunk of a young tree can severely retard the tree's growth, even if additional water and fertilizer are applied. A 30-inch-diameter ring of mulch around the tree can give it a good start. Keep the mulch away from the trunk, however.

Grade changes can kill many trees. Piling soil around the trunk can suffocate surface roots. Removing soil either damages roots or exposes them to drying. During the establishment of a lawn, make all grade changes around trees gradual. If the changes are more than a couple of inches, make retaining walls or dry wells; extend them to the drip-line of the tree.

Trees for Lawns
The following trees are especially adapted to lawns in those areas noted:

Species	Common Name	Northeast-Midwest	South	West
Acer spp.	(Maple)	•		•
Betula spp.	(Birch)	•		
Carya illinoinensis	(Pecan)		•	
Cercis canadensis	(Redbud)	•	•	
Chioanthus spp.	(Fringe tree)	•	•	
Cornus spp.	(Dogwood)	•	•	
Crataegus spp.	(Hawthorne)	•	•	•
Koelreuteria spp.	(Golden-rain tree)	•	•	•
Magnolia spp.	(Magnolia)	•	•	•
Maytenus boaria	(Mayten)			•
Pinus spp.	(Pine)		•	
Pistacia chinensis	(Chinese pistachio)			•
Pyrus spp.	(Pear)	•	•	•
Quercus spp.	(Oak)		•	
Tristania laurina	(Tristania)			•

GRASSES FOR YOUR REGION

Month by month, how to maintain your lawn's vitality and appearance, where you live.

Some grasses are naturally better adapted to specific climatic conditions. Each grass has an area where it is best adapted, but this is only a guide and not a set of rules. There are different recommendations for mowing and fertilization rates. These two differences indicate the high- and low-maintenance grasses. The grasses that require short mowing and frequent, heavy fertilization are only for dedicated lawn owners.

Another maintenance difference is the way grasses spread. For instance, Bermuda and zoysia grass spread from stems that run along the ground—beneath mower height. To keep these dense and smooth, mow them short.

Benefits of the New Varieties

The best of the improved Kentucky bluegrasses have dramatically increased disease resistance, compared to common bluegrass types. Some tolerate lower mowing (to ¾ inch), compared to the 2 to 3 inches required for the older types. However, as grasses are cut lower, their maintenance needs increase. The chart on page 139 describes the best Kentucky bluegrasses.

Probably the most significant breakthrough of recent years in lawn culture is the introduction of the turf-type perennial rye grasses. They are more persistent, more compatible with Kentucky bluegrass and fine fescue in both color and texture, and are cleaner mowing. (Common perennial rye has frayed tips that brown after mowing.)

Turf-type rye grass has revolutionized seed mixtures, and is now a common component of many mixtures. Because it can start as quickly as common perennial rye grass, it has been dubbed "crisis grass" by lawn professionals. Many of the turf-type ryes are described on page 140.

The lawn industry. Lawns are a big industry throughout this country, Canada, and Europe. A lot of the creeping red fescue seed planted around the world is grown in Canada. New varieties of bluegrass are being bred in Europe. Turf grass research is carried on in several locations in this country. The University of Georgia, Texas A&M, Michigan State, Penn State, Rutgers University in New Jersey, and areas in the Pacific Northwest are just a few of the locations familiar to the experts. Most state and land-grant colleges have at least one turf specialist on staff.

At the other end of the lawn-care spectrum are the lawn-service companies. These companies usually contract for specific jobs that homeowners do not want to do themselves or perhaps do not know how to do (e.g., weed, disease, and insect control, and renovation). Fertilization is often included in their programs. Some lawn companies provide their services on a once-a-year basis for special jobs; others will contract for year-round lawn care.

Keep your own lifestyle in mind. Of course, there can never be a perfect grass for every situation—that's why the decision as to what to plant is yours. But thanks to the work of the lawn experts, you can have a lawn that is perfect for you.

Lawn Grass Comparison

The following lists compare the specific types of grass in general terms. They are based on the personal observations of many specialists, and are not absolute. The specific qualities of one grass could vary, and newly developed varieties may enter at different positions in the lists.

A particular type of grass may seem perfect for your home lawn. However, you should consider adaptation to your climate and maintenance requirements, as well as other factors. For instance, where warm-season grasses are best adapted, the cool-season grasses naturally drop out of the lists and vice versa.

High temperature tolerance

zoysia grass
improved Bermuda grass
common Bermuda grass
St. Augustine grass
carpet grass
centipede grass
bahia grass
buffalo grass
tall fescue
dichondra
Kentucky bluegrass
perennial rye grass
colonial bent grass
creeping bent grass
roughstalk bluegrass

High temperature tolerance depends on variety and maintenance practices, and a whole range of climatic factors that affect growth habits. Raising the cutting height of a cool-season grass will improve its temperature tolerance. Also, tolerance to high temperatures is more important in transitional areas, since the grass is not as well adapted.

Accepts low mowing

creeping bent grass
(¼ inch or less)
improved Bermuda grass
colonial bent grass
common bent grass
common Bermuda grass
zoysia grass
buffalo grass
centipede grass
perennial rye gass
red fescue
roughstalk bluegrass
Kentucky bluegrass
St. Augustine grass
tall fescue
bahia grass

Mowing height is primarily determined by the growth habit of the grass. Those that spread horizontally can be clipped lower. There are certain cool-season varieties, such as 'Merion' Kentucky bluegrass, that can be cut at ¼ inch to ⅜ inch for backyard putting greens, but this is seldom recommended. In general, Kentucky bluegrass cut above 1½ inches is much easier to keep.

Drought tolerance

bahia grass
improved Bermuda grass
zoysia grass
buffalo grass
common Bermuda grass
blue grama
crested wheat grass
tall fescue
red fescue
carpet grass
centipede grass
St. Augustine grass
colonial bent grass
dichondra
creeping bent grass
roughstalk bluegrass
Kentucky bluegrass
perennial rye grass

A grass may tend to remain green and resist short periods of drought. However, this same grass may, if subjected to severe drought, die out completely.

Fertilizer requirements

buffalo grass
red fescue
bahia grass
zoysia grass
tall fescue
centipede grass
carpet grass
St. Augustine grass
perennial rye grass
Kentucky bluegrass
roughstalk bluegrass
common Bermuda grass
improved Bermuda grass
dichondra
colonial bent grass
creeping bent grass

While a lawn may exist on rather low amounts of fertilizer, high or desirable quality may only come with increased amounts. The variety, kind of soil, and climate greatly influence fertilizer needs.

Disease resistance

tall fescue
zoysia grass
buffalo grass
improved Bermuda grass
common Bermuda grass
bahia grass
carpet grass
St. Augustine grass
perennial rye grass
centipede grass
red fescue
Kentucky bluegrass
roughstalk bluegrass
dichondra
colonial bent grass
creeping bent grass

A grass may be indicated as having few disease problems, but this chart represents composite knowledge of the overall disease situation. Under the right environmental conditions, a single disease may be quite devastating.

Shade tolerance

red fescue
St. Augustine grass
roughstalk bluegrass
dichondra
colonial bent grass
tall fescue
creeping bent grass
bahia grass
centipede grass
perennial rye grass
Kentucky bluegrass
zoysia grass
buffalo grass
improved Bermuda grass
common Bermuda grass

Shade tolerance of turf depends upon many conditions. If the site is quite damp, roughstalk bluegrass could persist while red fescue would die out completely. On a dry site it would be the opposite. There often are also significant varietal differences.

Establishment time
from seeds or stolons

improved Bermuda grass
(stolons)
common Bermuda grass
perennial rye gass
creeping bent grass (stolons)
St. Augustine grass
carpet grass
roughstalk bluegrass
bahia grass
centipede grass
tall fescue
bent grass (seed)
buffalo grass
red fescue
Kentucky bluegrass
dichondra
'Emerald' zoysia grass

The point at which a new planting becomes a lawn depends upon the lawn owner. If it is only for appearance, and to keep the soil in place, a new seeding of perennial rye or tall fescue (at a heavy rate) can do the job, in as little as 2 to 3 weeks.

Wearability

zoysia grass
improved Bermuda grass
bahia grass
common Bermuda grass
buffalo grass
tall fescue
Kentucky bluegrass
carpet grass
perennial rye grass
red fescue
St. Augustine grass
centipede grass
colonial bent grass
creeping bent grass
roughstalk bluegrass
dichondra

In many situations traffic is much more than any turf grass can tolerate. Again, there is quite a lot of varietal variability. 'Benson', 'Baron', and 'Merion' Kentucky bluegrass take traffic rather well.

Starting from Seed

Seed is the most common and popular way to start a new lawn. Years ago, barn sweepings were scattered around the yard; eventually, a lawn would grow. Today, there is a very sophisticated industry that supplies around 120 million pounds of lawn seed each year. Starting from seed is economical. The cost of seed is usually no more than 5 percent of the total expense of a new lawn.

Of the millions of pounds of seed produced, Kentucky bluegrass is the most important. It is the most widely adapted grass of North America. Common Bermuda grass is also planted in large quantities; fine and tall fescue and the rye grasses are the other important lawn seeds.

The quality of seed is important. Quality seed is healthy, with a high percentage of germination. It is also weed and disease free. A few more dollars for five pounds of the highest possible quality seed can save hundreds of dollars in the years ahead. You'll have fewer weed and disease problems and, generally, a higher-quality lawn.

Choose your seed wisely. Experience has shown that the type of seed you select makes a difference. Make sure the grass type and variety are adapted to your area. Read the label on the seed container carefully. Prepare the soil well, and make sure there is good contact between the seed and the soil when planting. Sow the seed at the time of year most favorable to germina-

Top: A turf grass test plot. Choose a grass that's adapted to your area and that suits your lawn needs.

Left: Shade-grass research: shade cloths of varying densities are placed above test grasses to recreate the "shades of shade" found around the home. Researchers then record the respective tolerances.

tion (see pages 16–23). Keep the new seedbed moist until after germination. Before you buy the seed, ask yourself these important questions:

☐ Will your lawn be used primarily for decoration or for recreation?
☐ Which grasses are best adapted to your area?
☐ Will the lawn be partially shaded or will it receive full exposure to the sun?
☐ How much time and energy are you willing to put into lawn care?

These questions may seem obvious, but they are very important considerations. You can answer most of them by reading pages 132–141.

The importance of quality. Although some aspects of lawn seed production are under state and federal regulations, the seed producers' desire for quality is the only sure guarantee of good seed. But knowing how to read a seed label will enable you to compare various seeds, and therefore make a wise choice.

Most garden centers and hardware stores have so many different kinds of lawn seed that selecting lawn seed can be a bewildering experience. You can compare the colors, the size of the boxes, and the brand names, but the only real way to compare value is to read the label.

Seed box labeling is regulated by the government. The Federal Seed Act of 1939 determines the basic structure of seed labels. Many individual states have their own seed-labeling laws, but these tend to be largely identical to the federal standard. There is no real mystery to seed labels, but government regulations and the use of a technical vocabulary can make them difficult to understand. Seed labels are a legal document; each word has a specific meaning. The sample seed label illustrated here shows and briefly explains the major parts of a typical label.

The seed label.
How to use. Most commercial mixes will tell you how much seed to use and sometimes when to seed. Some will indicate the spreader setting to use.

The spreader setting is merely a guide, not a rule; however, it usually is an adequate guide. A more specific guideline is a statement like "enough seed for 1,000 square feet of new lawn." This tells you how far the seed will go, regardless of how you intend to spread it.

Experts have determined how many seeds per square inch are best for new seedings. These rates will vary according to many factors, such as the seed size and the growth habit of the grass. But most lawns get a good start if seeded at a rate of approximately 20 seeds per square inch—just under 3 million seeds per 1,000 square feet. Some quick multiplication will show that 3 million seeds per 1,000 square feet is the same as 1 pound of Kentucky bluegrass per 1,000 square feet, or as 5 pounds of fine fescue per 1,000 square feet. For more information, turn to "Seed Facts," page 96.

Different varieties of the same type of grass will vary in seed size. However, the difference is inconsequential when determining application rates. Naturally, the quantity recommended to sow is based on average conditions. If you expect a lot of the seeds to be eaten by birds or otherwise fail to survive past germination, sow at a heavier rate. But it isn't always wise to seed heavily just to be generous—grasses planted too closely together will produce weaker, slower-maturing plants.

"Fine-textured" and "coarse." The fine-textured grasses are the mainstay of a high-quality lawn seed mix. Kentucky bluegrass and the fine fescues are the most important fine-textured types.

Bluegrasses other than Kentucky types (*Poa pratensis*) are also legally considered fine-textured. Rough-stalk bluegrass (*P. trivialis*) is found in some shady lawn mixes. Bermuda grass is also listed as fine-textured. All other grasses must, by law, be listed as "coarse."

Bent grasses at one time were a component of all quality mixes. They are soft and their narrow leaf-blades qualify them as fine textured, but because of their different growth habit and management needs, they do not mix well with Kentucky bluegrass, fine fescue, or turf-type perennial rye grass. They form unattractive clumps in a bluegrass lawn if the lawn is mowed high. Mowed low, the bent grass will eventually predominate anyway by crowding out the others. Alone and properly cared for, however, the bent grass can make a handsome lawn.

Specifically, the coarse grasses are tall fescue, meadow fescue, redtop, timothy, and both annual and perennial rye. However, the ryes fit this category uncomfortably: While they are wide-bladed, clump forming, and coarse, the new varieties of perennial rye ("turf types") are as fine-bladed as Kentucky bluegrass. These turf-type ryes are premium-quality lawn grasses; some are labeled as coarse. Thus, the term "coarse" can be misleading, and can cause problems. Knowing something about the seed in the box and its potential is a better way to judge.

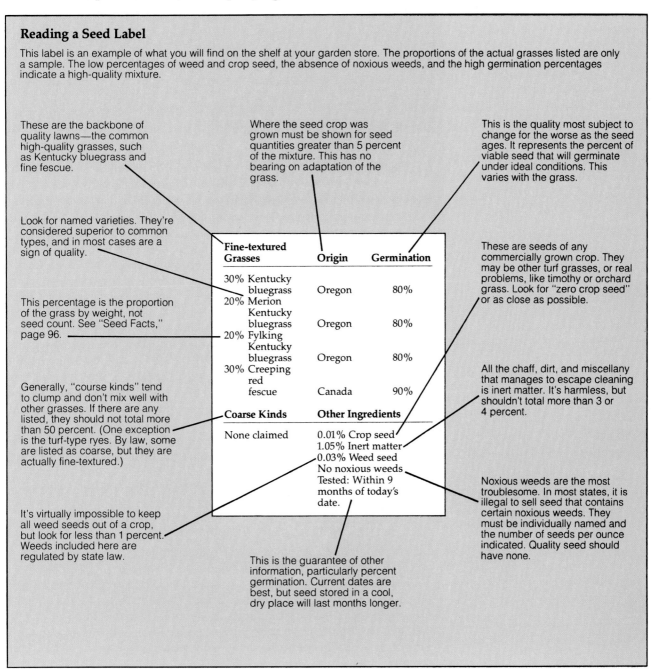

Reading a Seed Label

This label is an example of what you will find on the shelf at your garden store. The proportions of the actual grasses listed are only a sample. The low percentages of weed and crop seed, the absence of noxious weeds, and the high germination percentages indicate a high-quality mixture.

These are the backbone of quality lawns—the common high-quality grasses, such as Kentucky bluegrass and fine fescue.

Where the seed crop was grown must be shown for seed quantities greater than 5 percent of the mixture. This has no bearing on adaptation of the grass.

This is the quality most subject to change for the worse as the seed ages. It represents the percent of viable seed that will germinate under ideal conditions. This varies with the grass.

Look for named varieties. They're considered superior to common types, and in most cases are a sign of quality.

This percentage is the proportion of the grass by weight, not seed count. See "Seed Facts," page 96.

Generally, "course kinds" tend to clump and don't mix well with other grasses. If there are any listed, they should not total more than 50 percent. (One exception is the turf-type ryes. By law, some are listed as coarse, but they are actually fine-textured.)

It's virtually impossible to keep all weed seeds out of a crop, but look for less than 1 percent. Weeds included here are regulated by state law.

These are seeds of any commercially grown crop. They may be other turf grasses, or real problems, like timothy or orchard grass. Look for "zero crop seed" or as close as possible.

All the chaff, dirt, and miscellany that manages to escape cleaning is inert matter. It's harmless, but shouldn't total more than 3 or 4 percent.

Noxious weeds are the most troublesome. In most states, it is illegal to sell seed that contains certain noxious weeds. They must be individually named and the number of seeds per ounce indicated. Quality seed should have none.

This is the guarantee of other information, particularly percent germination. Current dates are best, but seed stored in a cool, dry place will last months longer.

Fine-textured Grasses	Origin	Germination
30% Kentucky bluegrass	Oregon	80%
20% Merion Kentucky bluegrass	Oregon	80%
20% Fylking Kentucky bluegrass	Oregon	80%
30% Creeping red fescue	Canada	90%

Coarse Kinds	Other Ingredients
None claimed	0.01% Crop seed 1.05% Inert matter 0.03% Weed seed No noxious weeds Tested: Within 9 months of today's date.

Rust disease can be devastating to seed growers, so naturally-resistant varieties are valued.

Percentages. When the label says that 60 percent of a given mixture is Kentucky bluegrass and 40 percent is red fescue, it means 60 percent and 40 percent by *weight* of the contents. If the meaning of this is not apparent, take a look at "Seed Facts" on page 96. Note that there are usually over 2 million seeds of Kentucky bluegrass in a pound, and approximately 600,000 seeds per pound of red fescue. When you plant a mixture labeled as 60 percent Kentucky bluegrass and 40 percent red fescue, in actual seed numbers you are planting 84 percent bluegrass and 16 percent red fescue. A red fescue seed weighs three times more than a seed of Kentucky bluegrass. The actual contents of a seed mixture would be more apparent if the percentages were in seed counts, rather than weight.

Germination percentages let you know how many of each seed type will germinate under ideal conditions, as of the test date. By multiplying the germination percent and the percent of the grass type in the mixture, you can determine how many seeds of that type have the potential to grow. This is called "percentage-pure live seed." This percentage is not listed on the label, but it's one (albeit complicated) way to figure the real value of the seed before buying.

Returning to the example of 60 percent bluegrass and 40 percent fine fescue mixture, if the germination percentage of the bluegrass is 80 percent, then 60 percent multiplied by 80 percent (.60 × .80) equals the percent-pure live seed of Kentucky bluegrass. Usually, 90 percent of the fine fescue will germinate, so 90 percent multiplied by 40 percent equals the pure live seed of fescue in the mixture. In these terms, the mixture is actually 48 percent viable Kentucky bluegrass and 36 percent viable red fescue. This leaves 16 percent non-viable seed, which is just filler. Obviously, as the germination percentage goes down, you are buying less viable seed.

If a container of seed is unmixed and unblended, it will list the percent "purity." Essentially, this means the same as the percentage of grass types in a seed mixture. A box of straight Kentucky bluegrass should be at least 90 percent pure. Again, by multiplying the percent purity by the germination percentage, you can determine how many viable seeds are in the box, and thus the value of the seed.

To make a quick field check of the seed production of a certain grass, the breeder removes the seed heads from the plant (left), and gently rubs them between the palms (middle). The seed separates easily from the hulls (right).

Percent-pure live seed is a good way to compare value, but it isn't the only measure. In terms of the label, judge quality primarily by comparing percent germination, percent weed and crop seed, and the occurrence (if any) of noxious weeds.

Crop seed vs. weed seed. Plants that are considered crop and those considered weeds are distinguished by agricultural laws of individual states. However, labeling laws were designed for farmers, not for buyers of lawn seed, so some of the most serious lawn weeds may not be listed under "weeds." Timothy, orchard grass, tall fescue, and brome grass—all serious lawn weeds—are usually classified as crop. Just 1 percent of a weedy fescue can contribute 10,000 seeds to every 1,000 square feet of new lawn. Both timothy and redtop have small, vigorous seeds. A small percentage of these can produce many established weeds in the new lawn.

Likewise, the percentage of weed seeds could represent a few large, harmless weeds, or it could indicate many serious, lightweight weed seeds. The quality of the producer is the only standard to judge by. At 0.27 percent of weeds, for instance, a homeowner can plant 30 unwanted chickweed seeds per square foot.

"Noxious" weeds. Once these weeds are established they can be hard to eliminate. Many spread just as aggressively with runners or bulbs as by seed. Each state has its own list of noxious weeds.

The specific noxious weeds, as set forth by the Federal Seed Act, are whitetop (*Lepidium draba, Lepidium repens, Hymenosphysa pubescens*); Canada thistle (*Cirsium arvense*); dodder (*Cuscuta* sp.); quackgrass (*Agropyron repens*); johnson grass (*Sorghum halepense*); bindweed (*Convolvulus arvensis*); Russian knapweed (*Centaurea picris*); perennial sowthistle (*Sonchus arvensis*); and leafy spurge (*Euphorbia esula*). These are primarily field crop weeds, but a few are serious lawn weeds.

In a few states, annual bluegrass (*Poa annua*) and Bermuda grass are considered noxious weeds. If noxious weeds are present in a seed mixture, they must be named, and the number of seeds per ounce must be shown. In a quality seed mixture, there should be no noxious weeds.

Straights, mixtures, and blends. The word "straight" is used to describe lawn seed that's composed of just one type of grass. Many warm-season lawns (for example, lawns of common or improved Bermuda, St. Augustine, or zoysia grass) are unmixed and unblended with other grass types. Tall fescue and bent grass are cool-season grasses that are sometimes used alone. For most cool-season lawns, a mixture or blend is preferred.

A mixture contains different varieties of seed that adjust individually to the varying soil conditions and sun or shade areas of typical lawns. The

Seed Facts

Name	Use	No. seeds per lb.	Lbs. seed per 1,000 sq. ft.	% purity	% germination	Days to germinate*
Bahia grass	Low maintenance. Gulf Coast.	175,000	8	75	70	21-28
Bent grass, creeping	Putting/bowling greens. Cool moist climates.	6,500,000	1	98	90	4-12
Bermuda, common	Good play lawn. Most important grass of southern states.	1,750,000	2	97	85	7-30
Blue grama	Low maintenance, drought tolerant. Northern Plains.	800,000	2	40	70	15-30
Bluegrass, Kentucky	Widely adapted, all-purpose.	2,200,000	1½	90	80	6-30
Buffalo grass	Central Plains, tough, drought tolerant, low maintenance.	290,000	5	85	—	20-30
Carpet grass	Tropical, wet soils, low maintenance.	1,300,000	2	—	90	21
Centipede grass	Gulf Coast, low maintenance.	410,000	½	50	70	14-20
Dichondra	Southwest. Lawnlike ground cover.		1			14-24
Fescue, fine	Widely adapted. Tolerant of shade. Takes dry soil.	615,000	5	97	90	5-10
Fescue, tall	Good transition zone grass. Tough play lawn. Use by itself.	230,000	12	97	90	7-12
Rye grass, annual	Quick cover for winter overseeding.	230,000	9	97	90	3-7
Rye grass, perennial	Improved types called "crisis grass." Good in mixes. Common kinds coarse and clumpy.	230,000	9	97	90	3-7

*Varies according to growing conditions

strength of one grass type compensates for another's weakness. A lawn of a single variety of Kentucky bluegrass could be wiped out if a potent disease swept through. Considerable amounts of fescue or rye in the lawn lessen the effect of the disease.

In the past, a little bit of everything was thrown into a bag of lawn seed. It was the shotgun approach—because growers weren't sure what would work, they tried a little of everything.

The idea of a "nursegrass" in a mixture is disregarded today, but once it was thought that the presence of a hardy, fast-growing grass made the way a little easier for the slower, more delicate premium grass. Actually, however, fast grasses compete too much with the others, slowing down the establishment of the premium grass.

The grasses that mix together best are those with similar color, texture, and growth rate, and that are roughly equal in aggressiveness. Of the grasses that are similar in these respects, the most important are Kentucky bluegrass, fine fescue, and the turf-type rye grasses. Seed formulators vary the relative amounts of these ingredients and sometimes add small amounts of other grasses, depending upon the intended use of the mixture. For instance, more fescue is added if the lawn will be partly shaded or if the soil is drought prone. More turf-type rye grass will get the lawn off to a fast start.

More Kentucky bluegrass will produce the show lawn. Opinions of many experts, as well as regional considerations, also play an important part in making up a seed mixture.

Many good packaged lawn seeds are a combination of a mixture and a blend. A blend is a combination of varieties from one species. Characteristically, a blend is between a regular mixture and a straight. Resistance to particular diseases is somewhat improved, and texture and color appear consistent. Seed containers that announce something like "an all-bluegrass mixture" are, technically, blends.

Certified seed. Almost every state has a program of seed certification. Technically, "certified" seed only guarantees varietal purity. In other words, if the label says "Certified 'Adelphi' bluegrass," the contents of the bag are guaranteed to be 'Adelphi' Kentucky bluegrass.

In most states, certified seed also ensures higher overall quality. It is also guaranteed to have fewer weed seeds and other crop contaminants, as well as less inert filler.

"Percent fluorescence" is a special rating of perennial rye grass. The photographs here show what fluorescing seed looks like. In 1929, it was discovered that annual rye grass secreted a fluorescent substance when it was germinated on white filter paper. By contrast, the improved, turf-type ryes secrete none of this substance.

A simple way to test for contamination of improved rye grass is to germinate a sample on filter paper. If there is any fluorescence when the sample is exposed to ultraviolet light, the presence of annual rye grass (or a hybrid of annual and perennial rye grass) is established. To date, only the Manhattan Ryegrass Growers Association requires that this test be indicated on the seed tab, by calling the fluorescing seedlings "other crop."

Germinating a sample of improved rye grass on filter paper (left) is a simple test of purity: If any of the germinating seeds show fluorescence when exposed to ultraviolet light, the presence of annual rye grass is confirmed (right).

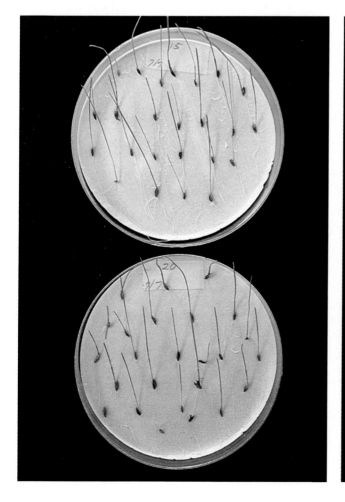
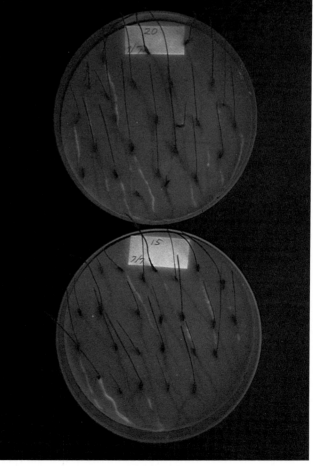

Germination time sequence: Four different grasses are sown in identical soil mixes and lightly covered with a mulch. From left to right: 'Manhattan', 'Merion', 'Fortress', and common Bermuda grass.

'Manhattan' rye grass was the first to germinate, followed closely by the fescue 'Fortress'. Both the Kentucky bluegrass 'Merion' and the common Bermuda grass took between 13 and 14 days to emerge.

'Manhattan' and 'Fortress' showed faster growth rates compared to the Bermuda and the bluegrass. The most rapid growth after germination of any type grass occurs if the soil is rich in nutrients and the time of year is most favorable.

Post-seeding care. A seeded lawn's success or failure depends on post-seeding care, especially watering, more than any other factor. The trick is to water enough to keep the soil moist, but not so much as to wash the soil away. This delicate nurturing period, during which watering can be a several-times-a-day chore, lasts from the time the seed is sown to the point when the grass becomes established. How long will this period last? The answer depends on the type of grass, its rate of germination and initial growth, and the daily temperature. An experiment conducted at the Ortho Test Garden in St. Helena, California illustrates this variability.

Four grasses were sown the same day: 'Manhattan' perennial rye grass; 'Merion' Kentucky bluegrass; 'Fortress' creeping red fescue; and common Bermuda grass. The accompanying photographs, taken at 15-day intervals, show what happened.

Actually, the rate of germination was surprising. The 'Manhattan' rye grass came up in less than five days. The others also germinated faster than expected. This extra-fast germination was probably due to an unexpected heat wave during the first week that sent temperatures into the mid-90s. Seed invariably germinates more slowly in the cool temperatures of late fall or early spring.

Regional Grasses

Which lawn you can grow depends on what the climate is like in your area. How much fertilizer your lawn will need each year is determined by the length of the growing season; whether your lawn needs irrigation systems or at least regular watering depends on summer rainfall patterns. And in terms of temperature, winter lows and summer highs dictate to a great extent which grasses can be grown where.

Lawn owners around the country revealed a strong desire for specific information concerning the lawns in their climates. As one person said, "Most lawn books are limited by various geographical problems. I would like a book on growing lawns where I live." An individual from Texas added, "None of the books about lawns have much use around here."

Climate Makes a Difference

Northeast/Midwest. The North is big, and the grass climate in North Dakota is very different from New Jersey. Compare the climate of Minot, North Dakota, in the Plains states to that of Atlantic City, New Jersey, in the Atlantic states. Minot receives an average of only 17 inches of rain per year. The average minimum temperature in January is −12°F. Only the hardiest of the cool-season grasses can be grown in this area. Quite a lot of watering is required to grow lawns in a climate this harsh, and lawns frequently experience winter damage.

Atlantic City, New Jersey, has a completely different set of climate circumstances. It receives an average of 45 inches of rain per year; the average minimum temperature in January is 24°F. While this is still cool-season grass country, some areas of New Jersey and other southern Atlantic states can grow some of the hardier varieties of Bermuda and zoysia grass.

Local characteristics, such as soil types and summer highs or winter lows, have a lot to do with which type of grass you can grow and what kind of care it needs. The more specific information you know, the better your lawn will be.

South. The grass climate in Tennessee is not the same as the grass climate in Florida. In Miami, Florida, for instance, the climate is almost tropical. Winter temperatures never drop anywhere near freezing, and Miami receives an average of 60 inches of rain per year. Warm-season grasses are the rule, and since the growing season occurs throughout the year, the need for fertilizer is also year-round.

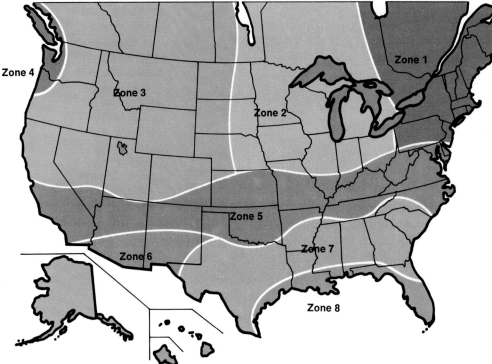

Zone 1
Zone 2
Zone 3
Zone 4
Zone 5
Zone 6
Zone 7
Zone 8

Zone 6—hot and dry summers: This zone is comprised of the arid Southwest, where rainfall is low and temperatures are high. All lawns here need some supplemental irrigation. Soils are usually alkaline. Lawns are primarily Bermuda grass with some St. Augustine and zoysia grass. In more northern areas, buffalo grass and wheat grass are sometimes used in low maintenance areas.

Zone 7—hot and humid: Most lawns in this zone are made up of warm-season grasses such as Bermuda, St. Augustine, and zoysia grass. Rainfall is high and summers are warm and humid. Kentucky bluegrass may be useful in shady situations.

Zone 8—tropical: This zone includes the Gulf Coast States, southern Florida, and much of Hawaii. Essentially a tropical climate, rainfall can be as high as 70 to 80 inches annually. Too much water is as much a problem here as too little water in the Southwest. In especially wet soils, carpet grass is a good choice. Centipede, zoysia, Bermuda, bahia, and St. Augustine grass can make good lawns throughout this region.

Zone 1—cold and humid: This zone includes northeastern United States and southeastern Canada. It is an area of abundant rainfall and acid soils. Summers are hot and humid; winters are cold and snowy. Cool-season grasses such as Kentucky bluegrass, bent grass, and fescue predominate. Zoysia and Bermuda grass lawns are occasionally found in southern portions along the Atlantic Coast.

Zone 2—cold winters and summer rains: Midwestern United States and central Canada make up this zone. Soils are not as acid and there is less rainfall compared to

zone 1. Zone 2 is more acid than zone 3, but the winters are less cold. Summers are warm and humid, with frequent thunderstorms. With the exception of a few zoysia grass lawns in the southern portion of this zone, cool-season grasses seem to predominate.

Zone 3—cold and arid: This is a large and varied zone. It is comprised of the Great Plains States, including parts of Montana, South Dakota, North Dakota, Nebraska, and Wyoming. This area is subject to drying winds in both winter and summer with relatively

little rain. Here, grasses are subject to the widest temperature fluctuation in the country. Aside from cool-season grasses, natives such as buffalo grass and wheat grass are utilized because of their drought tolerance and tenacity. The intermountain area supports fine fescues.

Zone 4—cool and humid: This is the Pacific Northwest, west of the Cascade Range. Rain is plentiful and soils are typically acid. Lawns are cool-season grasses and stay a beautiful green all year. Compared to the Northeast, both summers and winters are milder.

Zone 5—variable: This is a transition zone that runs across the entire United States. It is in this zone that the grass climates overlap, depending on many local factors. Both warm-season and cool-season grasses are common. Selection of a proper grass type is critical, since neither cool-season nor warm-season grasses are ideally adapted in many areas. Tall fescue makes a good lawn in many areas of this zone. Good maintenance practices can make the difference between success and failure. Smart lawn owners pay close attention to the many different micro-climates around their homes.

Jackson, Tennessee, on the other hand, has January low temperatures that average 15°F., which is much too low for most warm-season grasses. Although many of the zoysia grasses and hybrid Bermuda grasses can grow in Jackson, most of the beautiful lawns are made up of cool-season grasses— Kentucky bluegrass or fescues. This is the case with many northern or high-elevation areas of the South.

West. In the West, there are a variety of grass climates. Compare the climate of Casa Grande, Arizona, for instance, with that of Olympia, Washington. Total rainfall in Casa Grande averages only 8.1 inches per year. In July, temperatures go above 90°F. every day, and the average high temperature for the month is 106°F. Warm-season grasses are the rule. Obviously, such high temperatures necessitate quite a lot of lawn watering in Casa Grande.

The Olympia climate is the complete opposite. This area receives as much rain in July and August as Casa Grande gets all year. The total rainfall averages 51 inches annually. This is Kentucky bluegrass country, and if the rain falls at the right times Olympia lawns may not need any supplemental water to stay green the entire year.

Extension information. The recommended grasses that are listed for each region on pages 104–131 were compiled from extension bulletins from each state. They are the result of years of research and experience and are one of the best guides to a beautiful lawn in your area.

At the end of the information for each state or group of states are lists of addresses you can write to for additional local information. Most states produce high-quality pamphlets, brochures, or booklets that describe lawn growing. Don't hesitate to use these excellent resources.

The other addresses listed are for soil-testing facilities. Many of these facilities offer the test free; others may charge a nominal fee. Often, the most difficult part of getting your soil tested is knowing where to have it done.

About climate. Climate professionals use phrases such as "percent of sunshine" or "July days above 90°." Here is what they mean and how they relate to lawn growing.

Total inches rain. This is the average annual rainfall, including snow, hail, and sleet. Rainfall, within a wide range of temperatures, is the most important environmental factor promoting or restricting growth of all plants. In some areas, excessive water is a problem. Wet soil is caused by either too much rain or poor drainage, and will retard growth as surely as drought. In certain parts of the South, rainfall can be plentiful, but it comes all at once or within a short season, and is scant at other times of the year.

Too little rain is a more familiar problem. Soils that lose water rapidly through drainage (sandy soils) are more drought prone; while lawns in heavy soils (clay) are less likely to be damaged by short periods without rain.

In much of the West, drought is a familiar problem. Western drought is usually seasonal; winter rains supply all the lawn's needs and refill reservoirs. Supplemental irrigation in summer is essential, however. This seasonal characteristic for each state is revealed in the "Inches July/August" column, below.

Inches July/August. This figure refers to rainfall and tells how much water falls naturally when the lawn needs it most—during the hot months of the year. A lawn's water requirements during summer are determined not only by grass type and soil but also by the temperature and humidity.

July percentage of sunshine. Each day there is a certain amount of sunshine possible. This amount varies from the least on December 22 to the most on June 21. The actual number of sunshine hours also varies by latitude. In south Florida, December 22 is just less than 14. Percent of sunshine is figured by comparing the amount possible with the amount actually received. This figure indicates the number of cloudy, overcast days that occur in July.

July days above 90°F. The number of days in July when the temperature goes over 90°F. is one of the best indicators of which grass type you should grow. It also indicates the stress to which cool-season grass will be subjected. The best temperatures for growth of the cool-season grasses such as Kentucky bluegrass are between 60° and 75°F. Warm-season grasses grow best when temperatures reach into the 80s and 90s.

Average maximum/minimum temperatures. These are the monthly averages of the daily temperature extremes. As such, they are the best available guide to questions such as when to plant, water, and fertilize.

The best temperatures for growth of cool-season grasses is between 60° and 75°F. Warm-season grasses grow best at temperatures in the mid-80s and 90s.

Climate comparisons: South

cities	number of days growing season	average last frost	average first frost
Roanoke, VA	187	4/15	10/15
Lubbock, TX	205	4/10	10/30
Tulsa, OK	216	3/30	10/30
Louisville, KY	220	3/30	11/8
Knoxville, TN	220	3/30	11/8
Baltimore, MD	234	3/20	11/12
Raleigh, NC	237	3/17	11/12
Memphis, TN	237	3/15	11/7
Birmingham, AL	241	3/15	11/13
Little Rock, AK	244	3/10	11/11
Atlanta, GA	244	3/15	11/14
Dallas, TX	249	3/17	11/22
Norfolk, VA	254	3/15	11/24
Augusta, GA	260	3/8	11/17
Shreveport, LA	272	3/1	12/3
Savannah, GA	291	2/24	12/6
Charleston, SC	294	3/1	11/10
New Orleans, LA	302	2/10	12/10
Corpus Christi, TX	335	1/12	12/20
Miami, FL	365	—	—

Midwest/Northeast

cities	number of days growing season	average last frost	average first frost
Duluth, MN	125	5/22	9/24
Bismark, ND	136	5/11	9/24
Marquette, ME	159	5/13	10/19
North Platte, NE	160	4/30	10/7
Green Bay, WI	161	5/6	10/13
Minneapolis/ St. Paul, MN	166	4/30	10/13
Sioux City, IA	169	4/27	10/13
Peoria, IL	181	4/22	10/20
Detroit, MI	182	4/21	10/20
Springfield, IL	186	4/20	10/23
Pittsburgh, PA	187	4/20	10/23
Grand Rapids, MI	190	4/23	10/30
Cincinnati, OH	192	4/15	10/25
Charleston, WV	193	4/18	10/28
Springfield, MO	201	4/12	10/30
Evansville, IN	216	4/2	11/4
Louisville, KY	220	4/1	11/7

Lawn Care Calendar

January–February.
Snowmold. Take advantage of a midwinter thaw to treat a lawn that showed damage from this disease the previous spring.

March–April.
Where temperatures are favorable for lawn growth (e.g., Kentucky, West Virginia, and Maryland), begin planting and fertilizing.

Spring patching and rolling. If you live in an area where the ground is still frozen or covered with light snow, already-planted seeds won't sprout until the temperature rises. In established lawns after the spring thaw, roll fall-seeded lawns and areas raised by frost with a half-filled roller.

New lawns. Fall and spring are good times to start a lawn. The cool-season grasses (Kentucky bluegrass, fescue, bent grass, and rye grass) find temperatures of 70° to 75°F. ideal for growth. If seeding is done when the temperatures are favorable, lawns will become established quickly, overcoming much of the competition from weeds and avoiding erosion from heavy spring rains.

Sodding. You can do this any time during the growing season. However, spring and fall are ideal for quick establishment.

Fertilizing. If you missed fertilizing your lawn last fall, do it this spring, as soon as temperatures reach about 60°F.

Dethatching. Thatch slows air and water penetration, harbors pests and diseases, and slows growth by insulating roots and crowns against warming spring temperatures. Your lawn will recover in the shortest time from dethatching when temperatures are above 70°F. and the grass is growing vigorously.

Aeration. Early spring is a fine time to perform this chore. Aeration opens up the soil, thus providing roots with more water and air. If it is done prior to fertilizing, nutrients will reach the root zone quickly for spring green-up.

Crabgrass. Crabgrass seeds left over from the previous year will start to sprout when temperatures reach 65° to 70°F. for four to five consecutive days. Stop these seeds from coming up by applying a pre-emergent barrier *before* seeds germinate. Timing is important. If you plan to do any spring seeding, look for the word Tupersan (sideron) on the label. This product will not harm germinating grass seed.

Broadleaf weeds. Blooming dandelions are a sure sign of weeds, but other broadleaf weeds that aren't as obvious (e.g., plantain and knotweed) can be just as troublesome. There are two good reasons to control them now: (1) they are most susceptible to herbicides when young and actively growing, and (2) broadleaf weed killers work effectively in warm weather.

Grubs. As the soil warms up, grubs move up to the root zone from deep winter burrows. Treat them with an insecticide such as diazinon. Be patient—insecticides move slowly through the root zone. Follow label directions carefully.

Disease. The cool, moist weather of spring favors the development of several diseases. Leaf spot is a problem with bluegrass—look for it in fall as well as spring. A healthy lawn will usually make a strong comeback as the weather warms.

Stripe-smut symptoms are most pronounced during early to late spring, and again during similar periods of fall. Symptoms are almost nonexistent during midsummer. Dollar spot can occur anytime from now until late summer, especially when temperatures are up into the 80s and humidity is high.

May.
Feeding. If you think heavy rains have washed out nutrients, make a second application of fertilizer. May can be the first month for feeding if fertilizer was applied heavily the previous fall. Fertilize zoysia and Bermuda grass as they begin to green. Their best growing period is just ahead, and early feeding will speed recovery from winter dormancy. It also gives you a head start on weeds, thus preventing their growth. If you overseeded the lawn last winter, don't add fertilizer for a while; feeding now would only prolong the life of the overseeded winter grass.

Planting. When temperatures reach the mid-70s, sprigging and plugging weather has arrived in areas where Bermuda and zoysia grass are adapted. The hot weather ahead makes this the best time of year to plant these grasses.

Overseeding Bermuda grass. If you've overseeded your Bermuda grass lawn (zoysia grass doesn't lend itself well to this practice), now is the time to discourage the winter grass. Start mowing lower, less than 1 inch, to allow warmth and light to reach the Bermuda grass.

June.
Feeding. Do any feeding early in the month, before your cool-season grass begins to go dormant. During dormancy, grasses live off stored nutrients but actually manufacture very few. Continue feeding Bermuda and zoysia grass through the growing season until temperatures fall below 70°F. and your lawn begins to grow very slowly.

Crabgrass. If you didn't treat your lawn with a pre-emergent weed killer in the spring, crabgrass should be evident by now. Various sprays are available for selective control of crabgrass. Apply them as soon as you notice the crabgrass, and keep the soil moist.

Insects. This month, sod webworms may begin to cause irregular brown patches in the lawn. You'll probably see the adult moths fluttering around close to the lawn at dusk. Actually, it is the night-feeding larvae that do the damage. Armyworms also show up in summer. They're about twice as large as webworms, and they feed on the grass in broad daylight.

Chinch bugs are especially bad in warm dry weather in the Northeast. Discovering them is the first step toward control (see page 74). Hunt near the damaged area. Normal hatching times are often the first week in June and August.

Disease. Leaf spot disease continues to be a problem in southern areas. Brown patch is severe in hot weather. High humidity and temperatures of 60° to 80°F. are favorable for its development.

July–August.
Watering. It is the nature of cool-season grasses to go dormant in summer. Some people like it that way, but if you want to keep your lawn green, see pages 24 – 35.

Fertilizing. July and August are not the best months to fertilize cool-season grasses. Warm-season Bermuda and zoysia grass, however, grow most vigorously and may require additional nutrients.

Planting. The middle of August to the middle of September is one of the best times to reseed an old lawn or plant a new one. Summer heat will germinate the seed quickly, and the cooler weather that will soon follow will relieve you of the need for frequent watering.

Pests and diseases. A light case of brown patch can injure top growth, but the lawn should make a quick recovery in a few weeks if temperatures drop. If disease-favoring weather continues, so will brown patch. Chemical control may be necessary. In the Northeast, the small black and red chinch bug may have hatched a second generation, so be on the lookout. Continue to spot-treat crabgrass as it appears.

Grubs. In midsummer, adult beetles lay their eggs in the lawn. The tiny white grubs that hatch from these eggs feed near the surface until the first cold spell. Then they burrow into the surface more than a foot deep for overwintering. Control is most effective on surface-feeding young grubs.

September.

Cooler nights bring greater pleasure and fewer problems with lawn care. Grasses take on new life after the hard conditions of summer.

Broadleaf weeds. Now is a good time to begin controlling these vigorously growing weeds. Young weeds are most susceptible to chemical control. Remember, too, that chemicals designed for their control work best in warm but not hot weather.

Planting and dethatching. Planting weather, the year's best, continues into this

month. And as grasses perk up, consider removing thatch while favorable weather ensures quick recovery.

Overseeding Bermuda grass. Overseed Bermuda grass this month, as cooling weather favors germination and development of your winter grass and discourages further growth of the Bermuda grass. Mow first, then rake and mow again, removing the clippings. Rake seeds into the lawn and keep moist until they come up.

Fertilizer and lime. Discover the great response you get from a fall application of fertilizer. A lawn fed now spends less effort on top growth, more on root build-up. The result is a sturdier lawn going into winter and a stronger start next spring.

A fall application of lime is washed down into the soil by rains, where it is needed. Winter freezing and thawing further help the process.

Disease and weeds. Cool moist weather can bring problems, especially for Kentucky bluegrass, in the form of leaf spot disease. As in spring, it is the cool, moist weather that favors development.

October–December.

Where weather permits, the great opportunities of last month—planting, feeding, and weed killing—carry over for at least the first half of October.

If snowmold gave you trouble last spring, take precautions in November so it won't return. The disease organisms are still present; snow supplies the moisture to activate them. Infected grass develops patches several inches to several feet wide. Grass blades tend to form a mat or crust, and may show white to pink, or gray to black mold. Control once after frost (sometime in midwinter) when there is no snow on the ground, and again after snow melts next spring.

Climate comparisons: West

cities	number of days growing season	average last frost	average first frost
Albuquerque, NM	198	4/13	10/28
Phoenix, AR	295	2/14	12/6
San Diego, CA	365	—	—
Pasadena, CA	313	2/3	12/13
S. Barbara, CA	331	1/22	12/19
Bakersfield, CA	277	2/21	11/25
San Jose, CA	299	2/10	12/6
Sacramento, CA	307	3/8	11/20
Eureka, CA	328	1/26	12/20
Las Vegas, NV	239	3/16	11/10
Reno, NV	155	5/8	10/10
Medford, OR	161	5/3	11/14
Eugene, OR	205	4/14	11/4
Portland, OR	263	3/6	11/24
Vancouver, WA	226	3/30	11/11
Centralia, WA	173	4/27	10/17
Tacoma, WA	250	3/13	11/18
Spokane, WA	184	4/12	10/13
Boise, ID	177	4/23	10/17
Pocatello, ID	161	4/28	10/6
Salt Lake, UT	192	4/13	10/22
Provo, UT	171	4/26	10/14
Denver, CO	171	4/26	10/14
Pueblo, CO	174	4/23	10/14
Billings, MT	133	5/15	9/25
Casper, WY	133	5/19	9/29

Children don't need to be told about the pleasures of going barefoot in the grass, especially when it comes to playing lawn games.

Climates of the Midwest/Northeast

This section will help you determine the climate conditions that affect your ability to grow lawns in your region. Find the city closest to you on the chart, and note the information in each column. Check the information on the left-hand pages for specific information on soil conditions and lime requirements, recommended grasses, and suggestions for additional information.

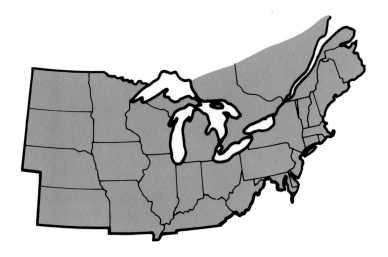

New England States

Soil and climate. Relatively moderate temperatures prevail throughout most of the region and make only occasional problems for lawn growing.

Rainfall is plentiful, rarely less than 30 inches in a year, but because of generally shallow soil, summer watering of lawns is usually necessary if they are to be kept green.

Lime is a must. Generally 50 to 200 pounds of ground limestone is necessary for every 1,000 square feet. A soil test will often recommend the appropriate quantity.

Soil testing
Maine Soil Testing Service
25 Deering Hall
University of Maine
Orono, Maine 04473

University of New Hampshire
Analytical Services Department
Durham, New Hampshire 03824

Soil Testing Laboratory
Regulatory Services
University of Vermont
Burlington, Vermont 05401

Soil Testing Service
Department of Plant and Soil Sciences
Stockbridge Hall
University of Massachusetts
Amherst, Massachusetts 01003

Agronomy Section
College of Agriculture and
   Natural Resources
The University of Connecticut
Storrs, Connecticut 06268

Rhode Island Soil Testing Service
District Office,
   Cooperative Extension Service
(check local telephone directory)

Recommended grasses. New England is solid Kentucky bluegrass territory. Fine fescues and a small percentage of turf-type rye grass are often included in mixtures. For low-fertility lawns, mixtures of fine fescues and colonial bent grass are well adapted.

Publications offices
Cooperative Extension Service
University of Maine
Orono, Maine 04473
Out-of-state requests: Yes.

Cooperative Extension Service
Plant Science Department
Durham, New Hampshire 03824
Out-of-state requests: Yes.

The Extension Service
University of Vermont
Burlington, Vermont 05401
Out-of-state requests: Yes.

Cooperative Extension Service
Stockbridge Hall
University of Massachusetts
Amherst, Massachusetts 01003
Out-of-state requests: Yes.

Agricultural Publications
The University of Connecticut
Storrs, Connecticut 06268
Out-of-state requests: Yes.

Resource Information Office
24 Woodward Hall
University of Rhode Island
Kingston, Rhode Island 02881
Out-of-state requests: Yes.

New York

Soil and climate. New York's climate, like most of the New England states, is humid and temperate. The quantity of rain is usually around 40 inches a year, most of which comes in summer. But it is not unusual for summer periods of high temperatures to coincide with short droughts. Lawns not watered during these times will suffer.

Throughout most of New York, the quantity of available sunshine is enough for excellent growth of grasses. During summer, about 60 percent of total possible sunlight is available. The growing season length varies from as few as 100 to as many as 180 days.

Most soil of the Northeast was developed under a natural forest cover. Most all of New York was also covered by glaciers. The topography is characterized by long ridges of low mountains and hills that extend in a northeasterly direction.

Lime is frequently necessary. If pH tests below 6.0, use a soil test to determine exact needs. See pages 18 – 20.

Soil testing. Contact the Cooperative Extension Agent in your county, or:
Agronomy Department
804 Bradfield Hall
Cornell University
Ithaca, New York 14853

Recommended grasses. Kentucky bluegrass blends are the best lawn grasses for New York. The red fescues are often mixed with Kentucky bluegrass for dry regions. Turf-type rye grass is also frequently used in mixtures. Zoysia grass is occasionally grown in warmer areas of the state.

The major lawn pests are white grubs, chinch bugs, and sod webworm. (See pages 70 – 77.) The disease, melting out or leaf spot, caused by *Helminthosporium,* is the primary disease. It can be prevented by using the new improved varieties of Kentucky bluegrass that are tolerant of this disease (see page 139). Dollar spot, *Fusarium* blight, and stripe smut are disease problems in the southern part of the state.

Publications office
Mailing Room
Building 7, Research Park
Cornell University
Ithaca, New York 14853
Out-of-state requests: Yes.

Far left: A smooth green lawn says "Welcome" to visitors and residents alike.
Left: A friendly talk takes on a special warmth when combined with a walk through the grass.

	TOTAL INCHES RAIN	INCHES JULY/AUG.	JULY % SUNSHINE	DEC. % SUNSHINE	JULY DAYS ABOVE 90°F.	AVERAGE MAXIMUM/MININUM TEMPERATURES											
						JAN.	FEB.	MARCH	APRIL	MAY	JUNE	JULY	AUG.	SEPT.	OCT.	NOV.	DEC.
New England States																	
Bangor, ME	44	10	62	48	—	28/12	32/14	38/22	52/34	64/44	72/52	78/58	77/56	68/49	57/39	46/31	32/17
Caribou, ME	36	7.7	60	40	1	20/1.5	23/2.7	33/14	45/28	60/39	70/49	76/54	73/51	65/43	53/35	38/25	24/8.2
Grnville, ME	43	10	60	48	—	24/4	29/7	35/14	49/28	63/38	72/48	78/52	75/50	66/43	54/34	41/25	27/10
Portland, ME	41	5.2	64	53	2	31/12	33/12	41/23	53/32	61/42	73/51	79/57	78/55	70/47	60/38	47/30	40/16
Berlin, NH	40	12	46	41	—	28/6	35/7	37/17	52/31	65/40	74/49	79/53	77/51	69/44	58/34	45/27	31/11
Concord, NH	36	6.0	62	47	5	31/10	34/11	42/22	58/32	69/41	78/52	83/57	80/54	72/46	62/36	48/28	35/15
Brlngtn, VT	33	7.2	65	33	3	26/8	28/9	38/20	53/33	60/43	76/54	81/58	78/56	70/49	59/39	44/30	30/15
St. Jhnbry, VT	38	10	52	38	—	29/7	34/11	40/19	56/32	69/42	78/51	82/55	80/53	72/47	60/36	46/28	32/13
Boston, MA	43	6.2	66	52	5	36/22	37/23	45/31	56/41	67/50	77/59	81/65	79/63	72/57	63/47	52/39	39/27
Milton, MA	47	6.8	57	46	2	34/19	35/19	43/27	56/37	67/46	75/56	80/62	79/60	71/53	62/44	50/35	37/22
Wrchstr, MA	45	7.8	62	50	1	31/16	33/17	41/25	55/36	66/45	75/55	79/61	77/59	70/52	61/42	47/32	34/20
Brdgprt, CT	39	7.2	62	52	3	37/23	38/24	45/31	56/40	67/50	76/60	81/66	80/65	74/58	65/48	53/39	40/27
Hartford, CT	43	7.3	62	48	8	34/16	36/18	47/27	59/36	70/46	79/56	84/61	82/59	74/51	64/41	51/32	37/20
Provdnce, RI	43	6.7	60	51	3	36/21	38/21	45/29	57/38	67/47	76/56	81/63	80/61	73/54	64/43	52/35	40/23
New York																	
Albany	33	6.0	63	38	4	30/12	33/14	43/24	58/36	70/46	79/56	84/60	81/58	74/50	63/40	48/31	34/18
Binghamton	37	7.4	65	27	1	29/15	30/15	39/24	54/35	65/45	74/55	78/60	77/58	69/57	59/41	44/32	31/19
Buffalo	36	6.5	69	27	1	30/18	31/18	39/25	53/36	64/46	75/56	79/61	78/59	71/52	60/43	46/33	34/22
Central Park	40	7.7	65	49	6	38/26	40/26	48/34	61/43	71/53	80/63	85/68	83/66	77/60	67/51	54/41	41/29
Elmira	37	6.7	60	40	6	22/4	35/15	50/26	59/33	73/39	73/48	82/56	80/56	72/53	59/37	50/37	35/19
Ithaca	35	7.2	62	35	2	21/5	31/16	47/29	57/35	71/44	71/51	79/58	77/57	70/52	56/37	49/36	34/20
Jamestown	53	1.5	65	30	2	19/0	32/13	49/25	58/32	73/39	72/45	81/54	76/51	71/49	58/35	48/35	33/19
Rochester	31	5.8	69	31	4	31/17	33/17	41/25	56/36	67/46	78/56	82/60	80/58	73/51	62/42	48/33	35/22
Syracuse	36	6.6	65	25	3	31/16	33/16	41/25	56/36	68/46	78/56	82/61	80/59	73/52	62/42	48/34	35/21
Utica	49	7.4	63	32	5	19/6	28/16	45/30	59/33	76/44	75/51	83/58	80/57	70/53	59/38	49/34	33/18

Atlantic and Transitional States

Soil and climate. This is a large, diverse area, complex because it is transitional. It includes the states of New Jersey, Delaware, Maryland, West Virginia, and Kentucky, and stretches over 600 miles east to west from Atlantic City on the coast, to Louisville, Kentucky.

In the western foothills of the Appalachian Mountains, Elkins and Beckley have cool summers. Baltimore and Washington typify the hot summer areas. Rainfall is plentiful. It averages around 45 inches on the coast, decreasing towards the west and north.

Soils are of different types; many are very good. Before planting, make sure soil structure is good. Add organic matter, if necessary, and then check the pH level. Some soil within this area is very acid, (pH of 5 or less), while some is alkaline.

Lime will be necessary in some areas. Adjust pH as per soil test recommendations.

Soil testing
University of Maryland
Soil Testing Laboratory
College Park, Maryland 20742

Soil Testing Laboratory
Cook College
Rutgers University
New Brunswick, New Jersey 08903

United States Department of Agriculture
Beltsville, Maryland 20705
(for Washington, D.C. residents)

Soil Testing Laboratory
University of Delaware
Newark, Delaware 19711

Soil Testing Laboratory
West Virginia University
Morgantown, West Virginia 26506

Soil Testing Laboratory
University of Kentucky
Lexington, Kentucky 40506

Recommended grasses. The cool-season grasses are by far the most common with tall fescue, a transition zone grass. Some of the hardy, warm-season grasses are also quite common.

A recommended cool-season lawn throughout the region is Kentucky bluegrass, or a mixture of Kentucky bluegrass, fine fescue, and turf-type rye. Depending on local conditions and soil types, proportions of each will vary.

If you are growing Kentucky bluegrass in a transition area where it is not really well adapted, here's what to do: (1) Set your mower as high as possible during summer. Don't mow lower than 2 inches. (2) Fertilize in early spring and again in fall as weather cools—but never in summer. Stimulating new succulent growth during hot weather invites disease. (3) Water in the morning and make sure the soil is getting wet to at least 6 inches. Proper watering will help avoid many problems. (4) Use disease-resistant varieties such as 'Adelphi' and 'Majestic' in mixtures with other bluegrasses, fine fescues, and turf-type rye. The other grasses will slow the spread of any disease. Good mixtures are available as seed or sod. (5) Dethatch every two or three years. A thick layer of thatch prevents air and water from reaching the roots and generally weakens the lawn. If attention to detail is not your style, consider another kind of grass.

Where higher summer temperatures and disease problems make growing the perfect lawn a full-time job, consider tall fescue. 'Kentucky 31', one of the most recommended varieties, originated from seed collected from William Suiter's farm in Menifee County, Kentucky. It makes a nice, tough (though coarse-textured) lawn.

Bermuda grass is sometimes used in southern and central New Jersey, southern Maryland, and in Delaware. 'Emerald' zoysia grass can be grown throughout the region. It's used in Baltimore, parts of Sussex County, Delaware, and is widely used along the south shore of New Jersey. Zoysia grass is less useful across the Appalachians; the growing season is often too short.

Publications offices
Agricultural Duplication Services
University of Maryland
College Park, Maryland 20742
Out-of-state requests: Yes.

Mailing Room
Agricultural Hall
University of Delaware
Newark, Delaware 19711
Out-of-state requests: Yes.

United States Department of Agriculture
Beltsville, Maryland 20705
(for Washington, D.C. residents)

Publications Distributions Center
Cook College, Dudley Road
Rutgers University
New Brunswick, New Jersey 08903
Out-of-state requests: No.

Mailing Room
Communications Building
Evansdale Campus
West Virginia University
Morgantown, West Virginia 26506
Out-of-state requests: No.

Bulletin Room
Experiment Station Building
University of Kentucky
Lexington, Kentucky 40506
Out-of-state requests: Limited quantities.

Pennsylvania

Soil and climate. The main geographic features of Pennsylvania are the Appalachian Mountains and somewhat lower Allegheny Mountains. The elevation changes and microclimates created by them are responsible for most climate distinctions. The city of Erie on the shore of Lake Erie and Wilkes-Barre in the Pocono Mountains are two of the consistently coldest cities of Pennsylvania. Summer rain is heavier in cities such as Philadelphia and Allentown, which are nearer the Atlantic Ocean.

Soil along the Allegheny Plateau is mostly stony and thin. This includes cities such as Clearfield, Greensburg, and Indiana. Soil of Harrisburg and Scranton is mostly clay. The pH level varies throughout the state and should be checked.

Lime is usually necessary in some quantity. Check with a soil test. Apply ground limestone in fall.

Soil testing. Check with your local County Extension Agent or write:
School of Agriculture
Pennsylvania State University
University Park, Pennsylvania 16802

Recommended grasses. Kentucky bluegrass is the best adapted and most widely used lawn grass in Pennsylvania.

Varieties tested in and recommended for the state are 'Fylking', 'Baron', 'Adelphi', 'Glade', 'Bonnieblue', and 'Victa'. Red fescue can be used in mixtures in the cooler regions of western and northern Pennsylvania, and especially where excessive shade is a problem. Tall fescue is a good, tough lawn grass for the transitional climates of Pittsburgh and Philadelphia.

Publications office
Agricultural Mailing Room
Agricultural Administration Building
University Park, Pennsylvania 16802
Out-of-state requests: No.

Atlantic and Transitional States

	TOTAL INCHES RAIN	INCHES JULY/AUG.	JULY % SUNSHINE	DEC. % SUNSHINE	JULY DAYS ABOVE 90°F.	AVERAGE MAXIMUM/MININUM TEMPERATURES											
						JAN.	FEB.	MARCH	APRIL	MAY	JUNE	JULY	AUG.	SEPT.	OCT.	NOV.	DEC.
Atlntc Cty, NJ	45	9.3	60	43	5	41/24	43/25	51/31	62/41	72/51	81/60	85/65	83/64	77/57	67/46	56/36	44/26
Newark, NJ	41	8.3	65	50	8	38/24	40/25	49/32	61/42	72/52	81/62	86/67	84/65	77/59	67/48	54/38	41/27
Trenton, NJ	40	8.9	65	48	7	39/25	41/26	49/33	62/42	72/52	81/62	85/67	83/65	76/58	66/48	51/39	41/28
Annapolis, MD	39	8	66	51	18	31/15	48/27	61/40	71/48	79/57	82/61	90/69	78/67	82/62	68/46	57/40	45/26
Baltmr, MD	40	8.3	65	48	11	42/25	44/26	53/32	65/42	75/52	83/62	87/66	85/65	79/58	68/46	56/36	44/26
Cmbrlnd, MD	29	4.9	59	39	21	30/11	47/22	64/35	72/42	80/50	83/56	93/63	89/63	82/58	67/40	54/38	42/23
Easton, MD	38	9.3	65	52	18	33/16	48/28	62/41	71/47	79/55	81/60	90/67	88/67	83/61	66/49	57/44	45/30
Frederick,MD	36	6	65	50	17	31/13	47/24	62/38	71/45	81/55	82/60	91/67	87/67	82/62	66/46	54/42	42/26
Hagrstn, MD	36	7.4	60	40	15	28/8	45/22	60/34	69/42	80/53	81/53	89/61	85/61	80/59	64/44	53/39	39/25
Hancock, MD	36	6.7	60	39	11	27/9	42/22	59/32	68/39	78/49	78/55	87/62	82/62	76/57	61/41	51/40	38/23
LaPlata, MD	42	8.9	67	51	12	34/14	51/27	64/40	72/44	78/54	80/59	88/67	88/66	82/59	67/46	58/42	46/27
Salisbury, MD	44	7.2	68	53	17	31/16	46/24	59/39	69/43	76/52	80/59	90/69	86/68	82/64	67/48	60/45	48/31
Brdgvl, DE	43	10	65	51	18	33/15	48/26	61/40	72/45	78/53	81/59	90/67	89/66	81/61	67/46	58/43	47/29
Dover, DE	42	8.7	65	51	18	34/16	49/27	62/40	71/44	79/54	83/60	90/68	88/68	82/62	68/47	59/42	47/29
Grgetown, DE	40	4.7	67	53	15	32/13	46/25	59/38	69/43	76/52	80/58	89/64	88/65	81/61	65/45	58/42	46/27
Lewes, DE	38	5.3	66	52	9	33/15	47/27	59/39	67/45	76/52	79/59	86/67	87/67	79/62	64/47	58/43	46/29
Middletwn, DE	41	6	65	51	12	32/14	46/26	57/37	70/44	79/53	81/58	88/65	86/65	81/60	66/45	56/41	44/27
Milford, DE	38	5	65	53	22	33/14	49/26	63/40	71/44	80/53	82/58	92/66	89/66	82/61	67/47	59/43	47/28
Newark, DE	41	8.7	64	51	13	31/13	45/24	60/36	69/43	79/52	81/58	89/65	86/65	80/60	66/44	57/44	43/26
Wlmngtn, DE	40	8.3	64	50	7	40/24	42/25	51/32	63/41	73/52	82/61	85/66	84/64	78/58	68/46	55/36	43/26
Wshngtn, DC	39	8.8	63	47	13	43/28	46/29	55/35	67/46	78/56	85/65	88/69	87/68	80/61	70/50	57/39	45/29
Beckley, WV	43	8.1	59	40	0	40/23	42/23	50/30	62/41	69/48	78/57	80/60	79/59	73/52	64/42	51/32	41/24
Charlestn, WV	41	8.1	60	39	7	44/25	46/27	55/34	68/44	77/52	83/61	86/64	84/63	79/56	69/45	56/35	45/27
Elkins, WV	43	9.0	59	40	1	41/19	42/20	51/27	63/37	71/45	78/53	80/57	79/55	74/49	65/38	52/29	42/21
Hntngtn, WV	39	7.5	60	39	7	43/26	45/27	55/34	67/44	76/53	83/61	86/65	85/63	79/56	69/45	55/36	45/27
Prksbrg, WV	38	7.6	62	29	8	41/24	44/26	53/33	66/43	75/52	83/61	86/65	85/63	79/56	68/45	54/36	43/27
Lxngtn, KY	44	8.2	70	42	6	41/24	44/26	53/34	66/45	75/54	83/62	86/66	85/64	80/58	69/47	54/35	44/27
Louisvle, KY	43	6.7	66	40	9	42/24	45/26	54/34	67/45	76/54	84/63	87/66	87/65	80/58	70/46	55/35	44/27

Pennsylvania

	TOTAL INCHES RAIN	INCHES JULY/AUG.	JULY % SUNSHINE	DEC. % SUNSHINE	JULY DAYS ABOVE 90°F.	JAN.	FEB.	MARCH	APRIL	MAY	JUNE	JULY	AUG.	SEPT.	OCT.	NOV.	DEC.
Allentown	42	8.5	60	39	7	36/20	38/21	48/28	61/38	72/48	81/58	85/63	83/61	76/53	66/42	52/33	39/23
Erie	38	6.9	63	30	0	32/18	32/18	40/25	53/36	64/45	73/56	77/60	76/59	70/53	60/43	46/34	35/23
Harrisburg	36	6.9	68	44	9	38/22	40/24	51/31	64/41	74/52	83/61	87/65	85/63	78/56	67/45	53/35	40/25
Philadelphia	40	8.2	63	49	7	40/24	42/25	51/32	63/42	74/52	83/62	87/67	85/65	78/58	68/47	55/37	43/27
Cty. of Ptsbrgh	36	6.9	53	23	6	37/24	39/24	49/32	62/42	72/52	81/61	84/65	83/63	77/56	66/45	52/36	40/27
Gtr. Ptsbrgh	36	7.0	60	30	3	35/21	37/21	47/29	61/39	71/49	79/58	82/61	81/59	75/53	64/42	49/33	37/24
Wilkes Barre	35	7.3	61	35	3	33/18	35/19	45/27	59/38	70/48	79/57	83/61	81/59	74/52	63/42	49/33	36/22
Williamsport	40	7.6	59	38	6	35/19	37/20	47/28	61/38	72/48	81/57	84/61	82/59	75/53	64/42	50/33	38/23

Ohio

Soil and climate. Ohio is the most eastern of the lake states. As such, its climate is similar to the neighboring states of Illinois and Indiana. Temperatures during the summer are high. Most climate variation is determined by latitude.

Topographically, northwestern Ohio is flat while the southeast is hilly. This is because the northwest was previously covered by a lake that was much higher than Lake Erie. Probably the best soil in the state is in this northwestern section.

More specifically, along the southeast through Portsmouth, Steubenville, and as far north as Youngstown, the soil tends to be stony and thin. North central soil is also stony but depth is more variable. The average statewide pH is 6.3, and around Toledo the pH averages about 6.5. These are near ideal conditions for Kentucky bluegrass.

Lime may be necessary, but the best advice is not to use lime unless need is indicated by a soil test.

Soil testing
Cooperative Extension Office
Ohio State University
2120 Fyffe Road
Columbus, Ohio 43210

Recommended grasses. The most used Ohio lawn grass is Kentucky bluegrass. For seeding, use a blend of improved varieties such as 'Fylking', 'Adelphi', 'Baron', or 'Sydsport'.

Use the fescues only in shaded, low maintenance areas, or in a mixture with Kentucky bluegrass.

Publications office
Extension Office of Information
Ohio State University
2120 Fyffe Road
Columbus, Ohio 43210
Out-of-state requests: Yes.

Indiana

Soil and climate. Indiana's climate is largely continental, with no large bodies of water (except in the extreme northwest) to moderate it. The northern half of the state is mostly level prairie but the south has many hills that contribute to a varying climate, even within short distances.

Generally, both temperatures and rainfall increase towards the south. The longest season is in the Evansville area. The shortest season in the west is in the Kankakee Valley area. Angola, Auburn, and Garrett have the shortest season in the northeast.

Lime. About a third of new lawns in Indiana need lime. Don't apply it unless pH has been checked and found to be lower than 6.0.

Soil testing
Plant and Soil Analysis Laboratory
Life Science Building
Purdue University
West Lafayette, Indiana 47907

Recommended grasses. Indiana is prime Kentucky bluegrass country, except for areas in the extreme south. Some of the newest improved varieties for Indiana are 'A-20' (available as sod), 'Adelphi', 'Baron', 'Victa', 'Bonnieblue', 'Glade', and 'Nugget'. Use a blend for an all-Kentucky bluegrass lawn or a mixture containing fine fescues and elite perennial rye grasses.

In the south, around Evansville, homeowners can plant tall fescue or even Bermuda or zoysia grass.

Publications office
Mailing Room
Agricultural Administration Building
Purdue University
West Lafayette, Indiana 47907
Out-of-state requests: Yes.

Illinois

Soil and climate. The range of climates in Illinois is wide, due to the state's north-to-south length. Climatologists have divided the state into three regions, all with a continental-type climate. The northern third has the coldest winters with warm summers; it extends as far south as Kankakee. The middle third stretches from Kankakee to Effingham. There, winters become progressively warmer toward the southern latitudes. The lowest third includes the rest of the state, from Effingham to Cairo.

In the north, the growing season averages 150 days. In Cairo the frost-free growing season is 200 days or more.

The northern two-thirds of Illinois soil is prairie. Prairie soil usually has a very dark brown or dark greyish-brown surface. It is deep and fertile, developed primarily from native grass vegetation.

Lime is often needed, especially in the southern part of the state. There, lime should be applied frequently. Before establishing a lawn, check the pH and add necessary limestone.

Soil testing. Soil testing is not offered by any public agency in Illinois. Check the telephone directory for private laboratories.

Recommended grasses. Kentucky bluegrass is the best lawn grass for most of Illinois. (Check the variety list on page 139.) It is often mixed with red fescue or turf-type rye grass, both of which enhance establishment vigor and mix well.

Tall fescue, planted alone, is a good, tough, play lawn for central and southern Illinois, although it may be injured during the coldest winters.

Publications office
University of Illinois
Agricultural Publications Office
123 Mumford Hall
Urbana, Illinois 61801
Out-of-state requests: No.

Iowa

Soil and climate. Iowa's climate is a continental type. That means most rain falls during the warm period of April to September. During the summer, periods of drought accompanied by hot winds will damage a lawn unless it is watered frequently. Northwood, near the Minnesota border, usually receives the heaviest snowfall. Bonaparte at the Missouri border receives the least.

Lime is often lacking, especially for soils where lawns have not been grown before. Check pH with a soil test.

Soil testing
Soil Testing Laboratory
Cooperative Extension Service
Iowa State University
Ames, Iowa 50010

Recommended grasses. Kentucky bluegrass is the dominant lawn grass of Iowa, as elsewhere in this climate. Common Kentucky bluegrass is acceptable in some situations, but the improved or elite types will not only provide greater beauty and utility, but also improved disease resistance. Turf-type rye grass may be a mix component. Tall fescues are coarse bladed but make a good, tough, play lawn.

Publications office
Bulletin Room
Cooperative Extension Service
Iowa State University
Ames, Iowa 50010
Out-of-state requests: Yes.

Ohio

	TOTAL INCHES RAIN	INCHES JULY/AUG.	JULY % SUNSHINE	DEC. % SUNSHINE	JULY DAYS ABOVE 90°F.	AVERAGE MAXIMUM/MINIMUM TEMPERATURES											
						JAN.	FEB.	MARCH	APRIL	MAY	JUNE	JULY	AUG.	SEPT.	OCT.	NOV.	DEC.
Akron	35	6.5	62	31	11	39/12	36/19	45/27	59/38	70/47	79/57	83/61	84/59	75/53	69/43	49/33	41/22
Cincinnati	40	7.0	68	38	10	40/24	43/26	52/33	65/45	75/54	84/62	87/66	86/64	80/57	69/47	53/36	42/27
Cleveland	35	6.4	68	26	3	33/20	35/21	44/28	58/38	68/48	78/57	82/61	80/60	74/53	64/44	49/34	36/24
Columbus	37	7.1	63	31	6	36/20	39/21	49/29	63/39	73/49	82/59	85/62	84/60	78/53	66/42	51/32	39/23
Dayton	34	6.1	68	37	7	36/20	39/22	48/30	62/41	72/51	82/61	85/64	83/63	77/55	66/45	50/33	38/23
Mansfield	34	6.4	65	32	4	35/21	38/22	47/29	60/40	70/50	80/59	84/63	82/62	76/55	65/44	50/34	38/24
Toledo	31	6.3	68	34	5	32/17	35/19	45/27	59/37	70/47	80/57	84/61	82/59	76/52	65/41	48/31	35/20
Youngstown	38	7.1	64	31	3	33/18	35/19	44/26	58/37	69/46	78/56	82/60	80/58	74/51	63/42	48/33	36/22

Indiana

	TOTAL INCHES RAIN	INCHES JULY/AUG.	JULY % SUNSHINE	DEC. % SUNSHINE	JULY DAYS ABOVE 90°F.	JAN.	FEB.	MARCH	APRIL	MAY	JUNE	JULY	AUG.	SEPT.	OCT.	NOV.	DEC.
Evansville	42	6.7	76	41	15	41/24	45/26	55/34	68/45	77/54	86/64	89/67	88/64	81/57	71/45	55/34	44/26
Fort Wayne	36	6.8	73	37	5	33/18	35/20	45/28	59/39	70/49	80/59	84/62	82/60	76/53	65/42	48/32	36/21
Indianapolis	39	6.5	70	40	6	36/20	39/22	49/30	63/42	73/51	82/61	85/64	84/62	78/55	67/44	50/33	39/23
Lafayette	37	11	70	43	14	17/-3	34/17	54/34	67/44	81/56	79/58	89/64	80/61	77/56	61/40	49/35	32/16
Muncie	38	6.8	68	43	19	18/-1	37/22	56/38	68/45	81/57	82/62	90/70	82/65	78/59	63/43	51/38	36/21
Oolitic	45	7.6	70	44	13	21/0	39/18	59/34	69/43	80/54	81/58	88/65	83/62	80/57	64/38	53/37	37/19
South Bend	36	6.9	72	37	4	31/16	34/18	44/27	58/38	69/47	79/58	83/62	82/60	75/53	64/43	47/32	35/21
Terra Haute	38	6.4	71	46	17	19/0	37/17	57/35	68/43	82/57	83/59	91/66	84/64	81/57	64/42	53/37	35/19

Illinois

	TOTAL INCHES RAIN	INCHES JULY/AUG.	JULY % SUNSHINE	DEC. % SUNSHINE	JULY DAYS ABOVE 90°F.	JAN.	FEB.	MARCH	APRIL	MAY	JUNE	JULY	AUG.	SEPT.	OCT.	NOV.	DEC.
Cairo	47	6.7	75	45	17	44/29	48/32	57/39	69/51	79/60	87/68	90/72	88/70	81/62	71/52	57/40	46/32
Carbondale	43	6.9	73	50	18	26/2	45/20	62/37	73/46	83/57	86/63	90/69	87/65	82/60	68/40	56/39	41/23
Chicago	34	7.2	70	38	9	31/17	35/20	45/29	59/40	70/50	81/60	84/65	83/64	76/56	65/46	48/33	35/22
Decatur	38	6.2	73	42	22	20/1	40/19	57/35	72/46	84/56	83/59	91/66	84/61	81/57	65/42	51/35	36/19
Moline	36	7.9	71	41	8	30/13	34/17	45/26	61/40	72/50	81/60	85/64	84/62	76/53	66/43	48/30	35/18
Peoria	35	6.8	69	40	7	32/16	36/19	46/28	62/41	72/51	82/61	85/65	84/63	76/55	66/44	49/31	36/20
Rockford	37	7.9	71	45	6	29/11	33/15	43/25	59/37	70/47	80/58	84/61	83/60	72/52	64/41	46/29	33/17
Springfield	35	8.5	73	42	10	35/19	39/22	49/30	61/43	74/53	83/62	87/66	85/64	79/56	68/45	51/33	38/23

Iowa

	TOTAL INCHES RAIN	INCHES JULY/AUG.	JULY % SUNSHINE	DEC. % SUNSHINE	JULY DAYS ABOVE 90°F.	JAN.	FEB.	MARCH	APRIL	MAY	JUNE	JULY	AUG.	SEPT.	OCT.	NOV.	DEC.
Burlington	35	7.1	77	51	11	32/14	36/18	47/27	62/40	73/51	82/61	86/65	85/63	77/54	67/44	49/30	36/19
Cedar Rapids	36	7.3	71	49	11	17/-3	36/15	50/32	67/42	79/55	81/57	86/65	77/59	72/55	58/40	42/27	25/12
Davenport	36	7.9	71	41	11	18/1	37/19	53/35	69/47	81/60	82/61	88/68	80/62	75/58	61/44	47/32	30/15
Des Moines	31	6.6	72	45	10	27/11	32/16	42/25	60/39	71/51	80/61	85/65	83/63	75/54	65/44	46/29	33/17
Dubuque	40	8.3	70	46	4	26/9	30/13	41/23	58/37	68/47	78/57	82/61	81/60	72/51	62/41	44/27	31/15
Ottumwa	37	8.3	72	50	15	19/1	38/19	53/36	69/47	79/60	84/62	91/68	80/62	75/58	61/43	47/31	30/16
Sioux City	26	6.2	76	51	10	28/8	33/13	43/23	61/37	72/49	81/59	87/64	85/62	75/51	66/40	47/26	33/14
Waterloo	38	8.2	71	48	6	26/7	30/11	41/22	58/36	70/47	79/58	84/61	82/59	73/50	63/40	45/26	31/13

North and South Dakota

Soil and climate. The climate of the Dakotas can be semi-arid and given to wide and rapid temperature fluctuation. Average rainfall is around 30 inches a year. The rain may fall gently, or as heavy cloudbursts. Some areas in western sections generally receive no more than 10 to 15 inches of rain in a year.

The eastern edge of the Dakotas have a generally fertile loam soil, though it may vary in depth. To the west, soils are far more variable, from very good to very poor.

Lime applications are rarely needed. A soil test will show need, if any, for lime as well as other characteristics of the soil.

Soil testing
Soil Testing Laboratory
Waldron Hall
North Dakota State University
Fargo, North Dakota 58102

Soil Testing Laboratory
South Dakota State University
Brookings, South Dakota 57007

Recommended grasses. The short, native grasses are the natural vegetation of the northern Great Plains. Blue grama, buffalo grass, wheat grass, and others are hardy and adapted to the dry, harsh climate.

Most home lawns, however, are

Kentucky bluegrass and fine fescue mixtures.

Publications offices
Department of Agricultural Communications
North Dakota State University
Fargo, North Dakota 58102
Out-of-state requests: Yes.

Bulletin Room
South Dakota State University
Extension Building
Brookings, South Dakota 57007
Out-of-state requests: Yes.

Nebraska

Soil and climate. Nebraska varies from the Dakotas by having a more mild climate: Summers are longer and winters are less cold.

Like the Dakotas, soil is on the average better toward the east. In many areas proper preparation of the soil before planting can be an important step towards establishment and maintenance of your lawn.

Lime applications are usually not necessary.

Soil testing. Check with your County

Extension Agent or write:
Soil Testing Laboratory
University of Nebraska-Lincoln
Department of Agronomy
Keim Hall, East Campus
Lincoln, Nebraska 68503

Recommended grasses. Kentucky bluegrass combined with the fine fescues makes a good all-around Nebraska lawn. The turf-type rye grasses are sometimes used. They have many advantages and mix well in a bluegrass-fescue lawn, but aren't quite as winter hardy.

Tall fescue, with winter hardiness roughly comparable to the rye grasses, is also a favorite in southern Nebraska. Zoysia and Bermuda grass are often grown south of the Platte in cities like Lincoln, Hastings, and McCook although they are at the northern limits of their range.

Publications office
University of Nebraska-Lincoln
Department of Agricultural Communications
Lincoln, Nebraska 68583
Out-of-state requests: Yes.

Missouri

Soil and climate. The geography and climate of Missouri is divided into three separate regions. The northwest is prairie, extending into neighboring Kansas, Nebraska, and Iowa. Cities like St. Joseph or Independence in the northwest are often dry and have cold winters. Soil in these cities may be slightly alkaline.

Extending through the center of the state from the northeast to the southwest is the Ozark Plateau. Springfield and Rolla are located here. The Ozarks have less severe winters than the prairies, and cooler summers compared to the southeast.

Cape Girardeau, Sikeston, and Poplar

Bluff are cities in the southeast lowlands. Growing seasons are around 200 days and rain is plentiful—about 45 inches a year. Soil here is acid. Most areas are well drained but some are swampy.

Lime is very likely needed, especially in the southeast. Check by testing the soil.

Soil testing
Soil Testing Laboratory
University of Missouri
Columbia, Missouri 65201

Recommended grasses. Kentucky bluegrass, fine fescue, and turf-type rye are the predominant cool-season grasses. The

highest quality lawns are usually a mixture of improved varieties of these three grasses.

'Meyer' zoysia grass grows well in the southern, long growing-season areas. It requires plenty of heat and a good, long season for best growth.

Bermuda grass is often grown in the southern areas.

Publications office
Extension Publications
206 Whitten Hall
University of Missouri-Columbia
Columbia, Missouri 65201
Out-of-state requests: Yes.

Kansas

Soil and climate. Kansas is the center of the United States. The slope of the land is gradual from the northwest to the southeast. This slope is apparent in measures of climate, too. The southeast—Independence, Parsonsville, Pittsburg, Chanute—receives about twice the rain, has a longer growing season (by 40 or more days), and has warmer winters and summers compared to northwestern Kansas. The soil also varies. Kansas City soil is frequently acid, as is soil in the above-named cities of southeastern Kansas.

Western Kansas is a part of the Great Plains. Here, wind erosion is a problem,

and blowing soil may make new lawn establishment difficult. The climate is quite variable month to month and year to year. Humidity is low and evaporation is fast.

The soil is sandy or fairly heavy (called "hard lands"). Both are fairly high in nutrients.

Lime may be necessary in the east, especially the southeast. West Kansas rarely needs lime.

Soil testing is available through local County Extension offices or write:
Agronomy Department
Kansas State University
Manhattan, Kansas 66506

Recommended grasses. Cool-season grasses are generally used, but in the south and western sections of the state, Bermuda grass and some of the native grasses, buffalo grass or blue grama, for instance, are useful. Buffalo grass will form a "lawn" on less than 15 inches of rain a year. Buy treated buffalo grass seed or establishment may be very slow and erratic.

Publications office
Publications Distribution Office
Umberget Hall
Kansas State University
Manhattan, Kansas 66506
Out-of-state requests: Yes.

	TOTAL INCHES RAIN	INCHES JULY/AUG.	JULY % SUNSHINE	DEC. % SUNSHINE	JULY DAYS ABOVE 90°F.	JAN.	FEB.	MARCH	APRIL	MAY	JUNE	JULY	AUG.	SEPT.	OCT.	NOV.	DEC.
										AVERAGE MAXIMUM/MINIMUM TEMPERATURES							

North and South Dakota

	TOTAL INCHES RAIN	INCHES JULY/AUG.	JULY % SUNSHINE	DEC. % SUNSHINE	JULY DAYS ABOVE 90°F.	JAN.	FEB.	MARCH	APRIL	MAY	JUNE	JULY	AUG.	SEPT.	OCT.	NOV.	DEC.
Bismark, ND	16	4.2	76	47	8	19/-3	24/2	35/15	55/31	67/42	76/52	84/57	83/55	71/44	60/33	39/18	26/5
Fargo, ND	20	6.0	71	43	5	15/-4	21/1	33/15	53/32	67/42	76/53	83/59	82/57	70/46	58/35	37/20	22/4
Minot, ND	17	4.5	69	53	5	8/-12	31/12	43/19	63/33	77/50	76/52	83/56	74/47	64/46	58/34	36/15	14/-2
Williston, ND	14	3.6	75	47	8	19/-3	26/3	36/14	55/30	67/41	75/50	84/56	83/54	70/43	59/32	38/18	26/5
Aberdeen, SD	19	4.8	72	50	2	12/-9	35/13	42/25	66/38	77/52	80/55	81/53	79/52	71/48	59/34	36/18	18/4
Pierre, SD	18	4.4	73	55	9	18/-4	41/19	47/26	67/39	79/52	85/58	86/56	84/55	76/49	60/36	42/22	26/11
Rpd City, SD	17	3.6	72	54	11	34/10	38/14	43/20	51/32	67/43	76/52	86/59	86/57	75/46	64/36	47/23	38/15
Sx Falls, SD	25	5.8	74	51	12	25/4	30/9	40/20	58/34	70/46	79/56	85/61	84/60	73/49	63/38	43/23	30/10

Nebraska

	TOTAL INCHES RAIN	INCHES JULY/AUG.	JULY % SUNSHINE	DEC. % SUNSHINE	JULY DAYS ABOVE 90°F.	JAN.	FEB.	MARCH	APRIL	MAY	JUNE	JULY	AUG.	SEPT.	OCT.	NOV.	DEC.
Lincoln	29	6.9	74	52	18	33/12	38/17	47/26	63/39	73/51	83/61	89/66	87/64	77/54	68/44	50/28	38/17
North Platte	20	5.0	74	60	12	37/10	41/15	47/21	61/34	71/45	81/55	88/61	87/59	77/48	67/35	50/22	40/14
Omaha	30	7.7	77	56	14	33/12	38/17	48/26	61/40	74/51	83/61	89/66	87/64	79/54	69/43	51/29	38/18
Chadron	16	3.1	73	60	17	30/3	48/23	49/23	64/38	74/48	86/58	90/61	81/55	80/49	65/36	46/24	35/13
Grand Island	23	5.5	78	60	18	29/6	49/19	53/29	68/45	77/57	85/62	91/67	82/61	77/54	65/40	50/29	41/15
Sidney	17	4.3	71	65	17	32/3	48/19	46/19	62/34	73/44	84/54	88/58	82/54	80/46	67/32	48/22	31/8
Valentine	18	4.9	75	59	16	30/4	49/21	46/24	65/40	76/52	86/59	90/62	83/55	79/50	65/39	48/28	37/16

Missouri

	TOTAL INCHES RAIN	INCHES JULY/AUG.	JULY % SUNSHINE	DEC. % SUNSHINE	JULY DAYS ABOVE 90°F.	JAN.	FEB.	MARCH	APRIL	MAY	JUNE	JULY	AUG.	SEPT.	OCT.	NOV.	DEC.
Columbia	37	7.0	75	46	16	38/21	43/24	51/32	65/45	75/54	83/63	87/67	86/65	79/57	69/47	54/34	41/24
Kansas City	37	8.2	82	59	19	36/18	41/23	51/31	65/44	75/54	83/63	88/67	87/66	79/57	68/47	51/33	39/23
Kirksville	36	7.7	72	50	22	22/2	41/20	57/36	69/46	80/57	85/61	92/69	83/63	78/57	64/43	50/33	34/18
Poplar Bluff	45	6.0	74	51	23	30/10	49/24	64/40	75/50	84/60	89/66	91/70	90/68	82/62	70/44	61/43	43/24
St. Joseph	36	7.8	77	55	20	25/4	45/24	58/38	70/48	77/59	86/64	91/70	84/65	78/59	66/43	51/34	38/20
St. Louis	36	6.6	72	43	14	40/23	44/26	53/33	67/46	76/55	85/65	88/69	87/67	80/59	70/48	54/36	43/26
Springfield	40	6.6	72	49	16	43/23	47/26	55/33	68/45	76/54	84/63	89/66	89/65	81/57	71/47	56/34	46/26
Vichy	42	4.5	75	50	17	27/9	46/26	60/39	72/50	79/60	82/64	89/71	86/67	80/62	67/47	52/38	41/24

Kansas

	TOTAL INCHES RAIN	INCHES JULY/AUG.	JULY % SUNSHINE	DEC. % SUNSHINE	JULY DAYS ABOVE 90°F.	JAN.	FEB.	MARCH	APRIL	MAY	JUNE	JULY	AUG.	SEPT.	OCT.	NOV.	DEC.
Chanute	40	8.6	78	60	21	31/11	53/26	61/37	72/50	80/59	87/65	90/70	86/67	81/62	70/47	55/37	45/23
Concordia	28	6.4	80	61	21	29/9	51/24	59/34	68/46	79/57	86/64	93/69	84/64	80/58	67/44	52/31	41/18
Dodge City	21	5.7	79	65	22	43/19	47/23	54/28	67/41	76/52	86/61	91/67	90/65	81/56	71/45	55/30	45/22
Goodland	17	4.8	75	68	19	36/9	53/21	52/25	65/39	74/50	86/58	91/62	83/59	82/52	67/38	53/25	46/16
Hill City	24	6.2	77	63	22	35/10	55/21	59/29	70/44	80/55	91/62	94/68	87/63	83/54	70/41	54/28	45/17
Salina	28	6.4	80	63	24	32/11	53/25	61/36	69/47	79/59	87/66	94/71	86/66	81/61	69/46	53/34	44/20
Topeka	35	8.4	69	51	15	38/18	44/23	53/30	66/43	76/53	84/63	89/67	88/66	80/56	70/45	54/32	42/22
Wichita	31	7.4	74	58	21	41/21	47/25	55/32	68/45	77/55	86/65	92/70	91/68	82/59	71/48	56/34	44/25

Michigan

Soil and climate. Along the shorelines, climate is dominated by the lakes. Both spring and fall arrive later than in the interior. Inland climate may be either continental or semimarine, depending on the direction of the wind.

Most Michigan soil is inherently acid and somewhat low in fertility. However, with the pH adjusted upwards and fertilizer added, it is quite productive.

Lime is not necessary unless a soil test indicates a pH of 5.7 or less. Most irrigation water used in Michigan contains enough lime to compensate for the naturally acid soil.

Soil testing
Crop and Soil Sciences Department
Michigan State University
East Lansing, Michigan 48824

Recommended grasses. According to lawn experts at Michigan State, mixtures of Kentucky bluegrass and fine fescues are the best for most parts of Michigan. Several varieties of Kentucky bluegrass have been tested under Michigan conditions and found to be quite good. They include: 'Baron', 'Fylking', 'Merion', 'Nugget', 'Adelphi', and 'Bonnieblue'. If possible, a blend of three or more bluegrass varieties is preferable.

'Pennlawn', 'Highlight', 'Jamestown', and 'Wintergreen' are among the varieties of fine fescue grown in Michigan.

The preferred time to seed is between August 15 and September 10 in southern Michigan, and between August 10 and September 1 in the northern part of the state.

Publications office
MSU Bulletin Office
P.O. Box 231
East Lansing, Michigan 48824
Out-of-state requests: Yes.

Wisconsin

Soil and climate. Wisconsin winters are cold and may reach −40°F. around Eau Claire and west-central parts of the state. Milwaukee winters are warmer and summers cooler due to the moderating influence of Lake Michigan. Summer thunderstorms are common. The wettest time of year is May to September.

Much of the soil in Wisconsin developed under an evergreen forest. Such soil is acid and generally low in nutrients. It must be adequately limed and fertilized for proper lawn growth.

Lime is often necessary.

Soil testing
Soil and Plant Analysis Laboratory
University of Wisconsin
806 S. Park Street
Madison, Wisconsin 53715, or,
State Soil Laboratory
Route 2
Marshfield, Wisconsin 54449

Recommended grasses. Blends of three or more Kentucky bluegrass varieties (see page 139) make a very handsome and hardy Wisconsin lawn. The fine fescues are used in sandy, dry soil or shady locations. Colonial bent grass will sometimes make a

good lawn (unmixed), especially along the lake shore.

Publications office
University of Wisconsin
Department of Agricultural Journalism
Agricultural Bulletin Building
1535 Observatory Drive
Madison, Wisconsin 53706
Out-of-state requests: Yes.

Minnesota

Soil and climate. Minnesota's climate is continental. Temperatures can swing widely within a short time and summer rain is often abundant. In general, there is a tendency towards climatic extremes. Rainfall is generally more plentiful moving south and east.

Minnesota soil varies from sandy and sandy loam to heavy clay. Tests of lawn soil in the Twin Cities area have shown that most are high in phosphorus.

Lime is usually applied every 6 to 10 years at rates of 50 to 150 pounds for every 1,000

square feet. The eastern half of the state commonly needs less liming. Make sure with a soil test.

Soil testing
Soil Testing Laboratory
University of Minnesota
St. Paul, Minnesota 55108

Recommended grasses. Most Minnesota lawns are either Kentucky bluegrass, red fescue, or a combination of the two. The more cold tolerant of the turf-type ryes, such as 'NK-200', are also used.

The bent grasses are difficult to maintain. The coarse fescues make good lawns in transitional climates but lack tolerance to Minnesota's winters. Zoysia grass is widely advertised but not adapted to Minnesota, since it requires a longer growing season.

Publications office
Bulletin Room
Coffey Hall
University of Minnesota
St. Paul, Minnesota 55108
Out-of-state requests: No.

Eastern Canada

Soil and climate. This region includes the provinces of Manitoba, Nova Scotia, Ontario, and Quebec. For climate and soil specifics, read about the most northern states of the United States. Soil and climate will also be essentially the same.

Lime. Necessary in Nova Scotia and most of eastern Quebec, less so traveling westward. A soil test is the only way to know for sure.

Soil testing
Department of Soil Science
University of Manitoba
Winnipeg, Manitoba   R3T 2N2

Soils and Crops Branch
Nova Scotia Agricultural College
Truro, Nova Scotia
B2N 5E3

Department of Land Resource Science
Ontario Agricultural College
University of Guelph
Guelph, Ontario
N1G 2W1

Canadian Industries Limited
Soil Laboratory, Beloiel Works
McMasterville, Quebec

Recommended grasses. A good home

lawn can be made throughout most of Eastern Canada using a mixture of Kentucky bluegrass and creeping red fescue. Turf-type rye may be included in such a mixture in order to speed establishment.

Publications offices
Contact the nearest Research Branch office of Agricultural Canada, a local provincial agricultural representative, or the Plant Science Department of a university for information about lawn growing in your area.

	TOTAL INCHES RAIN	INCHES JULY/AUG.	JULY % SUNSHINE	DEC. % SUNSHINE	JULY DAYS ABOVE 90°F.	AVERAGE MAXIMUM/MINIMUM TEMPERATURES											
						JAN.	FEB.	MARCH	APRIL	MAY	JUNE	JULY	AUG.	SEPT.	OCT.	NOV.	DEC.

Michigan

	TOTAL INCHES RAIN	INCHES JULY/AUG.	JULY % SUNSHINE	DEC. % SUNSHINE	JULY DAYS ABOVE 90°F.	JAN.	FEB.	MARCH	APRIL	MAY	JUNE	JULY	AUG.	SEPT.	OCT.	NOV.	DEC.
Alpena	28	5.2	68	29	2	27/9	29/8	37/16	52/28	64/37	74/47	79/52	77/51	68/44	59/36	43/27	31/16
Detroit	31	6.0	70	32	6	32/19	34/20	43/28	58/39	68/48	79/59	83/63	82/62	74/55	63/45	48/34	35/24
Flint	30	6.2	70	32	2	30/15	32/15	41/24	56/35	67/44	77/55	81/58	80/57	72/50	62/40	46/31	34/20
Grand Rapids	32	5.6	66	24	5	30/16	33/16	42/24	57/36	69/45	79/56	83/60	82/58	74/51	63/41	46/31	34/21
Lansing	30	5.6	71	29	4	30/15	32/16	42/24	57/36	68/45	78/56	83/59	81/58	73/50	62/41	46/31	34/20
Marquette	31	6.1	67	28	2	25/12	26/13	34/20	48/32	59/41	70/50	75/57	74/57	65/49	56/41	40/29	29/18
Muskegon	32	5.1	68	30	1	30/18	31/18	40/25	55/36	66/45	76/55	80/60	79/59	71/52	61/42	46/33	34/23
S. Ste. Marie	32	5.7	63	28	1	22/6	24/7	32/15	47/29	59/38	70/47	75/52	73/53	64/46	55/38	39/26	27/13

Wisconsin

	TOTAL INCHES RAIN	INCHES JULY/AUG.	JULY % SUNSHINE	DEC. % SUNSHINE	JULY DAYS ABOVE 90°F.	JAN.	FEB.	MARCH	APRIL	MAY	JUNE	JULY	AUG.	SEPT.	OCT.	NOV.	DEC.
Ashland	30	8.3	64	41	3	13/-8	30/9	43/24	56/30	72/45	74/49	80/56	74/50	65/47	57/34	40/23	24/10
Eau Claire	29	7.5	68	44	4	9/-11	29/9	46/28	64/40	79/53	77/55	84/62	77/54	69/51	57/36	39/23	22/7
Green Bay	27	5.7	65	37	3	24/7	27/9	37/20	54/33	66/43	76/53	81/58	79/56	70/48	60/39	42/26	29/13
Janesville	32	7.3	69	40	14	16/-6	34/13	51/31	68/41	82/52	81/54	88/63	80/58	74/55	61/39	45/29	30/13
La Crosse	29	6.5	69	46	6	25/7	30/10	40/22	58/37	69/49	78/58	83/62	82/61	72/52	62/42	43/28	30/14
Madison	30	6.9	69	39	5	25/8	29/11	39/21	56/35	67/45	77/55	81/59	80/57	71/48	61/39	43/26	30/14
Milwaukee	29	6.1	71	38	4	27/11	30/15	39/23	55/35	65/43	75/54	80/59	80/59	71/51	61/41	44/28	31/17
Wausau	32	7.8	65	42	4	12/-8	29/9	44/27	61/37	78/52	74/52	82/61	75/54	66/51	57/37	39/25	24/9

Minnesota

	TOTAL INCHES RAIN	INCHES JULY/AUG.	JULY % SUNSHINE	DEC. % SUNSHINE	JULY DAYS ABOVE 90°F.	JAN.	FEB.	MARCH	APRIL	MAY	JUNE	JULY	AUG.	SEPT.	OCT.	NOV.	DEC.
Austin	31	7.7	71	46	12	12/-10	25/5	49/32	67/43	80/56	82/56	87/63	78/55	74/50	59/36	42/24	23/10
Duluth	30	7.5	67	39	1	18/-1	22/2	33/14	48/29	60/39	70/48	76/55	74/54	64/45	54/36	35/21	22/6
Fergus Falls	25	6.4	72	49	4	4/-16	34/13	41/21	59/37	74/53	74/55	81/59	71/50	65/47	55/32	34/15	16/-3
Inter. Falls	26	7.3	46	33	2	13/-9	19/-5	32/9	49/27	62/38	72/48	78/53	75/51	64/42	54/33	32/17	18/-1
Mpls/St. Paul	26	6.7	71	40	7	21/3	26/7	37/20	55/35	68/46	77/57	82/61	81/60	71/49	61/39	41/24	27/11
Rochester	27	7.3	70	46	3	22/4	26/7	36/19	55/34	67/45	76/55	81/59	79/58	70/48	60/39	41/24	27/11
St. Cloud	27	7.1	72	48	4	19/-1	24/2	36/16	54/32	67/43	76/54	82/59	80/59	69/46	50/36	39/21	25/7

Eastern Canada

AVERAGE DEGREES CELSIUS

	TOTAL INCHES RAIN	INCHES JULY/AUG.	JULY % SUNSHINE	DEC. % SUNSHINE	JULY DAYS ABOVE 90°F.	JAN.	FEB.	MARCH	APRIL	MAY	JUNE	JULY	AUG.	SEPT.	OCT.	NOV.	DEC.
Frdrictn, N.B.	43	6.9	234*	91**	—	-9.2	-8.5	-2.6	4.0	10.5	15.7	19.1	18.0	13.6	7.9	1.8	-6.3
Montrl, Que.	39	7.3	264	77	—	-8.9	-7.6	-1.4	6.7	13.6	19.1	21.6	20.4	15.8	10.1	2.9	-5.7
No. Bay, Ont.	38	7.4	267	70	—	-12.8	-11.1	-5.4	3.2	10.1	15.8	18.3	17.1	12.4	6.9	-0.8	-9.4
Ottawa, Ont.	33	6.4	277	78	—	-10.9	-9.5	-3.1	5.6	12.4	18.2	20.7	19.3	14.6	8.7	1.4	-7.7
Quebec, Que.	43	8.3	233	65	—	-11.6	-10.6	-4.4	3.3	10.6	16.3	19.2	17.8	13.1	7.2	0.2	-8.6
St. Jhns, Nfld.	59	7.7	213	52	—	-3.8	-4.2	-2.4	1.1	5.5	10.4	15.3	15.4	11.9	7.1	3.5	-1.3
Thndr By, Ont.	29	6.3	302	92	—	-14.8	-13.0	-6.2	2.4	8.3	13.8	17.5	16.5	11.3	6.1	-2.5	-10.8
Toronto, Ont.	31	5.8	281	77	—	-4.4	-3.8	0.6	7.6	13.2	19.2	21.8	21.1	17.0	11.2	4.8	-1.8

*Total hours bright sun, July   **Total hours bright sun, December.

Climates of
the South

This section will help you determine the climate conditions that affect your ability to grow lawns in your region. Find the city closest to you on the chart, and note the information in each column. Check the information on the left-hand pages for specific information on soil conditions and lime requirements, recommended grasses, and suggestions for additional information.

This ingenious mosaic look is created by using centipede grass and pine straw.

Climates of the South

Virginia

Soil and climate. Much of Virginia is located in a transition zone where some kinds of both cool-season and warm-season grasses grow but where neither type is especially well adapted.

Lime. Normally needed if soil has not previously been limed. Apply lime as indicated by soil test results. One application lasts for at least three years and frequently much longer.

Soil testing. Check with your local County or City Extension Service office, or write:
Soil Testing Laboratory
Cooperative Extension Service

Virginia Polytechnic Institute and
State University
Blacksburg, Virginia 24061

Recommended grasses. West of the Blue Ridge Mountains and in the northern Piedmont area, the cool-season grasses should be planted. These include Kentucky bluegrass, tall fescue, the fine fescues, and turf-type perennial rye.

Warm-season grasses, such as Bermuda and zoysia, are best adapted in the southern Piedmont and much of the Tidewater area (Quantico through Farmville to Danville). Improved Bermuda grasses

such as 'Midiron' and 'Tufcote' are the better-adapted varieties for lawns.

Tall fescue makes a tough lawn and is a good compromise in a transitional area and is the most extensively used species for lawns in this area. 'Ky 31' is the best variety and has consistently remained better than other tall fescue varieties in Virginia trials.
Publications office
Bulletin Room
Extension Division
Virginia Polytechnic Institute and
State University
Blacksburg, Virginia 24061
Out-of-state requests: Yes.

North Carolina

Soil and climate. The state of North Carolina conveniently divides into geographic thirds.

In the west around Asheville and all the area west of the Blue Ridge Mountains, use Kentucky bluegrass in the higher elevations. Bermuda grass, zoysia, tall fescue, or Kentucky bluegrass is used at lower elevations.

For the Piedmont around Winston-Salem, Shelby, Hickory, and Eden, the main grasses are Bermuda grass, zoysia grass, and tall fescue. Centipede grass can be grown in the warmest sections, Kentucky bluegrass in the coldest.

Along the Coastal Plain, use Bermuda, centipede, or zoysia grass in dry, well-drained soil, and either carpet grass or tall fescue in soil that tends to stay wet. Zoysia and centipede grass are best in light shade. St. Augustine grass is all right near the coast.

Lime. The abundant rainfall the state receives combined with the natural soil makes an acid soil. Lime (natural ground limestone is best) is almost always necessary.

Soil testing. Check with local County Extension Agent offices for mailing kits

and directions, or write:
Agronomic Division
North Carolina Department of Agriculture
Raleigh, North Carolina 27611

Recommended grasses. The best-adapted grasses vary according to the three geographic regions.

Publications office
Publications Office
Department of Agricultural Information
Box 5037
State University Station
Raleigh, North Carolina 27607
Out-of-state requests: Yes.

	TOTAL INCHES RAIN	INCHES JULY/AUG.	JULY % SUNSHINE	DEC. % SUNSHINE	JULY DAYS ABOVE 90°F.	AVERAGE MAXIMUM/MINIMUM TEMPERATURES											
						JAN.	FEB.	MARCH	APRIL	MAY	JUNE	JULY	AUG.	SEPT.	OCT.	NOV.	DEC.

Virginia

Blacksburg	46	7.6	60	41	10	28/9	43/18	58/34	67/41	75/49	76/53	81/60	83/59	76/54	61/38	54/37	43/22
Charlottesville	44	9.9	64	41	21	33/17	49/22	63/41	72/46	80/56	81/60	93/67	89/64	82/62	66/45	55/40	44/27
Danville	43	8.6	63	50	24	37/17	51/23	66/39	76/46	82/56	84/60	95/68	92/67	85/61	66/43	60/40	48/27
Fredericksbg	40	9.2	68	52	26	36/13	54/25	65/38	75/42	82/53	86/58	95/66	92/65	85/59	69/44	55/40	46/28
Lynchburg	38	8.1	62	52	7	46/27	48/28	56/35	68/45	77/54	83/62	86/65	84/64	79/57	69/47	57/37	49/29
Norfolk	45	12	65	57	11	49/32	50/33	57/39	68/48	76/57	83/65	87/70	85/69	80/64	70/53	60/43	51/34
Richmond	43	11	65	51	13	47/28	50/29	58/35	70/45	78/54	85/63	88/67	87/66	81/59	71/47	61/37	49/29
Roanoke	39	7.9	61	41	9	46/27	48/28	56/34	68/44	76/53	83/60	86/64	85/63	79/56	70/46	58/36	47/28

North Carolina

Asheville	45	9.4	60	57	3	48/27	51/28	58/33	69/42	77/51	82/59	84/63	81/62	78/55	69/44	58/34	49/28
Charlotte	43	8.5	69	58	11	52/32	55/33	62/39	73/49	80/57	86/65	88/69	87/68	82/62	73/50	62/40	52/32
Elizabeth City	50	9.9	70	55	17	40/22	54/31	64/44	74/51	79/57	83/63	90/69	89/70	85/66	69/51	65/47	54/35
Fayetteville	47	11	65	55	25	42/22	57/28	67/44	78/51	84/59	87/65	94/71	90/70	86/64	71/47	66/44	54/32
Greensboro	41	8.7	62	54	11	49/28	51/30	59/36	71/46	79/55	85/63	87/67	86/66	80/59	71/47	60/36	50/29
Raleigh	43	10	61	56	10	51/30	53/31	61/37	72/47	79/55	86/63	88/67	87/66	81/60	72/48	62/38	52/30
Rocky Mount	46	11	67	54	26	41/23	56/31	67/43	78/49	82/58	86/64	94/69	91/68	86/64	71/49	66/45	53/34
Wilmington	54	15	63	59	15	57/36	59/37	65/44	74/52	81/61	87/68	89/72	88/71	83/66	75/55	67/44	58/37

Arkansas

Soil and climate. If you draw an imaginary dividing line from the southwest to the northeast, you'll notice most of the west is mountainous while the east is lowlands. The soil of the lowlands is very fertile and holds water well. Here, droughts rarely cause damage. The soil of the uplands is in many cases severely eroded, and is of low fertility. Lawns in the uplands will suffer during hot and dry summers unless watered.

Rain is evenly distributed throughout the year. Spring rain is usually heaviest, with May being, on the average, the wettest month. October is the driest month.

Lime needs to be added in most cases.

Soil testing. Contact your local County Extension Agent, or write:
Soil Testing Laboratory
Cooperative Extension Service
1201 McAlmont
P.O. Box 391
Little Rock, Arkansas 72203

Recommended grasses. Common Bermuda grass is the most widely used lawn grass in Arkansas. Mowed and fertilized on a regular basis, it makes a very attractive lawn.

Improved Bermuda grass is preferred by those desiring a very fine-textured, high-quality lawn. Use zoysia grass in areas of 30 to 40 percent shade. It requires less mowing and forms dense, weed-free lawns.

Centipede grass is slow to form a lawn, but can make an attractive turf. 'Oaklawn' is winter hardy throughout Arkansas.

Publications office
Cooperative Extension Service
Extension Publications Specialist
University of Arkansas
1201 McAlmont
P.O. Box 391
Little Rock Arkansas 72203
Out-of-state requests: No.

Oklahoma

Soil and climate. The climate of Oklahoma is continental, meaning it has pronounced seasonal and geographic ranges in both temperature and rain.

Vast open plains make up the central and western sections. The western parts of the state are relatively cool and dry, while the east is more hilly and the air more moist, with frequent showers.

Rain is fairly frequent throughout most of the state, though much less In the Panhandle.

The average length of the growing season varies from 180 days in the western part of Cimarron County to 240 days in the extreme southeast.

Droughts and dust storms in the western parts of the state sometimes occur, but are rarely damaging outside the Panhandle.

Soil in the bottom lands is the most fertile and is used extensively for agriculture. Upland soil is most similar to soil of the Plains states.

Lime is usually needed. Determine by testing the soil. Use finely ground limestone.

Soil testing. Contact your local County Extension office, or write:
Soil Testing Laboratory
Agronomy Department
Oklahoma State University
Stillwater, Oklahoma 74074

Recommended grasses. Bermuda grass is the lawn grass used most often. The common, seeded variety is most versatile, but some improved Bermuda grasses are available.

The native buffalo grass is well adapted to much of western Oklahoma. Buy seed that has been treated or else germination may be very slow and irregular.

Publications office
Central Mailing Service
Oklahoma State University
Cooperative Extension Office
Stillwater, Oklahoma 74704
Out-of-state requests: Yes.

Texas

Soil and climate. This state is so large and diverse that authorities have divided Texas into four regions of differing climates. In the southeast it's the Coastal Plains or East Texas Plains. This region extends from the coast to the Balcones Escarpment.

The north-central plains extend from the Black Lands westward to the Great Plains.

The Great Plains extend down from the north and northwest into Texas on the high ridge between the headwaters of the Canadian, Red, Brazos, and Colorado rivers.

The last division is called the Trans-Pecos Mountain area. It is a plateau lying west of Pecos Valley.

The growing season averages 185 days in the northern Panhandle, 230 days along the eastern and southern borders of the north-central divisions. From there to the coast, most of the counties have growing seasons over 300 days in length.

Rainfall averages over 50 inches in the east, but in the extreme west it averages less than 10 inches.

Soil in Texas varies in a similar degree. Generous amounts of organic matter are needed in most areas.

Lime is necessary in the eastern counties of the state.

Soil testing
Texas Agricultural Extension Service
The Texas A&M University System
Soil Testing Laboratory
College Station, Texas 77843

Recommended grasses. Common Bermuda grass and St. Augustine grass are the most widely used and practical warm-season grasses for Texas.

Buffalo grass is occasionally used in areas of the south and west where irrigation water is scarce.

Zoysia grass and centipede grass are grown in certain areas.

A Bermuda grass lawn is common in Texas. Drought tolerance is good and the lawn is relatively trouble free. Common Bermuda grass is easiest to plant and care for. Improved kinds, such as 'Tiflawn', 'Texturf-10', and 'Tifdwarf' are available.

St. Augustine grass is not as cold hardy or drought tolerant as Bermuda grass, so should not be planted west or north of Ft. Worth. It grows satisfactorily east of a line from Vernon to Brady to Del Rio. 'Floratam', selected through a combined effort of Florida and Texas agricultural scientists, has improved cold-hardiness and pest resistance. St. Augustine grass is sometimes confused with carpet grass, which is rarely grown in Texas.

'Emerald' zoysia grass is widely recommended for Texas. It is fine-leaved, dense-growing and dark green. Manila grass, or matrella (*Zoysia matrella*), is fine textured but is not recommended, except in the southern parts of the state. 'Meyer' zoysia grass accepts the cold.

Centipede grass is adapted to sandy, well-drained soils in east, south, and central Texas.

Tall fescue is a good lawn grass for north and west Texas. It requires watering but makes a year-around green lawn. 'Kentucky 31' and 'Fawn' are improved varieties.

Almost exclusively cool-season lawns are used in El Paso, Amarillo, and in parts of the Panhandle.

Publications office
Texas Agricultural Extension Service
The Texas A&M University System
College Station, Texas 77843
Out-of-state requests: Yes.

	TOTAL INCHES RAIN	INCHES JULY/AUG.	JULY % SUNSHINE	DEC. % SUNSHINE	JULY DAYS ABOVE 90°F.	AVERAGE MAXIMUM/MINIMUM TEMPERATURES											
						JAN.	FEB.	MARCH	APRIL	MAY	JUNE	JULY	AUG.	SEPT.	OCT.	NOV.	DEC.

Arkansas

Blytheville	48	6.6	72	50	28	34/16	55/34	68/45	78/54	89/65	93/68	95/73	93/69	84/66	72/49	60/45	47/30
El Dorado	49	6.9	71	48	28	46/25	63/34	72/47	79/54	87/64	95/71	96/75	91/71	89/69	77/50	65/43	57/34
Fayetteville	44	9.5	74	56	21	34/13	54/27	61/40	72/51	80/58	88/65	90/70	87/68	82/63	71/45	59/40	50/27
Fort Smith	42	6.1	71	51	22	50/28	55/32	62/38	74/50	81/59	89/67	94/70	93/69	86/62	76/50	63/38	52/31
Harrison	51	8.1	74	55	19	33/14	53/29	63/40	73/51	80/59	87/66	89/70	87/68	80/63	70/48	56/41	51/27
Little Rock	49	6.4	71	48	22	50/29	54/32	62/39	73/50	81/58	89/67	93/70	93/69	86/61	76/49	62/38	52/31
Pine Bluff	51	5.6	71	48	25	40/20	59/33	69/43	78/52	86/63	92/69	94/72	92/71	89/67	77/49	63/42	53/31
Texarkana	37	5.3	73	50	25	45/27	61/38	69/48	77/56	84/64	91/71	93/74	93/73	89/70	79/55	65/48	57/37

Oklahoma

Altus	24	4.1	79	61	31	47/20	64/33	71/39	76/48	82/62	96/68	100/71	95/69	94/64	83/50	67/38	60/30
Enid	30	5.5	76	60	28	41/18	60/33	67/40	73/50	82/62	93/69	97/72	91/70	89/66	77/51	60/39	51/28
Lawton	30	4.7	79	60	29	44/21	61/33	68/42	75/52	82/62	93/69	97/71	94/71	92/65	80/49	67/42	55/28
Muskogee	42	6.3	75	55	28	38/18	58/33	66/44	76/55	83/62	92/70	97/74	91/72	85/68	73/52	60/44	52/31
Okla. City	31	5.2	75	59	22	48/26	53/30	60/36	72/49	79/58	87/67	93/70	92/70	85/61	74/51	61/37	51/29
Ponca City	36	8.4	76	60	25	36/15	56/31	64/39	72/51	80/60	89/68	95/71	88/69	81/63	73/48	57/39	48/25
Stillwater	32	6.4	75	59	27	39/16	58/29	65/39	74/50	83/61	91/69	95/72	91/71	86/65	77/48	63/40	53/27
Tulsa	37	6.4	72	54	23	47/26	52/30	60/37	72/50	79/58	87/67	93/71	93/70	85/62	75/51	61/38	50/29

Texas

Abilene	24	4.4	78	67	26	56/32	60/36	67/42	78/53	84/61	92/69	95/72	95/72	87/65	78/54	66/42	58/34
Amarillo	20	5.9	77	68	21	49/22	53/26	60/31	71/42	79/52	88/61	91/66	90/65	83/57	73/46	60/32	51/25
Austin	32	4.1	76	51	27	60/39	64/43	71/48	79/58	85/65	92/71	95/74	96/73	89/68	81/59	70/48	63/42
Brownsville	25	3.8	81	45	25	69/51	73/54	77/59	83/67	87/71	91/75	93/76	93/76	90/73	85/67	77/59	72/53
Corpus Christi	28	5.1	82	48	27	66/46	70/49	75/54	82/63	87/69	91/74	94/75	95/75	90/72	84/64	75/55	69/49
Dals.-Ft. Wrth.	32	4.1	75	52	27	56/34	60/38	67/43	76/54	83/62	91/70	95/74	96/74	88/67	79/56	67/44	59/37
Del Rio	17	2.2	77	58	27	63/38	69/43	76/49	85/59	90/66	96/72	99/74	98/74	92/68	83/59	72/47	65/39
El Paso	7.8	2.6	79	78	27	57/30	62/34	69/40	78/49	87/57	95/66	95/70	93/68	87/61	78/49	66/37	58/31
Galveston	42	8.8	72	49	3	59/48	61/51	66/56	73/65	80/72	85/77	87/79	88/79	85/75	78/68	69/58	63/51
Houston	48	8.5	67	65	26	63/41	66/45	72/50	79/59	86/66	91/71	94/73	94/72	90/68	83/58	73/49	66/43
Lubbock	18	4.1	74	75	21	53/25	57/28	64/34	75/45	82/54	91/64	92/67	91/65	84/58	75/47	63/34	55/27
Midland	13	3.3	79	65	25	58/29	62/33	69/39	79/49	86/58	93/67	95/69	94/69	88/63	79/52	67/39	60/32
San Angelo	18	2.7	77	60	27	59/34	63/37	71/43	80/54	86/62	93/70	97/72	97/72	88/65	80/55	68/42	61/35
San Antonio	28	4.1	75	52	28	62/40	66/43	72/49	80/59	86/65	92/72	96/74	96/73	90/69	82/59	71/48	66/42
Waco	31	3.3	75	52	28	57/37	61/40	69/46	78/57	84/64	92/72	96/75	97/75	89/68	80/58	69/46	60/39
Wichita Falls	27	3.9	79	60	28	53/29	58/34	66/39	77/51	85/60	94/69	99/72	99/72	90/64	79/53	66/40	56/32

Alabama

Soil and climate. Northeastern Alabama is a part of the Appalachian and Cumberland-Allegheny Plateau. Huntsville and Gadsden are cities in this area. The 200-day growing season is long compared to the United States average but is among the shortest in Alabama. Most of the soils here are loams, stony loams, sandy loams, silt loams, or clay loams.

Central Alabama is a rolling to hilly region. The growing season is as long as 240 days. A part of the Piedmont soil is mostly clay or clay loams.

Southern Alabama is highly influenced by the Gulf of Mexico. Around Mobile, the growing season is 265 days. This climate extends as far north as Chatom in Washington County. In the southern counties, heavy frosts are irregular due to the flow of cold air into low areas and down river valleys. In certain areas, the growing season will be shortened by this effect.

Lime is usually but not always needed. Through Coosa Valley and the Black Belts, the soil pH may be naturally close to ideal, but have the soil tested to be certain.

Soil testing
Soil Testing Laboratory
Auburn University
Auburn, Alabama 36830

Recommended grasses. North of Goodwater, Mantevallo, and Panda, some cool-season grasses such as Kentucky bluegrass and tall fescue are grown, especially at higher elevations.

Most lawns in the state, particularly south of Jackson, Frisco City, Evergreen, and Ozark, are warm-season grasses.

Publications office
Head, Administrative Services
Alabama Cooperative Extension Service
Auburn University
Auburn, Alabama 36380
Out-of-state requests: No.

Mississippi

Soil and climate. The two most important factors controlling Mississippi's climate are the North American continent itself to the north and west, and the Gulf of Mexico. Because the land is fairly level, topography has little influence on the climate. The highest land in the state near the northern border is less than 800 feet above sea level. The northeastern prairie belt and the Delta section (between the Tallahatchie-Yazoo Basin and the Mississippi River) are level and very fertile.

Lime. Much of the state receives more than 50 inches of rain each year, producing an acid soil. Lime should be added to most Mississippi soil before any money or time is spent on fertilizers. About 90 percent of the sandy soil in southern Mississippi needs lime; more than two-thirds of Delta soil needs lime.

Soil testing. Check with your local County Extension Agent, or write:
Soil Testing
Box 5405
Mississippi State University
Starkville, Mississippi 39759

Recommended grasses. Bermuda grass is the most common choice. Common Bermuda grass can be seeded, but the improved 'Tif' Bermuda grass varieties are finer textured.

Zoysia grass is very slow to establish, but is attractive, and relatively problem free once it covers. 'Matrella' (same as manila grass), 'Meyer', and 'Emerald' zoysia grass are used, and are good performers in moderate shade.

St. Augustine grass is best for shady lawns, but lacks much cold tolerance.

Publications office
Chief Clerk
Mississippi State University
Starkville, Mississippi 39759
Out-of-state requests: Yes.

Louisiana

Soil and climate. Louisiana's climate is determined by its subtropical latitude and nearness to the Gulf of Mexico.

Rainfall is evenly distributed, with most falling in winter and midsummer. On the average, between 45 and 60 inches of rain fall each year. As much as 86 inches falls on New Orleans.

The western two-thirds of Louisiana is part of the Coastal Plain. It is mostly level country with sandy soil. The highest elevation in the northwest section is 400 to 500 feet above sea level.

Most Louisiana soil is very acid and needs regular lime applications.

Lime refers, of course, to materials such as ground limestone, ground dolomite, or ground seashells. Besides raising the soil pH, lime adds essential calcium and magnesium nutrients. Lime makes other fertilizers more effective and improves the structure of heavy clay soils.

Soil testing
Soil Testing Laboratory
Department of Agronomy
Louisiana State University
Baton Rouge, Louisiana 70803

Recommended grasses. Centipede grass is increasing in popularity in the Gulf Coast area. It will make a lawn in most any type of soil (even poor) in the lower South.

Bermuda grass is adapted to well-drained, fertile soils with full exposure to the sun. It will persist, however, in both acid and over-limed soils. One tip: Buy *hulled* Bermuda grass seed.

Publications office
Publications Librarian
Room 192
Knapp Hall
Louisiana State University
Baton Rouge, Louisiana 70803
Out-of-state requests: Yes.

Tennessee

Soil and climate. Tennessee is in a region that receives abundant rainfall, about 50 inches on the average. As much as 80 inches has been measured in some of the mountain areas. Even with such rainfall, summer droughts are rather common.

Tennessee topography is varied. The east is mostly mountains but has broad fertile valleys. These East Tennessee valleys are similar to Maryland's Cumberland Valley, and the Shenandoah Valley in Virginia.
The soil here is derived from limestone, sandstone, and shale and is very productive.

The Central Basin is a large section of central Tennessee that has rolling hills to 800 feet high. It is surrounded by hills several hundred feet higher called the Highland Rim. The Central Basin also has rich limestone soil, the same as the Kentucky bluegrass region of northcentral Kentucky.

Lime is very often necessary. A soil test will tell if your soil needs lime or any other nutrients.

Soil testing
Soil Testing Laboratory
University of Tennessee
P.O. Box 11019
Nashville, Tennessee 37211

Recommended grasses. Kentucky bluegrass is widely adapted in Tennessee. The variety 'Windsor' has been tested and judged superior by local experts.

Bermuda grass is the most drought resistant. It does brown in winter, but is easily overseeded with rye or other cool-season grass. Improved Bermuda grass may perform well in Tennessee.

Publications office
Agricultural Extension Service
University of Tennessee
P.O. Box 1071
Knoxville, Tennessee 37901
Out-of-state requests: Yes.

Alabama

	TOTAL INCHES RAIN	INCHES JULY/AUG.	JULY % SUNSHINE	DEC. % SUNSHINE	JULY DAYS ABOVE 90°F.	AVERAGE MAXIMUM/MINIMUM TEMPERATURES											
						JAN.	FEB.	MARCH	APRIL	MAY	JUNE	JULY	AUG.	SEPT.	OCT.	NOV.	DEC.
Anniston	62	7.0	59	46	27	42/23	58/30	68/46	79/52	84/59	92/66	93/70	91/71	85/66	72/48	65/47	56/33
Birmingham	53	9.5	59	46	14	54/34	58/36	65/42	75/51	82/58	88/66	90/69	90/69	85/63	76/51	64/40	55/35
Enterprise	50	13	60	51	20	50/29	62/36	74/50	78/55	85/61	92/68	91/69	88/69	85/67	73/49	68/48	60/36
Huntsville	52	8.3	70	48	15	50/31	54/33	62/40	73/50	81/58	89/66	90/69	90/68	84/62	74/50	62/39	52/33
Mobile	67	16	61	51	24	61/41	64/44	69/49	78/58	85/64	90/71	90/73	91/72	86/68	80/58	69/47	63/43
Montgomery	50	8.5	63	50	20	58/37	61/40	68/45	77/54	84/61	89/69	90/71	91/71	86/65	78/53	67/43	59/38
Selma	52	8.8	64	49	27	48/28	63/36	72/50	82/54	88/62	92/70	94/23	92/72	89/69	76/51	69/50	61/39
Tuscaloosa	50	12	68	47	19	42/24	57/32	71/49	77/51	84/60	93/66	92/70	90/70	87/66	71/46	63/45	53/32

Mississippi

	TOTAL INCHES RAIN	INCHES JULY/AUG.	JULY % SUNSHINE	DEC. % SUNSHINE	JULY DAYS ABOVE 90°F.	JAN.	FEB.	MARCH	APRIL	MAY	JUNE	JULY	AUG.	SEPT.	OCT.	NOV.	DEC.
Biloxi	62	13	65	50	25	55/34	63/42	71/52	79/55	86/66	91/75	92/75	88/74	87/73	79/58	72/55	64/46
Greenwood	51	7.1	71	45	19	39/22	56/32	69/48	76/56	87/64	92/70	91/73	91/72	87/69	74/51	64/47	54/37
Hattiesburg	59	11	65	49	26	49/25	63/36	72/48	78/53	87/61	94/69	93/71	91/71	88/69	76/49	70/48	60/38
Jackson	49	7.8	62	47	24	58/36	62/38	69/43	78/53	85/60	91/68	93/71	93/70	88/64	80/51	68/42	60/37
Meridian	52	9.0	68	48	23	58/35	62/38	69/43	78/52	85/59	91/67	92/70	92/69	87/64	79/51	68/41	60/36
Natchez	54	7.6	71	48	28	49/31	65/40	75/52	79/56	87/64	94/71	93/73	90/73	88/70	78/54	69/50	62/41
Tupelo	54	7.9	71	47	26	40/20	61/26	70/42	79/48	86/56	93/64	94/70	94/67	88/64	74/44	64/44	54/33
Vicksburg	52	6.6	70	48	28	46/27	65/35	73/48	79/54	86/62	94/69	93/72	92/72	89/69	77/52	70/47	62/38

Louisiana

	TOTAL INCHES RAIN	INCHES JULY/AUG.	JULY % SUNSHINE	DEC. % SUNSHINE	JULY DAYS ABOVE 90°F.	JAN.	FEB.	MARCH	APRIL	MAY	JUNE	JULY	AUG.	SEPT.	OCT.	NOV.	DEC.
Alexandria	56	8.6	71	48	27	49/29	65/37	72/49	78/57	87/65	94/71	95/74	91/73	89/70	79/54	69/49	60/38
Baton Rouge	54	11	61	49	24	61/40	64/43	71/49	79/58	85/64	90/70	91/73	91/72	87/68	80/57	70/47	64/42
Lafayette	60	15	70	47	27	53/35	65/43	74/55	80/59	87/68	92/73	93/76	88/73	88/71	79/55	72/53	63/41
Lake Charles	55	11	71	47	22	62/43	65/45	70/50	78/59	84/66	90/72	91/74	91/73	88/69	82/58	71/49	64/44
Monroe	50	7.1	72	48	19	47/28	65/40	73/49	78/56	87/64	94/71	91/73	90/71	88/68	77/50	65/45	56/38
Natchitoches	50	6.0	72	49	30	49/28	65/37	73/48	79/55	88/64	95/70	96/73	92/72	90/70	80/53	69/48	61/37
New Orleans	57	12	58	53	20	62/43	65/46	70/51	78/59	85/65	90/71	90/73	91/73	87/70	80/60	70/50	64/45
Shreveport	45	5.6	73	53	25	57/39	60/41	67/46	77/56	84/63	90/70	93/73	94/72	88/67	79/56	67/48	59/39

Tennessee

	TOTAL INCHES RAIN	INCHES JULY/AUG.	JULY % SUNSHINE	DEC. % SUNSHINE	JULY DAYS ABOVE 90°F.	JAN.	FEB.	MARCH	APRIL	MAY	JUNE	JULY	AUG.	SEPT.	OCT.	NOV.	DEC.
Bristol	41	8.7	60	43	5	46/27	49/28	57/34	68/44	77/53	84/61	86/64	85/63	80/57	70/45	57/34	47/28
Chattanooga	52	8.3	61	42	16	50/30	53/32	61/38	73/48	81/56	87/64	89/68	89/67	83/60	73/48	61/37	51/31
Knoxville	46	7.9	61	38	8	49/32	52/33	60/39	72/49	80/57	86/65	88/68	87/67	82/61	72/50	59/39	50/33
Memphis	49	6.9	73	50	21	49/32	53/34	61/41	73/52	81/61	89/68	92/71	91/70	84/63	75/51	61/40	52/34
Nashville	46	7.0	65	41	15	48/29	51/31	59/38	71/49	80/57	87/66	90/69	89/68	83/60	73/49	59/38	50/31
Oak Ridge	53	9.5	61	38	10	47/29	50/30	59/36	70/46	79/54	85/63	87/66	87/65	81/59	71/47	58/36	48/30
Jackson	49	7.0	72	49	21	32/15	52/24	66/42	75/51	84/60	88/65	92/71	89/68	84/65	70/44	60/42	47/29

South Carolina

Soil and climate. The general climatic patterns are very similar to those of North Carolina. However, the western mountains are not nearly as extensive, and the more southern latitude means a warmer climate.

South Carolina is divided into the two regions of the Piedmont and the Coastal Plain. The border of the two regions is roughly from the eastern boundary of Aiken County through central Chesterfield County, to the North Carolina border.

On the average, rainfall is heaviest in July, and least in November. Thunderstorms are frequent in summer.

The shortest season in the state is just under 200 days. Along the southern coast, the growing season averages 300 days.

Soils of the Piedmont and Coastal Plain are essentially the same as described for North Carolina.

Soil testing. Sample boxes and record sheets are available from local County Extension Agent offices, or write:
Soil Testing Laboratory
Clemson University
Clemson, South Carolina 29631

Recommended grasses. Bahia grass is well adapted in the Sandhills vicinity as well as in most of the rest of the South Carolina Coastal Plain.

Common Bermuda grass is one of the most widely used grasses. Improved types of Bermuda grass such as 'Tifgreen', 'Tiflawn', and 'Tifway' are often planted (see page 138).

Carpet grass is useful where soil is too wet or infertile for Bermuda grass, even though it does not make the most handsome lawn.

Centipede grass is frequently used in the Piedmont, Sandhills, and Coastal Plains areas.

St. Augustine grass is best, in sun or some shade, confined to the Coastal Plain.

Of the zoysia grasses, 'Meyer' is the easiest to maintain. 'Emerald' is the most beautiful, and 'Matrella' is the most widely adapted.

Tall fescue is the most heat tolerant of all the cool-season grasses.

Some of the improved Kentucky bluegrasses, such as 'Nugget', 'Adelphi', or 'Baron', are useful in partially shaded sites.

Use annual rye or a premium cool-season mixture to overseed dormant Bermuda grass.

Publications office
Agricultural Publications
Department of Public Relations
Clemson University
Clemson, South Carolina 29631
Out-of-state requests: Yes.

Georgia

Soil and climate. The climate in Georgia is controlled by the altitude, latitude, and proximity to the ocean. The state essentially has a warm, humid climate, modified considerably by the higher mountains in the northern parts of the state (from Atlanta to the Tennessee border).

More than half the state is included in the Coastal Plain. The soil is sandy and the land fairly level. Piedmont soil is mostly clay and clay loams, but some have a sandy surface in the top few inches. They will all be acid and not terribly fertile, though certainly capable of good production.

Lime is necessary in most cases, especially for new lawns.

Soil testing
Soil Testing and Plant Analysis Laboratory
2400 College Station Road
Athens, Georgia 30601

Recommended grasses. Common Bermuda grass is by far the most prevalent lawn grass in Georgia.

Dr. Glen Burton of the Georgia Coastal Plains Experiment Station developed several of the most-used improved Bermuda grasses such as 'Tiflawn', 'Tifway', 'Tifgreen', and 'Tifdwarf'.

Tall fescue is the most popular grass in the mountain and upper Piedmont areas.

Carpet grass is useful in wet soils, not infrequent in the central and southern parts of the state.

St. Augustine grass is the best shade-tolerant grass for most parts of Georgia.

Of the zoysia grass, 'Emerald' is most attractive and the best overall for Georgia.

Publications office
Extension Editor—Publications
University of Georgia
Athens, Georgia 30602
Out-of-state requests: Yes.

Florida

Soil and climate. The entire state of Florida is included within the Coastal Plain. Its climate is dominated most directly by the surrounding seas—no point in the state is more than 60 miles from the coast. Florida is very flat. The highest point in the state is 325 feet above sea level; the average elevation is somewhat less.

The soil is variable. Along the coast it tends to be sandy and marshy. Darker and more fertile soil occurs towards the interior. Muck soil reclaimed from the Everglades is among the most fertile. In a few areas, the soil is clay-like.

Lime is often necessary, but some soil is too "sweet." Check soil pH with a soil test.

Soil testing. Check with a County Extension Agent, or write:
Soil Testing Laboratory
University of Florida
Gainesville, Florida 32601

Recommended grasses. The grasses of Florida include St. Augustine, centipede, Bermuda, zoysia, carpet, and bahia grass.

Bahia grass is native to Brazil and better adapted to central Florida than anywhere else in the South.

Improved varieties of bahia grass are available. 'Argentine' is most popular for lawns. 'Pensacola' is used along highways. Common bahia grass is little used. Mole crickets are a major problem in bahia grass.

St. Augustine grass makes a beautiful lawn in many situations, especially in shady areas. It is the most popular lawn grass in the state. A good insect and disease program is necessary to keep it in good shape. The variety 'Bitter Blue', low-growing and dense, was developed on the lower east coast. It has an attractive color but will not tolerate heavy traffic.

'Floratine' is similar to 'Bitter Blue' in many respects but is even more dense. It can be mowed as close as ½ inch.

'Floratam' has shown some resistance to both chinch bugs and SAD disease (see page 84), but does not tolerate much shade.

Bermuda grass, especially the improved types like 'Tifgreen' and 'Tiflawn', will make a most attractive lawn but will require very high maintenance.

'Emerald' zoysia grass is often recommended for Florida gardeners. It will take a lot of shade, but is slow to cover.

Centipede grass makes a good, low maintenance lawn but may be seriously damaged by nematodes—especially in sandy soil. For this reason, it is rarely recommended for planting south of Orlando, where sandy soil is more commonplace. Ground pearls are also a problem.

Publications office
Bulletin Room
Cooperative Extension Service
University of Florida
Gainesville, Florida 32601
Out-of-state requests: Yes.

	TOTAL INCHES RAIN	INCHES JULY/AUG.	JULY % SUNSHINE	DEC. % SUNSHINE	JULY DAYS ABOVE 90°F.	AVERAGE MAXIMUM/MINIMUM TEMPERATURES											
						JAN.	FEB.	MARCH	APRIL	MAY	JUNE	JULY	AUG.	SEPT.	OCT.	NOV.	DEC.

South Carolina

Aiken	46	9.8	63	51	28	47/27	62/30	72/48	81/51	87/59	95/67	96/70	90/69	87/67	74/50	72/48	60/37
Anderson	40	3.7	61	50	28	41/22	59/27	69/46	79/54	85/62	91/68	95/73	91/72	85/68	72/51	65/49	54/36
Charleston	52	15	67	59	15	60/37	62/39	68/45	76/53	83/61	88/68	89/71	89/71	84/66	77/55	68/44	61/38
Clemson	51	9.4	60	52	26	41/20	56/26	66/42	76/49	82/58	89/63	93/68	89/67	84/64	70/45	61/43	51/31
Columbia	46	11	64	60	20	57/34	60/35	66/42	77/51	84/60	90/67	92/70	91/69	85/63	78/51	67/41	58/34
Georgetown	51	13	65	55	21	49/27	62/30	71/47	80/52	83/61	90/67	93/72	89/71	87/68	75/52	72/50	62/40
Greenville	47	8.2	59	54	11	52/33	54/35	62/40	72/50	80/58	86/66	88/69	87/68	81/62	72/51	62/40	52/33
Greenwood	46	8.3	62	51	27	43/20	57/23	68/41	78/48	83/55	91/63	95/68	90/67	85/63	71/45	65/41	54/30
Florence	46	10	64	54	24	43/24	59/30	68/47	79/53	84/60	88/66	94/72	88/70	87/68	72/48	67/45	56/35
Orangeburg	48	11	63	54	27	44/24	59/30	70/46	80/52	87/59	92/66	97/70	89/68	86/65	71/46	61/44	55/33
Spartanburg	46	5.1	60	50	26	42/23	58/30	69/44	77/51	83/55	89/64	94/66	88/67	84/63	72/47	64/43	54/31
Sumter	47	11	64	60	27	46/26	62/33	72/48	82/54	86/61	91/66	96/71	90/68	88/65	75/51	71/48	51/37

Georgia

Athens	51	8.8	62	51	15	53/33	56/35	63/40	74/50	82/58	88/66	89/69	89/68	83/62	74/51	63/40	54/34
Atlanta	48	8.4	62	50	7	51/33	54/35	61/41	71/51	79/59	85/67	86/69	86/69	81/63	72/52	62/41	53/34
Augusta	43	9.3	63	51	19	58/34	60/36	67/42	77/51	84/59	90/67	91/70	90/69	85/63	77/51	67/40	59/34
Columbus	51	10	65	51	20	58/36	61/38	67/43	77/52	85/60	90/67	91/70	91/70	86/65	77/53	67/42	59/36
Macon	44	8.2	64	56	21	59/37	62/39	68/45	78/53	86/61	91/68	92/71	92/70	87/65	78/53	68/42	60/37
Rome	53	8.2	66	48	17	52/30	56/32	63/37	74/47	82/55	82/63	90/67	90/66	85/60	75/47	63/36	53/31
Savannah	51	14	63	55	19	61/39	64/40	69/46	78/54	85/62	89/69	91/71	90/71	85/67	78/56	69/45	62/39
Tifton	47	11	63	54	28	48/28	61/34	71/52	80/56	86/63	98/69	93/72	89/71	87/69	76/50	69/50	60/37

Florida

Apalachicola	57	16	64	57	6	61/46	63/48	68/54	75/61	82/68	86/74	87/75	88/75	85/72	78/63	69/53	63/48
Daytona Bch.	50	13	60	59	16	69/48	70/49	74/53	80/59	85/65	88/70	90/72	89/73	87/72	81/65	75/55	70/49
Fort Meyers	54	17	64	65	22	75/52	76/53	80/57	85/62	89/66	90/72	91/74	91/74	90/73	85/67	80/59	76/54
Jacksonville	54	15	60	56	23	65/44	67/46	72/50	79/57	85/64	88/70	90/72	90/72	86/70	79/62	71/51	66/45
Key West	40	8.6	77	73	14	76/66	77/65	79/70	82/74	85/76	88/79	89/80	89/80	88/79	84/75	80/71	76/67
Lakeland	49	15	61	63	21	70/51	72/52	76/56	82/62	87/67	90/71	90/73	90/73	88/72	82/66	76/57	71/52
Miami	60	14	79	54	8	76/59	77/59	79/63	83/67	85/71	88/74	89/75	90/76	88/75	85/71	80/64	77/60
Orlando	51	15	61	60	24	70/50	72/51	76/56	81/61	88/66	89/71	90/73	90/73	88/72	82/66	76/57	71/51
Pensacola	64	14	57	49	17	61/43	64/45	69/51	77/59	84/66	87/72	90/74	90/74	86/70	80/60	70/49	63/44
Tallahassee	62	16	60	56	22	64/41	66/43	72/48	80/56	87/63	90/70	91/72	90/70	87/69	81/58	71/46	65/41
Tampa	49	16	61	62	19	71/50	72/52	76/56	82/62	87/67	90/72	90/74	90/74	89/73	84/65	77/56	72/51
W. Palm Bch.	62	13	65	67	15	75/56	76/56	79/60	83/65	86/69	88/73	90/74	90/74	88/75	84/70	79/62	76/57

Climates of
the West

This section will help you determine the climate conditions that affect your ability to grow lawns in your region. Find the city closest to you on the chart, and note the information in each column. Check the information on the left-hand pages for specific information on soil conditions and lime requirements, recommended grasses, and suggestions for additional information.

The rhythmical, almost fluid vertical lines of the trees contrast attractively with the horizontal of the sun-dappled lawn.

Climates of the West

Arizona

Soil. May be either heavy clay or very sandy. It is usually alkaline (pH 7.5 or higher).

The high pH causes problems with the nutrient iron (see pages 47 – 52). Iron-containing ferilizers are often necessary.

Lime is seldom needed but might be of some benefit in certain mountain areas.

Soil testing
Soil, Water, and Plant Tissue Testing Laboratory
Department of Soils, Water and Engineering
University of Arizona
Tucson, Arizona 85721

Recommended grasses. Warm-season grasses such as Bermuda, St. Augustine, and zoysia grass are best for southern

Arizona. Common Bermuda grass is usually planted April through August by seed. This grass is relatively pest free and will make a very attractive lawn. Overseed with rye in winter if you don't like the straw color of dormant bluegrass.

St. Augustine grass makes a good lawn. It is vigorous and tolerant of some shade, although it may become yellowish (chlorotic) in caliche soils. Don't overseed it and don't dethatch heavily. Start St. Augustine grass by sprigs; plant April through July.

Zoysia grass can also tolerate shade but is even more susceptible to chlorosis in caliche soils. It tends to have more pest problems than Bermuda grass. Overseeding zoysia grass does not work too well. Dethatching is recommended

about every two years. Plant from sprigs, stolons, or plugs May through June. It is slow to establish.

Dichondra is a good lawn grass substitute, but it doesn't stand up too well to foot traffic. It will take some shade. Plant plugs or seeds mid-April through mid-July. Flea beetles are a serious pest—see page 77.

Lippia (Phyla *Nodiflora* of the Verbena family) is another grass substitute. It's tough and takes either sun or shade, but one liability is that bees love the flowers. Start from sprigs April to July.

Publications office
Cooperative Extension Service
University of Arizona
Tucson, Arizona 85721
Out-of-state requests: Yes.

New Mexico

Soil is generally alkaline, and low in organic matter. Use generous quantities of amendments. Sulfur will lower pH. Occasional heavy watering (3 to 4 feet) will flush salts from the soil. Hard impenetrable soils, high in sodium salts, may benefit from heavy applications of gypsum.

Soil testing
New Mexico State University
Soil, Plant, and Water Testing Laboratory
Agronomy Department, P.O. Box 3Q
Las Cruces, New Mexico 88003

Recommended grasses. Bermuda grass is a common choice, particularly at lower elevations and towards the southern part of the state, where the growing season exceeds 200 days. Common Bermuda grass likes the heat and has deep,

drought-tolerant root systems. Improved varieties (see page 138) are fine-textured but are somewhat more pest prone. In high-altitude regions, Bermuda grass may be considered objectionable, due to its long dormant season.

Fall fertilizing of Bermuda grass can encourage later dormancy and earlier spring green-up.

Common Bermuda grass seed can be planted around April-May in Albuquerque. Improved Bermuda grass sprigs should be planted June-July.

Kentucky bluegrass does well in the cooler New Mexico climates such as around Santa Fe. Summer heat stress will be a factor. Plant disease-resistant varieties such as 'Baron' or 'Fylking', mixed with turf-type rye. Mow high in summer.

Tall fescue is sometimes used for lawns in cooler areas but the fine fescues are rarely used.

Native grasses such as buffalo grass are useful where water is scarce.

Lawns should be watered during extended dry periods in cooler times of the year.

Publications office
Bulletin Office
Department of Agricultural Information
Drawer 3-A1
New Mexico State University
Las Cruces, New Mexico 88003
Out-of-state requests: Yes.

	TOTAL INCHES RAIN	INCHES JULY/AUG.	JULY % SUNSHINE	DEC. % SUNSHINE	JULY DAYS ABOVE 90°F.	AVERAGE MAXIMUM/MINIMUM TEMPERATURES											
						JAN.	FEB.	MARCH	APRIL	MAY	JUNE	JULY	AUG.	SEPT.	OCT.	NOV.	DEC.

Arizona

Casa Grande	8.1	2.5	90	78	31	61/35	72/33	72/37	87/46	89/51	105/66	106/77	105/76	99/69	90/58	77/42	74/42
Douglas	16	7.4	85	75	23	57/32	68/32	65/34	77/45	85/49	93/61	91/66	94/64	89/57	78/47	71/35	67/30
Flagstaff	19.3	5.1	90	78	1	41/14	44/17	48/20	57/27	67/33	76/40	81/50	78/49	74/41	63/31	51/22	43/16
Globe	13	3.8	8.5	77	27	55/32	65/35	62/34	76/45	80/46	94/60	94/68	95/68	88/63	80/51	68/40	61/36
Phoenix	7	2	94	77	31	65/38	69/41	74/45	84/52	93/60	101/68	105/77	102/76	98/69	88/57	75/45	66/38
Sedona	16.7	3.8	90	78	26	52/28	63/30	62/29	77/38	78/44	95/55	98/63	96/63	89/57	79/48	64/36	60/32
Nogales	24	9.8	88	76	22	61/31	71/28	68/30	79/39	82/43	95/55	91/65	91/64	89/58	81/49	74/34	69/32
Tucson	11	4.7	78	80	29	63/38	67/40	71/44	81/50	90/57	98/66	98/74	95/72	93/67	84/56	72/45	65/39
Winslow	7.3	2.7	88	77	26	46/20	53/25	60/29	70/37	80/45	90/54	94/63	91/61	85/53	73/41	58/28	47/21
Yuma	2.7	.62	89	82	31	67/43	73/46	78/50	86/57	93/64	101/71	106/81	104/81	100/74	90/62	76/50	68/44

New Mexico

Alamagordo	10.2	3.8	81	72	30	57/28	63/30	67/34	77/44	85/54	97/63	96/64	97/66	92/60	80/49	70/37	63/32
Albuquerque	7.8	2.7	76	72	23	47/23	53/27	59/32	70/41	80/51	89/60	92/65	90/63	83/57	72/45	57/32	47/25
Carlsbad	10.8	2.4	75	70	29	52/26	64/32	69/35	79/48	89/59	97/65	97/69	99/71	95/65	77/51	71/37	66/34
Deming	6.8	3.0	80	71	27	54/28	64/29	64/32	73/42	80/46	93/60	94/65	96/67	90/59	77/47	69/34	61/30
Farmington	8.1	2.0	79	70	26	37/9	54/19	59/21	73/34	78/38	93/52	94/58	93/56	86/48	75/32	59/25	48/19
Gallup	9.1	3.6	81	71	7	39/6.9	50/16	52/19	65/28	71/36	85/48	85/57	85/56	78/49	70/35	56/25	51/23
Hobbs	14.4	4	79	70	30	54/24	65/34	69/36	76/46	86/58	94/64	93/65	95/67	92/62	78/50	70/37	65/33
Rosewell	10.6	3.1	75	71	30	52/25	63/33	68/36	77/48	87/59	96/67	97/71	95/71	92/65	77/51	69/37	63/31
Santa Fe	13.2	6.3	78	73	3	36/15	46/22	49/25	61/36	71/43	85/54	85/57	84/58	78/49	69/40	55/30	47/17
Socorro	7.9	2.9	81	73	24	49/19	60/24	63/27	74/37	81/42	92/54	92/60	91/61	86/55	76/39	66/27	59/25

Climates of the West

Nevada

Soil. Nevada soil is typically alkaline and low in organic matter. Generous additions of organic matter before planting will prevent potential lawn problems before they start.

Soil testing. Contact your local County Extension Agent, or write:
Nevada Soil and Water Testing Laboratory
College of Agriculture
University of Nevada
Reno, Nevada 89507

Recommended grasses. In northern Nevada, a Kentucky bluegrass-fine fescue mixture is the usual choice. There are commercial blends and mixtures that contain these grasses. Use 2 to 3 pounds of seed per 1,000 square feet, and never mow below 1½ inches. Quality bluegrass sod is also widely available.

Tall fescue makes a good lawn when planted unmixed. It's weedy when planted with bluegrass, growing in coarse, random clumps. Use lots of seed—about 7 or 8 pounds to 1,000 square feet.

In Las Vegas and the surrounding communities of Pahrump, Henderson, Border City, and Moapa, no grass makes a finer lawn than Bermuda grass. Improved Bermuda grass makes for good home putting greens but more maintenance is required than for common Bermuda grass. All Bermuda grass lawns should be periodically dethatched.

Lippia (see "Arizona") is grown occasionally in Las Vegas. Under the right conditions, it can make a fine lawn.

Zoysia grass is used to a limited extent. It makes a beautiful summer lawn but browns early and cannot be overseeded.

Publications office
Cooperative Extension Service
College of Agriculture
University of Nevada—Reno
Reno, Nevada 89507
Out-of-state requests: Yes.

California

Soil and climate. Within this large state, virtually all the grass climates are represented. There is the cool and humid northern coast, the cold mountain areas, the hot central valleys, and the southern coastal and southern interior valleys. The soil in California is as variable as the climate.

Lime will be necessary in the far northwest. Much of the rest of the state has alkaline soil. Organic matter should be incorporated before planting. Gypsum is useful in compacted soils with excess sodium salts. A soil test will show your soil's specific needs.

Soil testing is not provided by the state but there are many commercial soil laboratories. Check your telephone directory or your County Extension Agent.

Recommended grasses. The two most important California grasses are Kentucky bluegrass and common Bermuda grass. Kentucky bluegrass is grown throughout much of the state. It's well adapted in the north and does well in the higher elevations of the south. Don't try it in the San Joaquin or Imperial Valleys, unless you're prepared for a summer-long battle—it will then be disease prone. Along coastal and slightly inland areas stretching from Ventura to San Diego, bluegrass will be severely stressed during summer; disease can wipe it out fast.

If you are growing Kentucky bluegrass in a transition area where it is not really well adapted, here's what to do: (1) Set your mower as high as possible during summer. Don't mow lower than 2 inches. (2) Fertilize in early spring and again in fall as weather cools—but never in summer. Stimulating new succulent growth during hot weather invites disease. (3) Water in the morning, and make sure the soil is getting wet to at least 6 inches. Proper watering will help avoid many problems. (4) Use disease-resistant varieties such as 'Adelphi' and 'Majestic' in mixtures with other bluegrasses, fine fescues, and turf-type rye. The other grasses will slow the spread of any disease. Good mixtures are available as seed or sod. (5) Dethatch every two or three years.

A thick layer of thatch prevents air and water from reaching the roots and generally weakens the lawn. If attention to detail is not your style, consider another kind of grass.

Tall fescue grows well in California, and is more heat tolerant than most of the cool-season grasses. It should be 100 percent tall fescue or as close as possible. A small amount of tall fescue in a bluegrass lawn will appear after a couple of seasons as weedy clumps. Tall fescue has received attention lately because of its tolerance to drought. It's an upright-growing grass so it should be mowed high, about 3 inches.

'Kentucky 31' is the best known variety of tall fescue. Others include 'Alta', 'Fawn', and 'Goar'. Researchers hope to introduce finer-textured and spreading rather than clump-forming varieties of tall fescue soon.

Common Bermuda grass is the heat-loving grass that, if not chosen in the first place, often winds up in the lawn anyway. It spreads aggressively by seed, and by above- and below-ground runners. Where it's not wanted, it earns the name "devilgrass." Some choose to live with it. Fertilized and mowed frequently to about an inch, it makes a handsome and hardy summer lawn. After browning in the fall, it can be overseeded with rye grass. You can keep two lawns at once: A cool-season mix on "top" and the common Bermuda grass "below." So the Bermuda grass doesn't take over altogether, manage the lawn at all times to favor the cool-season grasses and discourage the Bermuda. Most importantly, mow as high as possible in summer and don't fertilize in summer.

Improved Bermuda grass varieties are another alternative. 'Tifgreen' is one favorite for home lawns. Beautiful when at their best, the improved Bermuda grasses are premium grasses that will require extra care.

Residents of Bakersfield, Fresno, Modesto, Stockton, Sacramento, Redding, and others in the San Joaquin Valley should consider a Bermuda grass first. The same is true for the Imperial Valley—El Centro, Brawley, and Indio. Most of the rest of the state is transitional, so you can choose between cool or warm-season grasses or any combination of both.

St. Augustine grass is another warm-season grass. It's coarse bladed and has rounded leaf tips. Kikuyu grass, a common southern California weed, is similar in appearance, but its leaves taper to a distinct point.

Unlike Bermuda grass, St. Augustine grass takes some shade, but is not as tough otherwise. Start it with sprigs, plugs, or sod.

Dichondra is not a grass but is a good lawn substitute, popular along the southern coast and in the San Joaquin Valley. The heat of the Imperial Valley is too severe unless it is filtered by some shade. Dichondra may need less mowing, but weeds are harder to get out once they're established.

Publications office
Agricultural Sciences Publications
University of California
1422 South 10th Street
Richmond, California 94804
Out-of-state requests: No.

	TOTAL INCHES RAIN	INCHES JULY/AUG.	JULY % SUNSHINE	DEC. % SUNSHINE	JULY DAYS ABOVE 90°F.	AVERAGE MAXIMUM/MINIMUM TEMPERATURES											
						JAN.	FEB.	MARCH	APRIL	MAY	JUNE	JULY	AUG.	SEPT.	OCT.	NOV.	DEC.

Nevada

	TOTAL INCHES RAIN	INCHES JULY/AUG.	JULY % SUNSHINE	DEC. % SUNSHINE	JULY DAYS ABOVE 90°F.	JAN.	FEB.	MARCH	APRIL	MAY	JUNE	JULY	AUG.	SEPT.	OCT.	NOV.	DEC.
Carson	11.5	.4	92	68	23	45/19	57/20	52/24	70/33	62/35	87/51	91/49	91/51	80/41	70/31	61/27	52/27
Elko	9.8	1.0	85	65	20	36/10	42/17	48/21	59/28	68/35	77/42	90/49	88/46	79/36	66/28	49/21	38/13
Ely	8.7	1.2	80	64	9	38/9	41/14	47/19	56/26	66/34	76/40	86/48	84/47	76/37	64/28	49/19	40/12
Hawthorne	5.9	.8	93	70	25	44/20	56/25	55/27	71/39	66/41	89/59	94/58	91/58	83/48	73/40	61/31	55/28
Las Vegas	3.8	.9	87	78	31	56/33	61/37	68/42	77/50	87/59	97/67	101/75	101/73	95/65	81/53	66/41	57/34
Reno	7.2	.5	92	64	22	45/18	51/23	56/25	64/30	72/37	80/42	91/47	89/45	82/39	70/30	56/24	46/20
Tonopah	4.2	.8	93	72	25	43/17	56/24	50/21	68/34	63/37	86/54	91/56	88/56	79/46	72/38	58/26	50/25
Winnemucca	8.5	.5	86	49	23	41/16	47/21	52/23	61/29	70/37	79/44	91/51	89/47	80/38	67/29	52/22	43/18

California

	TOTAL INCHES RAIN	INCHES JULY/AUG.	JULY % SUNSHINE	DEC. % SUNSHINE	JULY DAYS ABOVE 90°F.	JAN.	FEB.	MARCH	APRIL	MAY	JUNE	JULY	AUG.	SEPT.	OCT.	NOV.	DEC.
Bakersfield	5.7	.03	95	65	29	57/37	63/41	69/44	75/50	84/56	91/62	99/69	96/67	91/62	80/53	68/44	57/38
Eureka	40	.04	52	40	0	53/41	54/42	54/42	55/44	57/48	60/51	60/52	61/53	62/51	60/48	58/45	58/43
Fresno	10.2	.02	96	47	29	55/36	61/39	67/41	74/46	83/52	90/57	98/63	96/61	91/56	80/49	66/41	55/37
Lancaster	9.6	1.0	93	67	27	54/31	61/32	69/33	76/45	69/48	90/63	96/67	94/66	86/58	81/49	69/35	62/38
Long Beach	10	.02	70	68	6	68/47	73/46	66/44	72/53	71/55	77/61	84/64	85/68	81/62	80/61	80/53	69/53
Los Angeles	14	.04	82	71	4	66/47	68/48	69/50	70/53	73/56	76/59	83/63	84/64	82/63	78/59	73/52	68/48
Marysville	21	.07	90	52	25	51/35	66/40	66/41	80/50	74/50	94/61	95/60	94/61	86/57	80/51	67/42	58/43
Merced	22	.03	97	46	30	48/36	65/37	66/35	80/44	76/46	94/59	98/58	95/59	89/54	82/46	68/39	58/41
Mt. Shasta	37	4	90	48	9	42/25	47/28	51/30	58/34	67/40	74/46	85/51	83/49	78/44	65/38	52/32	44/27
Napa	24.8	.09	80	51	—	57/35	66/40	65/38	76/44	70/45	80/51	83/53	82/53	78/54	77/48	69/42	60/45
Oakland	19	.1	74	55	2	57/42	62/47	62/46	67/50	64/52	68/56	72/57	73/60	72/59	70/55	64/49	59/49
Palm Springs	5.3	.48	90	78	31	70/42	83/47	77/44	91/55	87/56	106/69	110/75	106/75	100/67	93/61	82/48	72/47
Pasadena	18.9	.07	87	72	—	67/45	76/48	68/43	75/50	71/50	82/57	—	88/63	84/59	82/56	79/51	69/50
Placerville	40	.1	68	52	22	52/30	61/33	57/32	72/40	65/41	88/62	93/65	92/64	82/57	78/54	62/45	55/42
Red Bluff	22	.22	96	51	28	54/37	59/40	64/42	72/47	81/54	89/62	98/67	96/64	91/60	78/52	64/43	55/38
Riverside	10.2	—	81	70	30	65/42	76/44	67/42	78/48	72/51	88/57	96/60	92/63	87/57	84/53	79/45	69/47
Sacramento	17.2	.06	97	46	23	53/37	59/40	64/42	71/45	79/50	86/55	93/57	91/57	88/53	77/49	64/42	53/38
San Bernar.	16.1	.14	82	70	30	68/42	78/44	68/41	80/49	71/50	91/58	99/62	96/64	90/58	87/54	81/47	70/46
San Diego	9.4	.08	67	71	0	65/46	66/48	68/50	68/54	69/57	71/60	75/64	77/65	76/63	74/58	70/51	66/47
San Frans.	20.6	.06	66	53	0	56/46	59/48	60/48	61/49	62/51	64/53	64/53	65/54	69/55	68/55	63/51	57/47
San Jose	13.6	.09	72	51	3	57/38	65/44	63/42	73/47	68/48	79/56	82/56	80/58	79/55	74/51	66/45	60/46
Sn. Luis Ob.	21.9	.05	65	58	5	64/44	71/47	64/42	70/44	65/47	73/52	79/53	79/56	77/52	75/49	—	67/49
Santa Ana	12.9	.06	79	67	—	70/47	75/47	68/45	74/53	71/54	77/60	84/61	83/65	82/62	79/59	79/50	70/52
Santa Barb.	17.4	.04	65	59	0	66/42	71/44	66/44	70/49	69/52	71/55	75/57	77/61	76/58	74/55	76/47	68/51
Santa Mon.	11.6	.03	71	68	0	63/45	64/47	64/49	66/52	68/53	70/59	75/62	76/63	76/62	73/57	70/51	66/47
Santa Rosa	30.5	.14	65	47	8	59/34	68/39	66/37	76/42	73/44	84/51	88/50	87/53	82/52	79/46	70/40	61/43
Stockton	14	1.4	97	46	25	53/36	59/39	65/41	72/45	80/50	88/55	95/59	93/58	89/55	78/49	64/41	53/38

Oregon

Soil. Lime will undoubtedly be necessary west of the Cascades but probably not to the east. In general, Oregon soils are fertile.

Soil testing
Soil Testing Laboratory
Oregon State University
Corvallis, Oregon 97331

Recommended grasses. Cool-season grasses such as Kentucky bluegrass, fine fescues, perennial rye grass, and sometimes bent grasses are used for home lawns in Oregon.

Basically, Oregon has two lawn climates. One, west of the Cascade Mountains, includes much of coastal Oregon and the great Willamette Valley. Reaching from the Portland-Vancouver area south to Roseburg, the Willamette Valley is a center of the lawn seed industry. Much of the Kentucky bluegrass, perennial and annual rye, and bent grasses planted throughout the country are grown here.

The other lawn climates west of the Cascade Mountains are more mild and humid. Improved rye grasses, sensitive to extreme cold, are more permanent here. Diseases like rust and red thread are common.

Eastern Oregon experiences shorter growing seasons, colder winters, and less humidity. Kentucky bluegrass makes up most of the home lawns. Gray snow mold can become a problem (see page 83).

Annual bluegrass is a serious weed problem west of the Cascades. The best control is proper maintenance of the desired grasses.

Publications office
Bulletin Mailing Service
Industrial Building
Oregon State University
Corvallis, Oregon 97331
Out-of-state requests: No.

Washington

Soil. All Washington soil benefits from the addition of generous quantities of organic matter before planting.

In the west, lime will likely be necessary for a good lawn. Have soil tested before planting. If an established lawn does not respond to fertilizer, lack of lime may be the problem.

Sulfur has been found to improve color and control certain lawn weeds and diseases. It is available as gypsum or as a component of common fertilizers.

Soil testing
Soil Testing Laboratory
Washington State University
Pullman, Washington 99163

Recommended grasses. Kentucky bluegrass, bent grass, and fine fescue are commonly planted in Washington. Turf-type perennial rye grass is a component of many seed mixtures and is sometimes used alone, particularly in the west.

Bluegrass is better adapted to eastern rather than western Washington, but with proper liming, fertilizing, mowing, and adequate drainage, it too makes a good lawn here.

Because of potential disease problems, Washington Cooperative Extension recommends *not planting* 'Nugget', 'Cougar', 'Delta', and 'Park' Kentucky bluegrasses in western Washington.

Bent grass is adapted to the cool, acid soil of western Washington. It will need close mowing and occasional thatch removal. 'Astoria', 'Highland', 'Exeter', and 'Holfior' are recommended varieties of colonial bent grass for western Washington. Do not use bent grass in a mixture with Kentucky bluegrass.

Turf-type perennial rye grass germinates fast and blends well with Kentucky bluegrass and fine fescue and has good performance records throughout the state.

Sod webworm, billbug, cutworm, and wireworms are common insect pests. Rust and red thread are common diseases. See pages 71 – 77.

Publications office
Bulletin Department—
Cooperative Extension
Publications Building
Washington State University
Pullman, Washington 99164
Out-of-state requests: Yes.

Idaho

Soil. Idaho soil is generally high in clay and has fairly moderate pH. In some areas, the soil is rocky and must be cleaned before planting. Also before planting, work plenty of organic material into the soil to a 6- to 8-inch depth.

Soil testing. Check with your County Extension Agent, or write:
Soil Testing Laboratory
Department of Plant & Soil Science
College of Agriculture
Moscow, Idaho 83843

Recommended grasses. Kentucky bluegrass is by far the most common lawn grass in Idaho. Use the fine fescues mixed with a shade-tolerant Kentucky bluegrass for a shaded lawn area.

Turf-type perennial rye grass has found favor in Idaho, particularly in the more southern regions where winter cold is not too intense.

Native grasses such as buffalo grass, blue grama, and wheatgrass can be considered as low-maintenance lawn grasses for areas that will not receive any extra water.

Make the spring fertilizer application around May 1 in Boise and a month later in Sandpoint. About 5 pounds of actual nitrogen for every 1,000 square feet of lawn should be applied over the course of the Idaho growing season. Apply no more than 1 to 1½ pounds at any single application.

The bluegrass billbug is a new pest to Idaho and has caused extensive damage, particularly in the Boise Valley. It is illustrated and described on page 75.

Powdery mildew, gray snow mold, and pink snow mold are troublesome diseases. See pages 80 – 85.

A fertilized lawn is a good method of stopping weed invasion.

Don't try to grow a more high-quality lawn than there is available water to support.

Publications office
Extension Bulletins
Agricultural Science Building
University of Idaho
Moscow, Idaho 83843
Out-of-state requests: Yes.

	TOTAL INCHES RAIN	INCHES JULY/AUG.	JULY % SUNSHINE	DEC. % SUNSHINE	JULY DAYS ABOVE 90°F.	AVERAGE MAXIMUM/MINIMUM TEMPERATURES											
						JAN.	FEB.	MARCH	APRIL	MAY	JUNE	JULY	AUG.	SEPT.	OCT.	NOV.	DEC.

Oregon

	TOTAL INCHES RAIN	INCHES JULY/AUG.	JULY % SUNSHINE	DEC. % SUNSHINE	JULY DAYS ABOVE 90°F.	JAN.	FEB.	MARCH	APRIL	MAY	JUNE	JULY	AUG.	SEPT.	OCT.	NOV.	DEC.
Astoria	66	2.4	45	27	–	46/35	51/37	52/37	56/40	60/44	64/49	68/52	68/52	68/49	61/44	53/40	49/37
Baker	12.7	2.7	79	42	9	28/11	48/23	48/25	68/30	62/36	82/47	84/46	86/49	72/40	63/32	46/25	40/26
Bend	12	.8	83	45	1	42/17	53/23	50/23	65/28	58/32	78/43	80/43	84/48	69/36	63/31	48/24	43/26
Corvallis	40	.9	58	29	1	46/28	54/34	52/35	63/38	62/41	75/48	79/49	86/53	71/48	64/43	52/37	50/39
Eugene	43	.8	60	30	6	46/33	52/35	55/36	61/39	68/44	74/49	83/51	81/51	76/47	64/42	53/38	47/36
Klamath Falls	14	.7	82	43	8	32/11	49/24	47/25	64/32	58/34	81/50	84/50	86/54	71/44	63/36	47/28	42/26
Medford	12	.6	70	34	15	39/25	46/31	53/34	62/40	70/46	78/53	88/59	85/57	78/51	63/42	49/34	42/30
Pendleton	38	1.3	81	35	3	44/32	50/35	54/37	60/41	67/46	72/52	79/55	78/55	74/50	63/45	52/38	46/35
Portland	34	.6	69	20	6	54/39	59/37	55/37	68/39	65/45	79/52	84/53	89/59	73/52	65/46	54/37	52/40
Roseburg	41	.9	72	32	6	45/32	51/34	55/35	61/38	68/43	74/48	82/51	81/51	76/47	64/42	53/37	47/35
Salem	21	.6	75	42	18	44/29	52/31	57/33	64/37	72/43	79/49	89/54	88/53	82/47	67/39	53/34	44/31

Washington

	TOTAL INCHES RAIN	INCHES JULY/AUG.	JULY % SUNSHINE	DEC. % SUNSHINE	JULY DAYS ABOVE 90°F.	JAN.	FEB.	MARCH	APRIL	MAY	JUNE	JULY	AUG.	SEPT.	OCT.	NOV.	DEC.
Bellingham	34	3.6	59	21	0	41/29	53/38	49/39	59/43	60/46	68/53	69/54	76/58	65/50	60/42	52/37	43/32
Centralia	46	2.1	65	26	2	44/31	54/37	52/35	64/39	63/42	74/50	76/50	82/56	68/49	61/42	53/39	46/36
Everett	35	2.2	60	22	0	42/31	55/38	51/39	61/44	62/47	70/54	70/54	78/58	67/49	60/42	54/39	47/36
Olympia	51	8.1	62	23	2	44/30	50/32	54/33	60/36	67/41	72/46	78/49	77/48	72/45	61/40	51/35	46/33
Seattle	36	1.7	63	23	1	45/35	50/37	53/38	59/42	66/47	70/52	76/56	74/55	69/52	62/46	51/40	47/37
Spokane	17.4	1	80	20	10	31/20	39/25	46/29	57/35	66/43	74/49	84/55	82/54	72/47	58/37	42/29	34/24
Tacoma	39	1.8	67	17	1	43/33	48/36	51/37	57/40	64/46	69/51	75/54	74/54	69/50	59/45	50/39	45/36
Vancouver	40	1.4	69	20	0	43/23	53/32	52/33	60/41	61/42	72/49	75/50	81/54	68/47	62/39	54/38	46/36
Walla Walla	16	.8	85	18	15	39/27	47/33	54/37	63/43	71/50	79/56	89/62	86/61	77/54	64/45	49/36	42/31
Wenatchee	9.4	.6	80	36	12	31/19	49/29	56/32	71/39	69/44	85/56	86/57	91/58	72/46	64/35	51/30	38/25
Yakima	8	.4	82	40	14	36/19	46/25	55/29	64/35	73/43	79/49	88/53	86/51	78/44	65/35	48/28	39/23

Idaho

	TOTAL INCHES RAIN	INCHES JULY/AUG.	JULY % SUNSHINE	DEC. % SUNSHINE	JULY DAYS ABOVE 90°F.	JAN.	FEB.	MARCH	APRIL	MAY	JUNE	JULY	AUG.	SEPT.	OCT.	NOV.	DEC.
Boise	11.5	.4	88	40	19	36/21	44/27	52/30	61/36	71/44	78/51	90/58	88/57	78/48	65/39	49/31	39/25
Burley	9.7	.8	78	47	5	32/13	47/19	47/25	67/34	62/40	82/53	84/54	84/53	74/43	67/32	48/26	41/27
Caldwell	10.8	0.5	84	44	20	27/14	44/24	55/30	74/41	69/43	89/58	91/58	91/58	79/47	67/36	50/29	44/31
Cr. D'Alene	26	1.7	80	22	6	35/20	46/27	47/30	67/35	65/42	80/51	82/53	88/54	69/45	60/37	43/29	37/25
Idaho Falls	8.9	1.0	74	47	8	19/0	30/7	42/21	64/31	61/38	82/50	85/52	83/48	73/41	63/30	43/22	34/20
Lewiston	13.2	1.1	77	29	16	38/24	46/30	53/33	62/39	71/45	78/52	89/58	87/56	78/49	63/40	48/33	41/29
Malad	14.3	1.5	75	48	6	32/11	44/18	45/22	66/33	65/37	84/51	85/53	85/48	74/42	66/31	46/23	38/21
Moscow	9.7	1.6	79	21	4	31/14	48/19	48/25	66/34	61/39	81/52	83/53	83/52	74/41	66/33	48/26	42/27
Pocatello	22.6	1.2	76	48	5	32/18	46/29	45/30	64/36	62/38	81/48	82/49	86/51	66/43	59/35	42/28	37/26
Twin Falls	10.8	1	83	37	16	32/14	39/20	46/25	58/33	68/41	76/47	89/54	86/52	76/43	63/34	46/25	35/18

Colorado

Soil. Most Colorado soil, such as around Denver, Pueblo, and Grand Junction, is alkaline with low levels of available iron. Lawns grown in these areas will likely benefit if iron-containing fertilizers are used.

In the mountains, soil is usually near neutral in pH, shallow, and droughty. For a good lawn, fertilize every 6 to 8 weeks during the growing season, applying about 1 pound of actual nitrogen per 1,000 square feet.

Soil testing. Contact your County Extension Agent, or write:
Soil Testing Laboratory
Colorado State University
Fort Collins, Colorado 80523

Recommended grasses. Kentucky bluegrass is the main lawn grass of Colorado. Common Kentucky bluegrass is frequently planted and does all right except for susceptibility to melting-out (also known as fade-out) disease.

'Merion' Kentucky bluegrass is a high-quality variety but it requires slightly more care. Stripe smut disease has become a problem of 'Merion' in Colorado.

Other good varieties for the state include 'Sydsport', 'Bensun', 'Baron', and 'Adelphi'. Plant a blend of three or more varieties and combine their strengths.

Problems may result from planting seed or sod on heavy, poorly drained soil. Organic soil amendments should be worked in before planting, to reduce future maintenance problems.

Thatch is common in many lawns and can be corrected by aerating and vertical mowing. See pages 54 – 59.

Inadequate watering causes, or is related to, many Colorado lawn problems. If you have questions, read pages 24 – 34.

Publications office
Extension-Experiment Station
Publications Office
Office of University Communications
Colorado State University
Fort Collins, Colorado 80523
Out-of-state requests: Yes.

Utah

Soil. Most Utah soil is naturally low in organic matter. Around the Salt Lake area, the soil is usually a heavy clay. If it is hard-packed because of a high sodium content, gypsum incorporated before planting will improve tilth.

If iron chlorosis (yellowing) is a problem and regular fertilizing has no effect, use fertilizers such as ferrous ammonium sulfate, known as FAS, or other fertilizers or products that contain available iron.

Soil testing
Soil, Plant, and Water Analysis Laboratory
Utah State University, UMC 48
Logan, Utah 84322

Recommended grasses. Kentucky bluegrass is most often planted. Look for the improved, lower-growing varieties. In shady areas, use varieties that have demonstrated some tolerance of shade such as 'Glade' or 'Bensun'. The fine fescues are widely used in the shade, usually mixed with Kentucky bluegrass.

Turf-type perennial rye grass is not generally as cold-tolerant as either Kentucky bluegrass or fine fescue, but some, such as 'NK-200', can be used in mixtures.

Clover is sometimes added to Kentucky bluegrass lawn seed mixtures. Considered a weed by some, it does reduce fertilizer need, and susceptibility to disease. But it is also slippery and stains clothes.

The best time to start a Kentucky bluegrass lawn is early spring, March to April. During midsummer, lawns can be planted, but will require frequent watering to compensate for the drying heat. Early fall, September to mid-October, is the other good time to plant lawns.

Fertilize 3 to 5 times per year with a high-nitrogen fertilizer. Use 1 pound of actual nitrogen per 1,000 square feet. The first application should be in April, the second around Labor Day. For infertile soil, a late May or June fertilization will encourage a deeper green growth. Fertilize again in fall.

Toward the Arizona border, in towns such as St. George, Bermuda grass and other warm-season grasses are sometimes planted.

Publications office
The Bulletin Room
UMC 48
Utah State University
Logan, Utah 84322
Out-of-state requests: Yes.

Montana and Wyoming

Soil. Few soils in the Montana and Wyoming areas are ideal, well-drained loams. Before planting, mix 2 or more inches of organic matter into the soil to a depth of 6 to 8 inches. The pH is usually alkaline.

Soil testing. Contact your County Extension Agent, or write:
Soil Testing Laboratory
Plant Science Division
University of Wyoming
Box 3354, University Station
Laramie, Wyoming 82071

Soil Testing Laboratory
Plant and Soil Science Department
Montana State University
Bozeman, Montana 59715

Recommended grasses. Throughout this region, Kentucky bluegrass is the most important lawn grass. It grows slowly during midsummer heat and rather fast in late summer. The late summer period—late August or very early September—is the best time to plant a new lawn. Apply 1 pound of actual nitrogen fertilizer per 1,000 square feet, 2 to 4 times each year. In the summer, grass may become yellowish. This can be treated with iron in the fertilizer or with a spray.

Fertilize first in early spring before new growth starts, then again six weeks after the spring flush of growth. Fall fertilization should be about six weeks before cold weather.

Fine fescue is also an important lawn grass. The blades are very fine textured, almost needlelike. It has good shade and drought resistance, and, if seeded heavily, will form a tough, wear-resistant sod. Fine fescue mixes well with Kentucky bluegrass.

Turf-type perennial rye grass is not as cold-hardy as Kentucky bluegrass or fescue, but is much more cold-tolerant than common perennial rye grass.

Crested wheat grass and buffalo grass are useful, long-lived grasses that survive with no supplemental water. 'Fairway' crested wheat grass is sometimes used for home lawns. Mow it no shorter than 3 inches and only 3 or 4 times per season. Clip buffalo grass about 1 inch high 2 or 3 times per season.

Publications office
Bulletin Room, College of Agriculture
University of Wyoming
Box 3354, University Station
Laramie, Wyoming 80271

Bulletin Room
Cooperative Extension Office
Montana State University
Bozeman, Montana 59717

	TOTAL INCHES RAIN	INCHES JULY/AUG.	JULY % SUNSHINE	DEC. % SUNSHINE	JULY DAYS ABOVE 90°F.	AVERAGE MAXIMUM/MINIMUM TEMPERATURES											
						JAN.	FEB.	MARCH	APRIL	MAY	JUNE	JULY	AUG.	SEPT.	OCT.	NOV.	DEC.

Colorado

Alamosa	7	2.3	76	71	1	35/-7	40/5	47/15	58/24	68/33	78/41	82/48	80/46	74/36	63/25	48/12	37/60
Boulder	19	3.4	71	68	—	41/16	44/19	48/23	59/33	68/43	78/51	84/57	82/56	75/47	64/37	50/25	43/19
Colo. Spr.	15.7	5.7	76	72	8	43/16	46/19	50/24	61/34	70/44	80/52	87/59	86/57	78/48	67/37	53/25	46/19
Denver	15.5	3.1	71	68	15	44/14	52/24	54/26	63/39	75/46	86/57	88/61	83/57	81/49	69/37	51/20	49/21
Durango	18.5	4.2	77	70	10	36/4	50/17	51/19	66/31	70/35	86/46	86/53	86/52	80/45	69/30	54/23	45/18
Ft. Collins	15	2.9	70	66	12	40/10	51/22	53/24	63/36	73/46	79/45	86/59	80/56	80/49	67/37	52/25	47/21
Grand Junc.	8.4	1.5	77	60	26	37/16	44/23	53/30	65/39	76/48	86/57	93/64	89/62	81/53	68/42	51/29	39/20
Greely	12.2	2.4	71	67	22	41/10	53/22	57/23	66/37	77/47	90/56	91/59	85/56	85/48	72/35	54/24	47/19
La Junta	14	8.3	78	72	21	44/11	56/22	61/27	73/42	83/54	93/62	94/64	88/61	87/52	72/36	58/22	50/16
Pueblo	11.9	3.8	78	73	22	43/12	57/19	60/24	70/39	81/49	91/57	94/61	88/60	86/49	72/35	59/23	52/19
Sterling	15	4.0	72	65	—	36/6	51/21	51/24	65/38	76/49	89/59	92/62	85/59	83/50	69/34	50/24	43/16

Utah

Beaver	11.3	2.4	78	60	12	42/12	51/16	51/19	65/30	65/37	86/46	87/52	86/51	78/44	69/34	56/24	50/20
Cedar City	10.3	2.2	79	63	19	45/18	54/21	51/23	68/35	67/41	87/54	89/59	89/58	80/49	72/37	58/27	52/27
Logan	17.6	1.2	76	49	6	30/13	39/19	44/25	63/38	62/41	83/57	85/59	82/58	74/49	64/40	47/29	41/26
Moab	7.9	1.4	77	66	—	44/17	58/23	61/30	77/43	80/49	98/59	—	96/64	88/56	76/40	61/30	53/25
Mexican Hat	3.0	1.3	78	69	27	33/13	55/24	57/24	73/38	78/46	96/60	96/65	95/62	90/52	76/36	59/27	52/25
Ogden	16.2	1.3	81	43	18	36/18	47/25	48/28	68/42	65/43	88/60	91/62	86/59	78/51	68/41	51/31	43/28
Price	8.4	3.5	75	50	17	35/9.7	52/22	52/22	67/37	67/40	88/55	88/58	88/58	78/49	—	—	44/24
Spanish Fork	18	1.6	—	—	24	36/17	45/21	49/25	68/37	67/41	89/55	92/60	89/58	81/50	70/42	53/32	45/28
S.L. City	15.2	1.6	84	45	25	37/18	43/23	51/28	62/37	72/44	81/51	91/60	90/59	80/49	66/38	50/28	39/21
Vernal	7.8	1.1	—	—	15	35/12	46/18	48/19	67/34	69/38	90/50	89/53	86/53	79/44	65/33	48/21	40/17

Montana and Wyoming

Billings, MT	14.1	1.9	78	45	12	31/12	37/18	42/23	56/33	66/43	74/51	86/58	84/56	71/46	61/37	45/26	36/18
Cheyne, WY	14.6	3.3	68	59	6	38/15	41/17	43/20	55/30	65/40	74/48	84/54	82/53	73/43	62/34	47/23	40/18
Glsgw, MT	10.9	2.9	75	55	9	19/-5	25/5	36/15	55/31	67/42	74/50	84/57	83/55	70/44	59/34	39/19	26/7
Gt. Falls, MT	15	2.3	80	45	9	29/12	36/17	40/21	54/32	65/41	72/49	84/55	82/53	70/48	59/37	43/26	35/18
Helena, MT	11.4	1.9	79	43	7	28/7.8	36/15	42/19	55/30	65/39	72/47	84/52	82/50	70/41	59/32	43/21	33/13
Casper, WY	11.2	1.5	72	62	11	34/13	38/16	43/19	55/30	61/39	76/47	87/55	86/53	74/43	61/34	45/23	36/16
Jacksn, WY	15.2	1.9	68	48	—	28/0.2	37/5.2	41/14	61/20	59/32	79/40	—	78/39	71/32	61/21	41/19	33/17
Laramie, WY	10.1	2.5	65	46	—	33/6.2	40/9.3	40/13	53/26	64/33	80/46	81/49	76/46	72/39	60/28	44/18	38/16
Missla, MT	13.3	1.8	79	25	10	29/13	36/19	44/23	57/31	66/38	72/45	84/49	83/47	71/40	57/31	41/24	32/17
Rawlins, WY	9.8	3.1	74	62	—	30/9.2	41/15	38/17	57/30	64/36	82/49	82/53	77/50	72/41	59/32	42/21	35/20
Rck. Sps, WY	8.8	1.2	74	60	6	34/11	44/17	39/16	60/31	64/35	84/50	84/52	79/49	74/39	62/31	43/21	36/19

Hawaii

Soil. Most Hawaiian soils do not have ideal characteristics for lawn grasses. They need to be amended with organic matter such as manure, leaves, grass clippings, compost, bagasse, peat moss, or hapuu.

Soil testing
Soil Testing Service
Cooperative Extension Service
University of Hawaii
Honolulu, Hawaii 96822

Recommended grasses. Bermuda grass, known locally as *manienie* or *mahiki*, is commonly planted. Don't try to grow it where there's shade—it won't work. Bermuda grass is tough and takes heavy traffic in stride. 'Sunturf' improved Bermuda grass is endorsed by Hawaii Cooperative Extension.

'Emerald' zoysia grass is very slow to establish—it may take two or three years

to form a good lawn. Once filled, it makes a dense, weed-choking turf. 'Emerald' will also tolerate some shade.

Temple or Korean grass is another kind of zoysia. It's more of a ground cover than lawn grass. When mature it makes a bumpy, wavy surface.

St. Augustine grass is known as buffalo grass to some Hawaiians. It's definitely not the same buffalo grass native to the continental Great Plains. St. Augustine is coarse bladed, tough, and shade tolerant.

Hilo grass is the grass to plant if you live in Makiki, Lihue, Wahiawa, Kaneohe, or other cities that receive about 150 inches of rain each year. Hilo grass probably won't survive in areas receiving less than 50 inches of rain annually.

McCoy grass makes a beautiful lawn. Actually it's a sedge, not a grass. Roll it between your fingers and you can feel

the three distinct sides characteristic of all sedges. Originally imported from Australia, the blades are delicate and light green in color. It will thrive at any elevation, sun or shade.

Publications office
Cooperative Extension Service
College of Tropical Agriculture
University of Hawaii
Honolulu, Hawaii 96822
Out-of-state requests: Yes.

Alaska

Soil. If you're in a low, swampy area, haul in soil to improve drainage. Incorporate organic material into the soil before making the seedbed.

Interior Alaska soils are generally low in nitrogen, phosphorus, and potassium. A complete fertilizer such as 10-20-20 should be added prior to seeding. About 12 pounds of this formula fertilizer for 1,000 square feet is usually adequate.

A soil test will indicate if lime is necessary and how much to use.

Soil testing
Palmer Plant and Soils Analysis Laboratory
Agricultural Experiment Station
Palmer Research Center
P.O. Box AE
Palmer, Alaska 99645

Recommended grasses. Kentucky bluegrass and red fescue do quite well

in Alaska. Certain varieties of Kentucky bluegrass, such as 'Adelphi', 'Nugget', and 'Park' have good winter hardiness. Consider other varieties too, as components of blends. Snow mold is a serious disease of bluegrass in Alaska, so it is important to use varieties resistant whenever possible, such as 'Nugget'.

'Arctared' red fescue is superior to the other varieties of fine fescue. It has good winter hardiness, it's fairly snow-mold resistant, greens up early in the spring, and is drought resistant. 'Boreal' is all right where little or no snow accumulates, but it's highly prone to snow-mold damage.

Perennial rye grass is recommended for areas such as steep slopes where a quick cover is needed, but winter survival is poor.

Lawns can be planted anytime after spring break-up until about August 1. Plantings between July 1 and August 1

usually have fewer weed problems and are more successful.

Publications office
School of Agriculture and Land Resources Management
Agricultural Experiment Station
University of Alaska
Fairbanks, Alaska 99701
Out-of-state requests: Yes.

Western Canada

Soil. Generally very fertile. Lime is often necessary along coastal British Columbia. A soil test will show needed amounts.

Soil testing
Soil Testing Unit
British Columbia Department of Agriculture
1873 Small Road
Kelowna, British Columbia
V1Y 4R2

Soil and Feed Testing Laboratory
University of Alberta
O. S. Longman Building
6906 116 Street
Edmonton, Alberta
T6G 2M7

Recommended grasses. Of the many grasses tested at the research stations of Sidney and Agassiz, bent grass, fine fescue, Kentucky bluegrass, and turf-type perennial rye are the ones most often

recommended for coastal British Columbia.

Colonial bent grass makes a beautiful, fine-textured lawn. It thrives in cool, wet climates and is adapted to heavy moist soil. It requires attention to maintenance practices, such as periodic dethatching, and close mowing to remove the thatch accumulation.

Fine fescue is also well adapted to coastal conditions. It tolerates shade and rather poor soil.

The new, turf-type ryes such as 'Manhattan' also grow well along the coast. Inland, they don't have the necessary winter hardiness.

Kentucky bluegrass is the prime grass of interior parts of Canada. Generally, it does not do as well as bent grass and fescue under coastal conditions. Seed or sod of red fescue and Kentucky bluegrass mixtures do best throughout central British

Columbia and Alberta. A late fall fertilization that stimulates new succulent growth tends to promote snow mold disease.

Publications offices
The Publications Office
Department of Agriculture
Parliament Buildings
Victoria, British Columbia
V8W 2Z7

Bulletins
University of Alberta
O. S. Longman Building
6906 116 Street
Edmonton, Alberta
T6G 2M7

	TOTAL INCHES RAIN	INCHES JULY/AUG.	JULY % SUNSHINE	DEC. % SUNSHINE	JULY DAYS ABOVE 90°F.	AVERAGE MAXIMUM/MINIMUM TEMPERATURES											
						JAN.	FEB.	MARCH	APRIL	MAY	JUNE	JULY	AUG.	SEPT.	OCT.	NOV.	DEC.

Hawaii

	TOTAL INCHES RAIN	INCHES JULY/AUG.	JULY % SUNSHINE	DEC. % SUNSHINE	JULY DAYS ABOVE 90°F.	JAN.	FEB.	MARCH	APRIL	MAY	JUNE	JULY	AUG.	SEPT.	OCT.	NOV.	DEC.
Halawa, Oahu	18	1.6	—	—	0	81/64	81/66	81/67	82/68	83/70	84/70	85/71	86/71	87/71	86/70	85/68	82/66
Hilo, Hawaii	133	20	42	35	0	80/63	79/63	79/63	80/64	81/66	83/66	83/67	83/68	86/69	84/68	81/66	80/64
Hnolulu, Oahu	23	1.3	73	75	0	79/65	79/65	80/66	81/68	84/70	86/72	87/73	87/74	87/78	86/72	83/70	80/67
Kahului, Maui	18	.7	75	67	2	79/64	79/64	80/64	82/66	84/67	86/69	86/70	87/71	87/70	86/69	83/68	80/65
Kealakekua	32	6.9	—	—	0	78/58	78/60	76/61	76/62	76/62	77/63	79/64	80/65	81/63	81/65	80/62	79/60
Kaneohe, Oahu	70	8.4	—	—	0	80/68	79/68	77/68	77/68	79/70	80/70	81/72	83/73	83/73	82/73	80/71	79/69
Lihue, Kauai	44	4.1	62	47	0	78/64	78/64	78/65	79/67	81/69	83/72	84/73	85/74	85/73	83/71	81/70	78/67
Molokai (AP)	33	.3	—	—	0	82/63	81/64	82/65	80/65	83/66	84/69	86/70	—	—	—	85/69	81/66
Waialua, Oahu	29	2.2	—	—	0	81/60	81/61	80/64	80/63	82/64	84/65	84/65	87/67	87/67	86/65	85/64	81/62
Waikiki, Oahu	16	.3	—	—	0	83/65	83/66	82/68	82/68	84/68	86/69	86/70	89/71	89/70	89/69	86/67	83/64
Wmnalo, Oahu	34	1.6	—	—	0	80/65	80/66	79/67	78/67	80/68	82/71	83/72	85/73	85/73	84/73	82/70	80/67

	TOTAL INCHES RAIN	INCHES JULY/AUG.	JULY % SUNSHINE	DEC. % SUNSHINE	JULY DAYS ABOVE 90°F.	JAN.	FEB.	MARCH	APRIL	MAY	JUNE	JULY	AUG.	SEPT.	OCT.	NOV.	DEC.
Anchorage	15	4.4	45	33	8	20/3	27/9	33/15	44/27	55/37	63/46	66/50	64/48	56/40	42/28	28/14	21/5
Annette	114	13	—	—	7	38/29	41/32	44/33	49/37	52/43	61/48	64/52	65/52	60/48	52/42	44/35	40/32
Cold Bay	33	6.1	—	—	0	33/24	33/24	34/24	38/28	44/35	50/41	54/46	55/47	52/43	44/35	39/30	33/24
Fairbanks	11	4.1	—	—	21	-2/-21	9/-14	23/-4	40/17	59/36	71/47	72/50	66/45	54/34	33/17	12/-6	-1/-19
Homer	23	4.2	—	—	1	28/15	32/18	35/20	42/28	50/34	57/41	60/44	60/45	55/39	44/30	34/22	28/15
Juneau	55	9.7	31	20	7	29/18	34/22	38/26	46/31	55/38	62/44	64/48	62/46	56/42	47/36	37/27	32/22
Kodiak	57	7.8	—	—	2	34/26	36/27	37/27	42/32	48/38	55/45	59/49	60/50	55/45	46/36	39/30	34/25
Nome	16	6.0	35	34	3	13/-2	14/-3	16/-2	27/11	41/28	52/39	56/44	55/44	48/36	34/23	22/9	12/-3
Talkeetna	29	8.3	—	—	13	19/0	26/5	33/7	44/21	56/33	66/44	67/48	64/45	56/37	41/24	26/9	18/0
Valdez	59	10	—	—	3	25/11	30/15	35/18	44/27	52/35	60/43	61/45	60/44	54/39	44/31	32/20	26/13
Yakutat	132	19	—	—	2	31/17	35/21	38/23	44/28	51/36	56/43	59/47	60/46	55/41	47/34	38/26	33/21

Western Canada

AVERAGE DEGREES CELSIUS

	TOTAL INCHES RAIN	INCHES JULY/AUG.	JULY % SUNSHINE	DEC. % SUNSHINE	JULY DAYS ABOVE 90°F.	JAN.	FEB.	MARCH	APRIL	MAY	JUNE	JULY	AUG.	SEPT.	OCT.	NOV.	DEC.
Calgry, Alta.	17.2	4.9	317*	94**	—	-10.9	-7.4	-4.3	3.3	9.3	13.2	16.5	15.2	10.7	5.7	-2.6	-7.6
Edmtn, Alta.	18.3	6.1	306	80	—	-14.7	-10.5	-5.4	4.0	10.9	14.7	17.5	15.9	10.9	5.4	-4.2	-10.7
Kmlps, B.C.	10.2	2.1	308	43	—	-6.0	-1.3	3.6	9.3	14.3	18.0	20.9	19.7	15.0	8.4	1.7	-2.6
P. A., Sask.	15.3	4.6	303	72	—	-21.0	-16.9	-10.4	1.7	9.5	14.3	17.7	16.2	10.2	3.9	-7.1	-16.4
P. Grge, B.C.	24	5.2	279	39	—	-11.8	-6.2	-2.1	3.9	9.4	13.0	14.9	13.7	9.8	4.7	-2.8	-7.6
Rgna, Sask.	15.6	4.2	337	83	—	-17.3	-14.3	-8.3	3.3	10.6	15.3	18.9	17.9	11.6	5.3	-5.2	-12.9
Skatn, Sask.	13.8	3.9	341	84	—	-18.7	-15.1	-8.7	3.3	10.6	15.4	18.8	17.4	11.3	5.0	-5.8	-14.0
Vancvr, B.C.	42	2.6	305	44	—	2.4	4.4	5.8	8.9	12.4	15.3	17.4	17.1	14.2	10.1	6.1	3.8
Victoria, B.C.	34	1.7	338	60	—	2.9	4.7	5.8	6.8	11.9	14.5	16.4	16.1	13.9	10.0	6.2	4.2
Wnpeg, Man.	21	6.1	331	86	—	-18.3	-15.7	-8.1	3.3	10.6	16.5	19.7	18.7	12.6	6.6	-4.4	-13.7

*Total hours bright sun, July   **Total hours bright sun, December.

ENCYCLOPEDIA OF MAJOR GRASSES

Your lifestyle—and the facts about seeds given here—will help you decide which type of grass will give you most satisfaction.

This listing of the 15 most important lawn grasses is intended to help you select just the right grass for your lawn. The grasses are described in similar terms to make comparison easier: strengths and weaknesses, shade tolerance, water and fertilizer needs, wearability, recommended mowing heights, most suitable climate, and growing conditions. Varieties and scientific names are also listed.

Bahia Grass

☐ *Strengths:* Low maintenance. Extensive root system valued for erosion control and drought tolerance. Moderately aggressive.
☐ *Weaknesses:* Forms a coarse, open lawn. Tall, fast-growing seed stalks need frequent mowing to remain attractive. Considered a weed in fine lawns. May turn yellow from chlorosis. Dollar spot and especially mole cricket may be a problem.
☐ *Shade tolerance:* Fair to pretty good.
☐ *Water needs:* Good drought resistance, but performs best where rain is plentiful and evenly distributed over the season.
☐ *Fertilizer needs:* Medium, about 4 to 6 pounds of actual nitrogen per 1,000 square feet per year.
☐ *Wearability:* Good.
☐ *Mowing height:* High, to 3 inches.
☐ *Best adapted:* Infertile, sandy soils. Central coast of North Carolina to east Texas. Popular in Florida.
☐ *Varieties:* 'Argentine', 'Pensacola'.
☐ *Scientific name: Paspalum notatum.*

Creeping Bent Grass

☐ *Strengths:* The grass of choice for golf course putting greens, lawn bowling, and similar uses. Can be mowed very low.
☐ *Weaknesses:* Requires low mowing or else it quickly builds extensive thatch layer. Creeping bent grass, like all bent grasses, is susceptible to several diseases.
☐ *Shade tolerance:* Somewhat tolerant, but best in full sun.
☐ *Water needs:* High. Poor drought tolerance.
☐ *Fertilizer needs:* Medium to high. Needs 6 to 12 pounds of actual nitrogen per 1,000 square feet per year for highest quality.
☐ *Wearability:* Fair to good.
☐ *Mowing height:* Keep it low, between ¼ inch and 1 inch.
☐ *Best adapted:* Grows without special care in sandy-loam soils of northern U.S. and Canada. Extensively used in Pacific Northwest and Northeast.
☐ *Varieties:* 'Penncross' is quick to establish, repairs itself fast. 'Penncross', 'Emerald', 'Seaside', and 'Penneagle' start from seed. From sprigs: 'Cohansey', 'Congressional', and 'Toronto' creeping bent grass.
☐ *Scientific name: Agrostis stolonifera.*

Bahia grass.

Creeping bent grass.

Bermuda Grass

- ☐ *Strengths:* Likes heat, easy to grow in most soils, takes considerable abuse. The most widely adapted warm-season grass. Tolerates little maintenance but makes a handsome lawn when given extra care.
- ☐ *Weaknesses:* Invasive, poor shade tolerance, often browns in fall until spring.
- ☐ *Shade tolerance:* Poor.
- ☐ *Water needs.* Very drought tolerant but needs extra water in dry periods to look good.
- ☐ *Fertilizer needs:* Moderate to high (4 to 12 pounds of actual nitrogen per year per 1,000 square feet).
- ☐ *Wearability:* Good.
- ☐ *Mowing height:* About 1 inch.
- ☐ *Best adapted:* Lower elevations of the Southwest, Maryland to Florida in the east, then west to Kansas, Oklahoma, and Texas.
- ☐ *Varieties:* Common.
- ☐ *Scientific name: Cynodon dactylon.*

Bermuda Grass (Improved)

- ☐ *Strengths:* Most of the same virtues of common Bermuda grass, but softer and finer-textured. Generally shorter dormant season.
- ☐ *Weaknesses:* More water, fertilizer, and mowing needed compared to common Bermuda grass. Also more disease and insect prone. Requires regular thatch control.
- ☐ *Shade tolerance:* None. Does not grow in the shade.
- ☐ *Water needs:* Relatively drought tolerant but should get more water than common Bermuda grass.
- ☐ *Fertilizer needs:* High: Up to 12 pounds or more of actual nitrogen per 1,000 square feet per year.
- ☐ *Wearability:* Excellent.
- ☐ *Mowing height:* ½ inch to 1 inch.
- ☐ *Best adapted:* Very popular in the South and Southwest for a fine-quality lawn.
- ☐ *Varieties:* See chart, page 138.
- ☐ *Scientific name: Cynodon species.*

Kentucky Bluegrass (Common)

- ☐ *Strengths:* The standard against which other grasses are measured. Looks the way most people think a lawn is supposed to look—dark green, dense, with a medium texture. Easy to grow where adapted. The most important lawn grass in North America.
- ☐ *Weaknesses:* Most varieties are weakened if mowed too short. Disease prone during summer periods of high heat.

Below: Bermuda grass.
Below right: Improved Bermuda grass.

- ☐ *Shade tolerance:* Not too good, but certain varieties have shown some shade tolerance.
- ☐ *Water needs:* High. Will recover from drought (except in semi-arid regions) as rainy season begins.
- ☐ *Fertilizer needs:* Medium. Between 2 to 4 pounds of actual nitrogen per 1,000 square feet per year.
- ☐ *Wearability:* Medium.
- ☐ *Mowing height:* 2 to 3 inches. In summer, mow at highest level.
- ☐ *Best adapted:* Grown in every northern state. Northcentral and Northeast is Kentucky bluegrass heartland.
- ☐ *Varieties:* Several—see page 139.
- ☐ *Scientific name: Poa pratensis.*

Kentucky bluegrass, common.

Kentucky Bluegrass (Improved)

- ☐ *Strengths:* As a group, color and density are superior to common Kentucky bluegrass. Improved resistance to diseases such as leaf spot (*Helminthosporium*), stripe smut (*Ustilago striiformis*), and *fusarium* blight. Some varieties take heat better; some can be mowed shorter.
- ☐ *Weaknesses:* Usually higher maintenance than common Kentucky bluegrass; more fertilizer is needed and more thatch build-up.
- ☐ *Shade tolerance:* Improved in some varieties.
- ☐ *Water needs:* Most varieties are more drought sensitive than common Kentucky bluegrass.
- ☐ *Fertilizer needs:* Medium to high. About 6 to 12 pounds of actual nitrogen per 1,000 square feet per year. Some new varieties will do well on as little as 1 or 2 pounds of nitrogen per 1,000 square feet per year if established in good soil.
- ☐ *Wearability:* Better than common Kentucky bluegrass.
- ☐ *Mowing height:* Check the variety list on page 139.
- ☐ *Best adapted:* Same as common Kentucky bluegrass.
- ☐ *Varieties:* See page 139.
- ☐ *Scientific name: Poa pratensis.*

Kentucky bluegrass, improved.

Centipede Grass

- ☐ *Strengths:* Makes a good, low-maintenance, general purpose lawn. Adapts to poor soil. Aggressive enough to crowd out weeds. Needs less mowing than most grasses. Resistance to chinch bugs and *Rhizoctonia* disease provides an alternative to St. Augustine grass.
- ☐ *Weaknesses:* Coarse texture. Color is not dark green. Tends to yellow from chlorosis. Sensitive to low temperatures.
- ☐ *Shade tolerance:* Fair.
- ☐ *Water needs:* Shallow root system is sensitive to drought, but recovery is fast.
- ☐ *Fertilizer needs:* Low—2 pounds of actual nitrogen per 1,000 square feet per year.
- ☐ *Wearability:* Not too good. Recovers slowly from damage.
- ☐ *Mowing height:* To 2 inches.
- ☐ *Best adapted:* Southern U.S. The northern limit would be a line drawn between northern Alabama and Raleigh, North Carolina.
- ☐ *Varieties:* 'Centiseed' is a trade name for common centipede grass that can be grown from seed. 'Oaklawn', developed in Oklahoma, can be established by sprigs.
- ☐ *Scientific name: Eremochloa ophiuroides.*

Centipede grass.

Dichondra

- ☐ *Strengths:* Dichondra is not a grass, but a broadleaf plant. It makes a lush, dense, bright green carpet when well maintained. Needs less mowing than most grasses. Attacked by few diseases.

Dichondra.

- [ ] *Weaknesses:* Cutworms, flea beetles, snails and slugs prefer it to grass lawns. Hard to get weeds out once they invade.
- [ ] *Shade tolerance:* Pretty good: better than bluegrass.
- [ ] *Water needs:* High. Shallow roots cannot tolerate prolonged drought.
- [ ] *Fertilizer needs:* High. Likes frequent, light feeding of ½ to 1 pound of actual nitrogen per 1,000 square feet per month during growing season.
- [ ] *Wearability:* Poor.
- [ ] *Mowing height:* Depends on use. In shade where traffic is rare, mow a few inches high. Lower height to about 1 inch is best for most other lawn areas and helps keep out weeds.
- [ ] *Best adapted:* Dichondra likes heat. Not adapted to cool, foggy climates or where temperatures drop below 25°F.
- [ ] *Varieties:* None.
- [ ] *Scientific name: Dichondra micrantha.*

Chewing Fescue

- [ ] *Strengths:* Will tolerate close mowing in cool climate areas. Usually persistent in mixtures with Kentucky bluegrass.
- [ ] *Weaknesses:* Same as red fescue. Competitiveness can be a disadvantage in mixtures with Kentucky bluegrass.
- [ ] *Shade tolerance:* Same as red fescue.
- [ ] *Water needs:* Low.
- [ ] *Fertilizer needs:* Low. About 2 to 4 pounds of actual nitrogen per 1,000 square feet per year.
- [ ] *Wearability:* Same as red fescue; may form clumps.
- [ ] *Mowing height:* About 1 inch or higher.
- [ ] *Best adapted:* Same as red fescue.
- [ ] *Varieties:* See pages 140–141.
- [ ] *Scientific name: Festuca rubra* var. *commutata.*

Chewing fescue.

Red Fescue, Creeping Red Fescue

- [ ] *Strengths:* Frequent component of bluegrass mixtures. Blends well and does what some bluegrasses can't do—grows well in shade or drought-dry soil. Fine texture, deep green color. Tolerates acid soil.
- [ ] *Weaknesses:* Very susceptible to summer diseases in hot climates, especially in moist fertile soil.
- [ ] *Shade tolerance:* Usually the best cool-season grass for dry shady lawns.
- [ ] *Water needs:* Good drought tolerance.
- [ ] *Fertilizer needs:* Low. 2 to 4 pounds at most of actual nitrogen per 1,000 square feet per year.
- [ ] *Wearability:* Poor. Slow to recover if damaged.
- [ ] *Mowing height:* Normally, mow 2 inches or higher. After establishment it can be left unmowed for a "meadow look."
- [ ] *Best adapted:* Where summers are cool, such as coastal northwest, or at higher elevations.
- [ ] *Varieties:* See pages 140–141.
- [ ] *Scientific name: Festuca rubra* var. *rubra.*

Red fescue, creeping red fescue.

Tall Fescue

- [ ] *Strengths:* A good, tough, play lawn. Some disease and insect resistance. Green all year. Good transition zone grass.
- [ ] *Weaknesses:* Coarse textured, tends to clump. Not good in mixtures unless it comprises 80 or 90 percent of the mix. Must be seeded at a heavy rate.
- [ ] *Shade tolerance:* Okay in partial shade.
- [ ] *Water needs:* Good drought tolerance.
- [ ] *Fertilizer needs:* Medium. Between 4 and 6 pounds of actual nitrogen per 1,000 square feet per year.

Tall fescue.

- ☐ *Wearability:* Good in spring and fall when growth is fast. Less acceptable in summer.
- ☐ *Mowing height:* Mow high—about 3 inches.
- ☐ *Best adapted:* The best cool-season grass for transition areas. Takes heat.
- ☐ *Varieties:* 'Kentucky 31'. 'Fawn' texture is less coarse. 'Alta' is wear resistant. 'Goars' is most tolerant of poor soil.
- ☐ *Scientific name: Festuca elatior.*

Annual Rye

- ☐ *Strengths:* Aggressive, fast-germinating, quick to establish. Best use is overseeding in warm-winter areas.
- ☐ *Weaknesses:* Poor cold and heat tolerance. Doesn't mow clean. Some perennial rye seed is usually mixed with annual rye, which grows in weedy clumps.
- ☐ *Shade tolerance:* Medium.
- ☐ *Water needs:* High.
- ☐ *Fertilizer needs:* Low to medium. Between 4 to 6 pounds of actual nitrogen per 1,000 square feet per year.
- ☐ *Wearability:* Medium.
- ☐ *Mowing height:* Around 1½ to 2 inches.
- ☐ *Best adapted:* Same as perennial rye. Use for overseeding dormant Bermuda grass.
- ☐ *Varieties:* None.
- ☐ *Scientific name: Lolium multiflorum.*

Annual rye.

Perennial Rye (Turf-Type)

- ☐ *Strengths:* Fast seed germination and establishment. Compatible in mixes with Kentucky bluegrass and fine fescues. Greater persistence than common perennial rye. Cleaner mowing. Improved heat and cold tolerance. Tough play lawn.
- ☐ *Weaknesses:* Suffers from winter kill in coldest climates. If it comprises more than 25 percent of a seed mix, it will impair establishment of the other grasses.
- ☐ *Shade tolerance:* Medium.
- ☐ *Water needs:* Intermediate.
- ☐ *Fertilizer needs:* Medium. Apply between 4 to 6 pounds of actual nitrogen per 1,000 square feet per year.
- ☐ *Wearability:* Fairly good.
- ☐ *Mowing height:* 1 to 2 inches.
- ☐ *Best adapted:* Coastal regions with mild winters and cool moist summers. Excellent for overseeding dormant Bermuda grass in the South.
- ☐ *Varieties:* See page 140.
- ☐ *Scientific name: Lolium perenne.*

Perennial rye, turf-type

St. Augustine grass.

St. Augustine Grass

- ☐ *Strengths:* The best warm-season lawn grass for shade. Tolerates salty soil.
- ☐ *Weaknesses:* Chinch bug is a serious pest. Susceptible to several diseases, including St. Augustine grass decline (SAD) virus. Tends to thatch badly.
- ☐ *Shade tolerance:* Good.
- ☐ *Water needs:* High.
- ☐ *Fertilizer needs:* Medium high—4 to 7 pounds actual nitrogen per 1,000 square feet per year.
- ☐ *Wearability:* Poor.
- ☐ *Mowing height:* Between 1½ and 2½ inches.
- ☐ *Best adapted:* Mild areas of the Southwest; Gulf Coast states.
- ☐ *Varieties:* 'Floratine', 'Bitter Blue', and 'Floratam'.
- ☐ *Scientific name: Stenotaphrum secundatum.*

Zoysia grass.

Zoysia Grass

- *Strengths:* Forms dense, fine-textured lawn, resistant to weeds. Good heat and drought tolerance. Relatively free of disease and insect pests, though chinch bugs may bother it.
- *Weaknesses:* Very slow to establish. Does not thrive where summers are too short or too cool. Wiry blades tough to mow if left too long. Tends to build thatch.
- *Shade tolerance:* Slow in shade but much better than Bermuda grass.
- *Water needs:* Good but needs more than Bermuda grass.
- *Fertilizer needs:* Medium-low—between 2 and 6 pounds of actual nitrogen per 1,000 square feet per year.
- *Wearability:* Outstanding.
- *Mowing height:* ½ inch to 1½ inches.
- *Best adapted:* Throughout the South. Occasionally used in the Northeast.
- *Varieties:* 'Emerald' (see photo) is a hybrid (*Zoysia japonica* × *Z. tenuifolia*) and probably the best. *Zoysia japonica* 'Meyer' or *Z. tenuifolia* are least cold tolerant but the finest textured.
- *Scientific name: Zoysia* species.

Varieties of Bermuda Grass

Variety	Description	Strengths	Comments
'Midiron'	Medium texture, dark green.	Most winter hardy of the Bermuda grasses. Best tolerance to winter traffic. Vigorous, fast rate of coverage.	Tends to go dormant earlier. Develops a purplish cast in the fall. In South, used primarily in upper South and transition zones for tees and fairways. Also—as in West—used on athletic fields. Useful at higher elevations (above 4,000 feet).
'Midiron'– 'Tifway' Blend	Medium texture, dark green.	Combines vigor and winter hardiness with frost resistance and dense growth for wear resistance and longer period of color retention.	Used on tees, fairways, and athletic fields in the upper South and the West.
'Ormond'	Medium fine texture, blue-green.	Vigorous, rapid spreading and wear tolerant. Doesn't tend to thatch as much as other Bermuda grasses. Is subject to winterkill, mites and diseases.	Used mostly in Florida for golf-course fairways, athletic fields, and home lawns.
'Santa Ana'	Fine textured, dark green.	Short dormant season and very vigorous growth. Has shown high tolerance to air pollution.	A seedling selection made in Los Angeles, California. Grows very dense and requires regular dethatching. Generally recommended for athletic fields rather than home lawns.
'Tifdwarf'	Fine texture, dark green.	Tolerates consistent low mowing down to ⅛ inch.	Used primarily on golf greens and home lawns.
'Tifgreen'	Fine texture, medium green.	Tolerates close mowing and heals rapidly.	Most popular grass for putting greens in the southeast and some golf courses of the southwest. Also used for home lawns and grass tennis courts.
'Tiflawn'	Medium fine texture, bright green.	Accepts a lot of traffic, fast recovery from wear. Performs reasonably well under low maintenance. Good tolerance to herbicides.	Used primarily for athletic fields. Tends to form more seedheads and has the feel of common Bermuda. One of the first 'Tif' hybrids released. Is subject to winterkill in upper South.
'Tifway'	Fine texture, dark green.	Forms a dense, weed-resistant turf. Frost tolerant; withstands a lot of wear. Overall, less maintenance requirements than other Bermuda grasses. Good tolerance to herbicides.	Most popular tee and fairway grass in the southeast. Most popular grass for athletic fields, as well as the most popular Bermuda grass for home lawns. In the upper South, is subject to winterkill. May be subject to winterkill at higher elevations.

The improved Bermuda grasses of the 'Tif' series were developed or discovered and released through the University of Georgia's Coastal Plains Experiment Station and the U.S.D.A. In contrast to common Bermuda grass, the 'Tif' varieties are more disease resistant, have greater density, better weed resistance, fewer seed heads, and finer, softer textures with better color. They are especially well suited to playgrounds, football fields, and golf courses.

Varieties of Kentucky Bluegrass

Variety	Description	Strengths	Comments
'Adelphi'	Very dark green with good density and medium texture.	Good summer performance and spring greenup; widely adapted.	Good resistance to leaf spot, stripe smut and *Fusarium* blight.
'Baron'	Dark green with medium texture and density.	Moderately good summer performance and widely adapted.	Moderately good resistance to leaf spot and stripe smut.
'Bensun (A-34)'	Light green with good density and fine texture.	Good shade performance and wear resistance. A very aggressive variety.	Good resistance to stripe smut and moderately good resistance to leaf spot.
'Birka'	Moderately dark green with good density and fine texture.	Moderately good shade performance.	Good resistance to leaf spot, stripe smut, powdery mildew.
'Bonnieblue'	Moderately dark green with medium texture and good density.	Good winter color and spring greenup.	Good resistance to leaf spot and stripe smut.
'Bristol'	Dark green with a medium coarse texture and good density.	Moderately good shade tolerance.	Good resistance to leaf spot, stripe smut and powdery mildew.
'Columbia'	Moderately dark green with good density and fine texture.	Good winter color and spring greenup; moderately good heat tolerance.	Good resistance to leaf spot, stripe smut and *Fusarium* blight.
'Delta'	Medium green with an upright growth habit and moderate density.	Moderate drought tolerance.	Very susceptible to leaf spot. Prone to chlorosis in alkaline soils.
'Fylking'	Moderately dark green with fine texture.	Good sod former.	Good resistance to leaf spot, moderately resistant to stripe smut but susceptible to *Fusarium* blight. Best kept mowed 1½ inches or lower.
'Glade'	Dark green with very good density and fine texture.	Moderately good shade tolerance.	Moderately good resistance to leaf spot and good resistance to stripe smut and powdery mildew.
'Kenblue'	Medium green with an upright growth habit and moderate density.	Best at low maintenance levels—high cutting and low fertility.	Susceptible to leaf spot.
'Majestic'	Dark green with a medium texture and good density.	Good winter color and spring greenup.	Good resistance to leaf spot; moderately good resistance to stripe smut.
'Merion'	Dark green with a medium coarse texture with good density.	Good heat and drought tolerance and transplanting ability in the heat.	Good resistance to leaf spot; susceptible to stripe smut, powdery mildew, and rust. Not good in the shade.
'Newport'	Moderately dark green with medium texture and density.	Good winter color.	Susceptible to leaf spot and *Fusarium*.
'Nugget'	Dark green with very fine texture and high density; poor color in winter.	Very good cold hardiness.	Good resistance to leaf spot and powdery mildew; susceptible to dollar spot.
'Parade'	Medium green with good density and fine texture.	Good winter color and spring greenup.	Good resistance to leaf spot, stripe smut, and *Fusarium* blight.
'Park'	Moderately dark green with an upright growth habit and moderate density.	Best performance at low maintenance levels which includes high cutting and low fertility.	Susceptible to leaf spot and *Fusarium* blight. Prone to yellowing in alkaline soils.
'Sydsport'	Medium green with good density and fine texture.	Good sod former; wear tolerant, widely adapted.	Moderately good leaf spot, stripe smut, and powdery mildew.
'Touchdown'	Moderate dark green with very good density and fine texture.	Moderately good tolerance of low mowing and shade; good winter color and spring greenup.	Good resistance to leaf spot, stripe smut, and powdery mildew.
'Victa'	Dark green with a medium texture and density.	Moderately good summer performance; widely adapted.	Moderately good resistance to leaf spot and stripe smut.
'Warrens A-20'	Dark green with a medium texture and good density.	Good spring greenup.	Good resistance to leaf spot and stripe smut.
'Windsor'	Moderately dark green with moderately good density and texture.	Good spring greenup.	Susceptible to stripe smut; moderately resistant to leaf spot.

Varieties of Turf-Type Perennial Rye Grass

Variety	Description	Strengths	Comments
'Birdie'	Medium green with good density and fine texture.	Good heat tolerance.	Good resistance to brown patch; moderate resistance to crown rust. Good mowing qualities with stemming period in the spring.
'Citation'	Dark green with good density and fine texture.	Good heat tolerance.	Good resistance to brown patch; moderate resistance to red thread. Good mowing qualities. Stemming period in the spring.
'Derby'	Moderately dark green. Good density and texture.	Moderately good heat and cold tolerance.	Good resistance to brown patch; good mowing qualities.
'Diplomat'	Moderately dark green; very good density and fine texture.	Moderately good heat and cold tolerance.	Good resistance to brown patch; good mowing qualities.
'Loretta'	Light green with very good density and fine texture.	Moderately good cold tolerance and very good mowing qualities.	Good resistance to crown rust; no stemming period in spring and lower performance in the summer.
'Manhattan'	Medium green with good density and fine texture.	Good cold tolerance and good performance in the spring and fall.	Moderately good resistance to brown blight; good mowing qualities and no stemming period.
'NK-200'	Moderately dark green with moderately good density and texture.	Good cold tolerance.	Moderately good resistance to *Fusarium* patch.
'Norlea'	Dark green; intermediate density and texture.	Good cold tolerance.	Moderately good resistance to *Fusarium* patch. Mowing quality less desirable than other varieties. Susceptible to crown rust.
'Omega'	Moderately dark green with good density and texture.	Moderately good heat and cold tolerance.	Good resistance to brown blight and moderate resistance to brown patch. Good mowing qualities with short stemming period.
'Pennfine'	Moderately dark green with good density and texture.	Good heat tolerance.	Good resistance to brown patch and moderately good resistance to brown patch. Good mowing qualities with stemming period in the spsring.
'Regal'	Dark green with moderately good density and texture.	Moderately good heat tolerance.	Moderately good brown patch resistance. Moderately good mowing qualities.
'Yorktown I'	Dark green with good density and texture.	Moderately good heat and cold tolerance.	Moderately good brown patch and brown blight resistance. Good mowing qualities.
'Yorktown II'	Dark green with very good density and fine texture.	Moderately good heat and cold tolerance.	Good resistance to brown patch and crown rust; very good mowing qualities.

Varieties of Fine Fescues

Variety	Description	Strengths	Comments
'Banner'	Chewings type, dark green, good density and fine texture.	Moderately good disease resistance and tolerant of close mowing.	Very competitive with Kentucky bluegrasses in mixtures. Susceptible to powdery mildew.
'Boreal'	Creeping type, moderately dark green. Medium texture and density.	Good seedling vigor.	Has good winter hardiness.
'Cascade'	Chewings type. Medium green with very fine texture.	Good establishment rate.	Susceptible to leaf spot.
'C-26'	Hard fescue type, dark green, fine texture, and good density.	Good disease resistance compared to the other fine fescues. Good drought tolerance.	Should perform well in mixtures with Kentucky bluegrass.
'Dawson'	Semi-creeping type, medium green, good density and fine texture.	Moderately good leaf spot resistance and tolerant of close mowing. Good for overseeding Bermuda grass.	Can be damaged severely by dollar spot.
'Fortress'	Creeping type forming extensive rhizomes. Dark green with medium texture and density.	Good resistance to powdery mildew and good seedling vigor.	Blends well with Kentucky bluegrasses and recovers well from summer injury.
'Highlight'	Chewings type. Medium green with fine texture and good density.	Moderately good disease resistance and tolerant of close mowing.	Very competitive with Kentucky bluegrass in mixtures.

Varieties of Fine Fescue, Continued

Variety	Description	Strengths	Comments
'Illahee'	Creeping type. Dark Green, medium texture and density.	Good seedling vigor.	Blends well with Kentucky bluegrasses.
'Jamestown'	Chewings type. Dark green, good density and fine texture.	Moderately good disease resistance and tolerant of close mowing.	Very competitive with Kentucky bluegrass in mixtures. Susceptible to powdery mildew.
'Pennlawn'	Predominantly a creeping type. Medium dark green, good density and fine texture.	A widely adapted variety with moderate disease resistance.	Used widely in mixtures with Kentucky bluegrasses.
'Ruby'	Creeping type. Dark green, medium texture and density.	Good seedling vigor.	Blends well with Kentucky bluegrasses.
'Wintergreen'	Chewings type. Moderately dark green, fine texture and good density.	Good winter color and rust resistance.	Good winter hardiness, used in northern areas.

Varieties of Tall Fescue

Variety	Description	Strengths	Comments
'Alta'	Upright growing and coarse texture. Medium green.	Drought tolerant. Moderately persistent in turf.	Has performed equal to 'Kentucky 31' in Northern California.
'Fawn'	Upright growing and coarse texture. Medium green.	Drought tolerant.	Susceptible to crown rust. Not as persistent in turf as 'Alta' and 'Kentucky 31'.
'Goar'	Upright growing and coarse texture. Medium green.	Drought tolerant.	Lacking competitive ability compared to 'Alta' and 'Kentucky 31'.
'Kentucky 31'	Coarse texture and somewhat lower growing than 'Alta' and 'Fawn'. Medium green.	Drought tolerant. Widely adapted to many soil types. Moderately disease resistant.	Good persistence in turf in transition zone. Good winter recovery and spring greenup.
'Kenwell'	Slightly lower growing than 'Kentucky 31' with coarse texture. Medium green.	Drought tolerant. Better fall color than 'Kentucky 31' in fall.	Similar to 'Kentucky 31' with slightly better disease resistance.

Northern Native Grasses

	Description	Culture	Comments
American beach grass (*Ammophila breviligulata*)	A tough grass that grows tall, to about 5 feet. Deep root system and aggressive underground runners allow rapid growth and spread in shifting, infertile beach sand. Very similar to European beach grass but has a longer planting season and greater persistence.	Dig old clumps in fall just before complete dormancy. Cut stems back to about 2 feet. Plant clumps about 8 inches deep. Addition of fertilizer at planting time will promote more rapid growth.	Used for first-stage stabilization of shifting dune areas. As soon as the grass covers, begin planting more permanent woody plants. Beach grass grows naturally on the shores of the Great Lakes, along the Atlantic Coast from Newfoundland to North Carolina and along the Pacific Coast.
Blue grama (*Bouteloua gracilis*)	Grayish green and fine-textured. Excellent heat and drought tolerance. Used in rangeland seedings or similar never-water situations.	Use 1 to 3 pounds of seed per 1,000 square feet. Slow to establish. Sow fall or spring, about 30 days to germination. Mow to 2 or 3 inches. Very little fertilizer required.	Basically a warm-season grass but hardy to −40°F. An important native of the Great Plains, it's found in Wisconsin, Manitoba, Alberta, and south to Arkansas. Good in arid-alkaline soil.
Buffalo grass (*Buchloe dactyloides*)	Fine textured blades are grayish green. One of the most dominant grasses of the short-grass prairie. Grows during summer and has outstanding heat tolerance. Only green during growing season which is often short.	Easily started from seed. Use 3 to 5 pounds per 1,000 square feet in fall. Should come up in about 30 days. Water deep to establish, then little is needed. Give ½ to 2 pounds of actual nitrogen per 1,000 square feet per year. Mow to about 1 inch.	Favored by settlers for building sod houses, it makes a dense turf. Thrives in areas that receive 12 to 25 inches of rain per year (Minnesota to central Montana; south to Iowa, Texas, Arizona, and northern Mexico). Does well in heavy soil.
Fairway wheat grass (*Agropyron cristatum*)	Not a true native—introduced from Russia. Very tolerant of high temperatures, takes up to 110°F. Okay in cold to −20°F. and lower. Related to the nuisance weed, quackgrass.	Low 3 to 5 pounds of seed per 1,000 square feet. Germination in 14 to 30 days. Water deeply until established then no supplemental water should be necessary. Mow to 2 inches.	Grows best in moist alkaline soil. Commonly found throughout much of western Canada, the northern Great Plains, and other northern mountain regions of the U.S. Sometimes grows as far south as Texas and as west as northeast California, Oregon, and Washington.

Native grasses make excellent low-maintenance ground covers. They don't make the most attractive home lawn, but can be used to stabilize banks, and roadsides. Fertilizer and water needs are minimal. Growth is slow, so mowing is usually done three or four times per season. Some native grasses may be difficult to find, but if they are adapted to where you live and are useful in your area, they will be available. Check with your nurseryman or local seed supplier.

Lawn Measurements and Conversions

The lawn keeper is asked to be a measurer in almost every operation—"Apply 2# of nitrogen per 1,000 square feet," "Mix two tablespoons per gallon," "Spread two or three inches of organic matter over the soil," "Determine the area of your lawn," "Add lime if soil tests show the need." In these directions we find the elements "How much," "How wide," "How long."

How many square feet?

Irregular shapes
(within 5% accuracy)
Measure a long (L) axis of the area. At every 10 feet on the length line measure the width at right angles to the length line.
Total all widths and multiply by 10.

$$\text{Area} = (A_1 A_2 + B_1 B_2 + C_1 C_2 \text{ etc.}) \times 10$$

$A = (40' + 60' + 32') \times 10$
$A = 132' \times 10'$
$A = 1,320 \text{ square feet}$

Unusual shapes
Calculations can be made by sections and totaled.

In this case calculate and add together:
    Area of triangle
    Area of rectangle
    One-half area of circle
TOTAL = square feet in area

Square or rectangle
Area = LW
  L = Length
  W = Width
  A = 90' x 60'
  A = 5,400 square feet

Triangle
Area = 0.5 BH
  B = Base
  H = Height
  A = 0.5 x 60' x 120'
  A = 3,600 square feet

Circle
Area = πR²
  π = 3.14
  R = Radius
  A = 3.14 x 20' x 20'
  A = 1,256 square feet

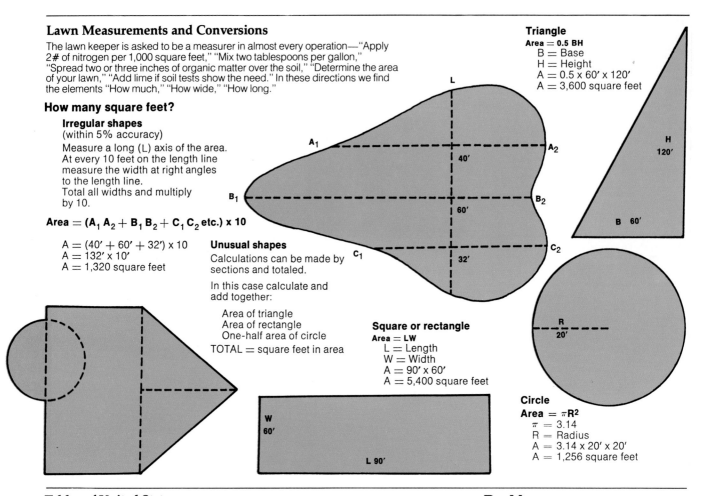

Tables of United States Customary Weights and Measures

Linear measure

12 inches (in.)	= 1 foot (ft.)
3 feet	= 1 yard (yd.)
5½ yards	= 1 rod (rd.), pole, or perch (16½ ft.)
40 rods	= 1 furlong (fur.)
	= 220 yards
	= 660 feet
8 furlongs	= 1 statute mile (mi.)
	= 1,760 yards
	= 5,280 feet
3 land miles	= 1 league
5,280 feet	= 1 statute or land mile
6,076.11549 feet	= 1 international nautical mile

Area measure

Squares and cubes of units are sometimes abbreviated by using "superior" figures. For example, ft² means square foot, and ft³ means cubic foot.

144 square inches	= 1 square foot
9 square feet	= 1 square yard
	= 1,296 square inches
30¼ square yards	= 1 square rod
	= 272¼ square feet
160 square rods	= 1 acre
	= 4,840 square yards
	= 43,560 square feet
640 acres	= 1 square mile
1 mile square	= 1 section (of land)
6 miles square	= 1 township
	= 36 sections
	= 36 square miles

Cubic measure

1,728 cubic inches	= 1 cubic foot
27 cubic feet	= 1 cubic yard

Calibrating Equipment

Not all fertilizers come with spreader calibrations listed on the bag. Here are some ways to check the actual amount of fertilizer that will be dropping on your lawn.

Spreaders, drop spreaders using a collection pan.
Attach collection pan to spreader.
Fill spreader.
Operate spreader a known distance.
Weigh amount of fertilizer in collection pan.
Measure width of spreader drop.
The distance traveled times the width of the spreader equals the number of square feet material has been applied to.

Example:
Spreader travels 100 feet, is 4 feet wide, delivers 3 lbs. of material.
Area covered = 100 × 4
    = 400 square feet.
Set up proportion.

$$\frac{3 \text{ lbs.}}{400 \text{ square feet}} = \frac{X}{1,000 \text{ square feet}}$$

$400\,X = 3,000$
  $X = 7.5$ lbs. per 1,000 square feet.

Readjust spreader and continue by trial and error until desired rate is obtained. Keep records of spreader settings for various materials.

Drop spreaders with no collection pan.
Procedure and calculation methods are the same except material is run out on wrapping paper, plastic, or a smooth clean concrete floor, swept up and weighed.

Dry Measure

When necessary to distinguish the dry pint or quart from the liquid pint or quart, the word "dry" should be used in combination with the name or abbreviation of the dry unit.

2 pints = 1 quart	
(= 67.2006 cubic inches)	
8 quarts = 1 peck (pk.)	
(= 637.605 cubic inches)	
= 16 pints	
4 pecks = 1 bushel (bu.)	
(= 2550.4 cubic inches)	
= 32 quarts	

Liquid Measure

Teaspoons
3 tsp. = 1 Tbs.

Tablespoons
2 Tbs. = ⅛ cup or 1 fl. oz.
4 Tbs. = ¼ cup or 2 fl. oz.
8 Tbs. = ½ cup or ¼ pint
16 Tbs. = 1 cup or ½ pint

(Measurements in cups and spoons mean level measuring cup and level measuring spoon.)

Cups, pints, quarts
2 cupfuls = 1 pint or 16 fl. ozs.
2 pints = 1 quart
4 quarts = 1 gallon

Watering Your Lawn

To cover 1,000 sq. ft. with an inch of water takes 625 gallons.
One gallon/min (gpm) = 1,440 gallons/day
10.4 gallons/min applies one inch of water over 1,000 sq. ft. every hour.
Gallons/minutes × 8.03 = cubic ft./hour.
One gallon of water weighs 8.34 pounds.

Index

Italicized page numbers refer to illustrations.